HIKE LIST

W9-AXQ-561

ANNE ARUNDEL COUNTY
1 Baltimore and Annapolis (B&A) Trail
2 BWI Trail
3 Downs Memorial Park
4 Kinder Farm Park

CITY OF BALTIMORE
5 Baltimore Inner Harbor–Waterfront Promenade
6 Cylburn Arboretum
7 Druid Hill Park Lake Loop
8 Fort McHenry
9 Gwynns Falls Park
10 Gwynns Falls Trail from Leon Day Park to Cherry Hill Park
11 Lake Montebello–Herring Run Park
12 Leakin Park
13 Patterson Park
14 Wyman Park–Stoney Run Trail

BALTIMORE COUNTY
15 Banneker Historical Park–No. 9 Trolley Line Trail
16 Cromwell Valley Park with Loch Raven Add-on
17 Double Rock Park
18 Eastern Regional Park
19 Fort Howard Park
20 Gunpowder Falls State Park (Hereford Area): Gunpowder North–South Circuit
21 Gunpowder Falls State Park: Jerusalem Village Trail with Jericho Covered Bridge Trail
22 Irvine Nature Center
23 Loch Raven Reservoir: Deadman's Cove Trail
24 Loch Raven Reservoir: Glen Ellen–Seminary Trail
25 Loch Raven Reservoir: Merryman Trail
26 NCRR (Northern Central Railroad) Trail
27 North Point State Park
28 Oregon Ridge Park
29 Patapsco Valley State Park: Glen Artney Area
30 Patapsco Valley State Park: Hilton Area
31 Patapsco Valley State Park: McKeldin Area

32 Prettyboy Reservoir: CCC (Civilian Conservation Corps) Trail
33 Prettyboy Reservoir: Gunpowder River
34 Prettyboy Reservoir: Hemlock Trail
35 Robert E. Lee Park–Lake Roland
36 Soldiers Delight Natural Environmental Area

CARROLL COUNTY
37 Gillis Falls
38 Hashawha Environmental Appreciation Area
39 Liberty Reservoir: Liberty West–Morgan Runs
40 Liberty Reservoir: Middle Run Trail
41 Morgan Run Natural Environmental Area
42 Piney Run Park
43 Union Mills

CECIL COUNTY
44 Elk Neck State Forest
45 Elk Neck State Park

HARFORD COUNTY
46 Gunpowder Falls State Park: Lost Pond Trail
47 Gunpowder Falls State Park: Sweet Air Area
48 Rocks State Park
49 Rocks State Park: Falling Branch Area
50 Susquehanna State Park: River Trails
51 Susquehanna State Park: Woodland–Farm Trails

HOWARD COUNTY
52 Centennial Park
53 Lake Kittamaqundi
54 Middle Patuxent Environmental Area
55 Patapsco Valley State Park: Hollofield Area with Pickall Area Add-on
56 Patapsco Valley State Park: Orange Grove–Avalon Areas
57 Patapsco Valley State Park: Unmaintained Area—Granite–Woodstock
58 Patuxent Branch Trail
59 Rockburn Branch Park
60 Savage Park

i

60 Hikes within 60 MILES

BALTIMORE

INCLUDING ANNE ARUNDEL, CARROLL, CECIL, HARFORD, AND HOWARD COUNTIES

Evan Balkan

MENASHA RIDGE PRESS
Birmingham, Alabama

ISBN 10: 0-89732-623-7
ISBN 13: 978-0-89732-623-0

Library of Congress Cataloging-in-Publication Data is available
from the Library of Congress.

Cover design by Grant M. Tatum
Text design by Karen Ocker
Cover photo © Evan Balkan
All other photos by Evan Balkan
Maps by Evan Balkan, Jennie Zehmer, and Steve Jones

Menasha Ridge Press
P.O. Box 43673
Birmingham, AL 35243
www.menasharidge.com

To Amelia and Molly—
don't let anyone teach you to be afraid of the woods.

TABLE OF CONTENTS

TABLE OF CONTENTS

ACKNOWLEDGMENTS

I want to thank the many people who create and maintain the trails and areas around them. Their services to the community are invaluable.

I am sorry I did not catch the names of everyone who answered my many questions: the young woman at Irvine Nature Center who identified flowers and birds, another young lady at Hashawha Environmental Appreciation Area who did the same for me there, and the elderly lady cleaning the floors at North Point State Park who told me about her grandchildren. These interactions remain as memories every bit as pleasant as the hikes I did in these places. Of course, these three are by no means an exhaustive list of the many people I came in contact with at the locations in this book. Thanks to all of you.

Special thanks goes to Cheryl Farfaras at the Middle Patuxent Environmental Area. Thanks also to friends Doug Lambdin and Jack Broderick, who accompanied me on some of the hikes. A debt of gratitude goes to Russell Helms at Menasha Ridge, whose exceedingly patient tutorials in the tricky ways of topo software and willingness to make the hard changes in the text that I couldn't bring myself to do were invaluable. A very sincere debt of thanks goes to my wife, Shelly, whose patience and encouragement during this project are extremely appreciated, and also to Amelia, whose smiling face looked out at me from the digital camera I lugged along and often kept me going when my knees began to ache. My family deserves thanks for their general encouragement. I owe my father the biggest debt of gratitude for exposing me to the great outdoors when I was just a boy and for instilling in me a lasting love and awe of the natural world around me. Lastly, I need to acknowledge the best companion a man can ever hope for and who now remains forever in one of our favorite spots—17 years was a good run.

—*Evan Balkan*

FOREWORD

Welcome to Menasha Ridge Press's *60 Hikes within 60 Miles*, a series designed to provide hikers with information needed to find and hike the very best trails surrounding cities usually underserved by good guidebooks.

Our strategy was simple: First, find a hiker who knows the area and loves to hike. Second, ask that person to spend a year researching the most popular and very best trails around. And third, have that person describe each trail in terms of difficulty, scenery, condition, elevation change, and all other categories of information that are important to hikers. "Pretend you've just completed a hike and met up with other hikers at the trailhead," we told each author. "Imagine their questions, and be clear in your answers."

An experienced hiker and writer, author Evan Balkan has selected 60 of the best hikes in and around the Baltimore metropolitan area. From urban hikes through the heart of Baltimore to the isolated and rural places of Carroll and Baltimore counties, along beaches, rivers, Chesapeake Bay, piedmont foothills—even a prairie—Evan Balkan provides hikers (and walkers) with a great variety of hikes, all within roughly 60 miles of Baltimore.

You'll get more out of this book if you take a moment to read the Introduction explaining how to read the trail listings. The "Topographic Maps" section will help you understand how useful topos will be on a hike, and will also tell you where to get them. And because this is a "where-to," not a "how-to" guide, those of you who have hiked extensively will find the Introduction of particular value.

As much for the opportunity to free the spirit as well as to free the body, let these hikes elevate you above the urban hurry.

All the best,
The Editors at Menasha Ridge Press

ABOUT THE AUTHOR

Evan Balkan teaches writing and literature at the Community College of Baltimore County–Catonsville. His fiction and nonfiction, mostly in the areas of travel and outdoor recreation, have appeared in numerous publications throughout the United States, as well as in Canada, England, and Australia. He holds degrees from Towson, George Mason, and Johns Hopkins universities, and he lives in Lutherville, Maryland with his wife, Shelly, and daughters, Amelia and Molly.

PREFACE

A good walk is therapy. The fresh air, the sights, sounds, and smells of the natural world: these things can fill a person's senses better than any artificial stimulant. Maryland has long been a leader in programs combating urban sprawl and preserving open spaces. Indeed, what makes Maryland and specifically the Chesapeake watershed the "Land of Pleasant Living" is the wonderful mix of urban and rural. There is nothing you could want, whether a cultural or historical attraction or a solitary walk in the woods, that you can't find in and around Baltimore.

Maryland is a varied state topographically, packing extraordinary diversity into a relatively small area. Home to mountains in the west, Atlantic coastline in the east, and the country's largest estuary splitting the state in the middle, everything a nature lover could want is within a few hours' drive. This diversity led Gilbert Grosvenor, the editor of *National Geographic,* to nickname Maryland "America in Miniature."

This legacy can apply specifically to the Baltimore area. A good-sized city (once the country's second largest), Baltimore is endowed with many fine attractions. But surprisingly to many—even many who live in the city—Baltimore is also home to an abundance of hiking opportunities. Before I began working on this book, I thought I was familiar with most, if not all, of these opportunities. I couldn't have been more wrong. It has been an incredible thrill to discover the multitude of places nearby where I can go for a great hike, and in many of these locations I had the place to myself. This is an astounding surprise in an area where millions of people make their homes.

The idea of this book is to catalog 60 hikes within 60 miles. As you'll notice when you look at the locations of these hikes, virtually all of them are within 30 miles. This is intentional. First, you don't need to travel very far from the city center to find great places to hike. Further, within all this laudation of Baltimore, a truth must be acknowledged: traffic can be tough, and as anyone who has sat for hours on I-695 can tell you, 60 miles often does not equal an hour. Only two of the hikes, Elk Neck State Park and Elk Neck State Forest, push the 60-mile limit. But anyone who has hiked in these locations can certainly attest to their deserved inclusion in this book.

It would be an impossible task to include every great hiking destination within 60 miles, and surely at least a few readers will be chagrined to see that their favorite spot was not included. Certainly Catoctin Mountain Park and Cunningham Falls State Park, outside Frederick, are within 60 miles of Baltimore and are fantastic places for hiking, but these locations are covered in Paul Elliott's excellent book *60 Hikes within 60 Miles: Washington, D.C.* Because of the thoroughness of that book,

Trailside turtles

I concentrated most of the hikes in this book in the city and north of Baltimore, in Baltimore County. Nevertheless, many hikes in northern Howard and Anne Arundel counties are represented here. In addition, you will find hikes in Harford, Carroll, and Cecil counties.

My goal in choosing the hikes was to create as much of a spectrum as possible. You will find very short 1-mile hikes (walks, really) as well as a few that stretch more than 10 miles and can be extended even more (the NCRR Trail, which stretches a total of 40 miles, comes to mind). I chose each hike for its special historical and/or natural interest. The result is 60 hikes that offer a wide array of geographical and topographical differences.

Several locations intentionally have more than one hike, with Patapsco Valley State Park topping out with six. It would have been very easy to include 60 hikes in Patapsco Valley and Gunpowder Falls state parks alone. Throw in the reservoir watersheds of Liberty, Loch Raven, and Prettyboy, and a hiker could keep himself busy and sated for years. In these cases I tried my best to provide the same diversity within each repeated area as I did in the 60 hikes as a whole. One location—Susquehanna State Park—has two hikes because of the very different nature of their main attractions, and the hikes can be combined in one ambitious and strenuous day. Lastly, I should note that I chose many of the hikes because of their proximity to other attractions, many of which are perfect for family outings. So by all means, grab the kids and go! There are few better ways to spend a day.

A quick note: all of the hike directions begin at I-695 (Baltimore Beltway), I-95, or I-83 (Jones Falls Expressway or Harrisburg Expressway, depending on what portion you're driving). Check the directions carefully; depending on where you're coming from, there very well may be quicker and easier routes. I made every effort to be as accurate and thorough as possible; if you see any mistakes or omissions—or if you simply have any comments for me—please contact me at e.balkan@worldnet.att.net.

Jastrow Trail

▶ BALTIMORE

Baltimore's rises and falls have been well documented. Bustling in the 1700s, all but leveled in the Great Fire of 1904, and sunk into economic depression for decades after, the city's rise at the tail end of the 20th century is often cited as a leading example of urban renewal. Sparked by the development of the Inner Harbor, as well as the country's first of the now ubiquitous downtown "old-style" baseball stadiums, many grand old neighborhoods that had fallen into decay have rebounded as well. Not surprisingly, many of these border popular urban green spaces.

Baltimore, which is virtually unmatched in this area, constantly surprises and delights visitors with the large amount of green inside this Eastern, industrialized city. This didn't happen by accident. From early on, city leaders recognized the need for and value of open spaces. In 1859 they passed a park tax and raised enough revenue to create and preserve a park system, eventually bringing in famed landscape architect Frederick Law Olmstead to design the city's green spaces. Continued attention to these spaces has resulted in the protection and maintenance of more than 7,000 acres of city parklands, much of it in the adjacent parks at Leakin and Gwynns Falls. These two parks make up part of the largest unbroken urban forest in America, no small feat for a city that is one of the country's oldest.

The plethora of green space within the city perfectly complements what makes Baltimore so attractive: the eminently walkable city features a patchwork of unique neighborhoods within easy distance of each other. Beyond the glitz of Harborplace, Baltimore's uniqueness can be found in its diverse neighborhoods: the stateliness of Mount Vernon, the historicity and funkiness of Fells Point and Federal Hill, the grittiness and renewal of Hamden, the beauty and elegance of Guilford, the energy of Charles Village and Johns Hopkins, and the cultural attractions (and restaurants) in Little Italy and Greektown. The list goes on. I've heard many first-time visitors exclaim, "I had no idea how charming Baltimore is!"

All of this charm came somewhat slowly, however. For much of Baltimore's history, the city remained first and foremost a maritime destination. Beginning in the 1600s, its deep and wide natural harbor attracted shippers. This attraction grew as Baltimore did, and its position farther inland than any other major Atlantic port allowed for easier delivery to western locations. Likewise, the system of railways and waterways spreading from the city made its allure as a port almost unparalleled for both cargo and people. Indeed, Baltimore Harbor ranked second only to Ellis Island as a port of entry for New World immigrants.

The city played a well-documented part in the War of 1812. The defeat of the British at Fort McHenry prompted Francis Scott Key to pen the words that served as a rallying point for embattled American militiamen and later became our national anthem. Baltimore's proximity to Chesapeake Bay made it a logical location for canning factories, which packed and exported the bounty of the bay to other parts of the country. Things waxed and waned in Baltimore for years, but recently another renaissance has begun with major development projects spreading out from the harbor, which remains the city's major compass point. A concerted effort to lure high-tech and Internet businesses to the old maritime industrial areas has people in the city looking forward to a Silicon Valley East, the so-called Digital Harbor.

Enjoy all the city has to offer, but don't forget about the hiking. The numerous opportunities afforded by our watersheds, rural spaces, and many parks in and around the city help put the charm in Charm City.

▶ THE MECCAS

As I mentioned above, I chose the hikes in this book primarily for their variety in location and topography, but certain locations feature more than one hike, including the state parks at Patapsco Valley and Gunpowder Falls and the reservoir watershed areas of Liberty, Loch Raven, and Prettyboy. These hiking meccas deserve extra attention from the dedicated hiker.

PATAPSCO VALLEY STATE PARK

Patapsco Valley State Park (PVSP) extends along 32 miles of its namesake, the Patapsco River, encompassing more than 14,000 acres in four counties with more than 170 miles of trails, enough to satisfy any hiker. Surprisingly, many of the trails are empty, and you may see 20 times more deer than people. The park has six developed, maintained sections: Hilton, McKeldin, Hollofield, Avalon, Glen Artney, and Orange Grove (the last three share an entrance). Here you will find ball fields, campgrounds, picnic areas, disc golf, and playgrounds. A network of maintained trails exists in each of these areas, and I have taken all the separate blazed trails to create long hikes, usually a loop, through each area (a combined hike traverses the Orange Grove and Avalon areas). I've also included a hike in an unmaintained section of the park, which I've called Granite-Woodstock for its location between those two towns.

GUNPOWDER FALLS STATE PARK

Gunpowder Falls State Park (GFSP) extends almost 18,000 acres along the Big and Little Gunpowder Falls and Gunpowder River. This long, narrow park, which is not always contiguous, envelops a stunning array of topography ranging from tidal marshes and wetlands to steep, rugged slopes. Including the 21-mile Maryland portion of the Maryland–Pennsylvania NCRR Trail, which is maintained by Gunpowder Falls State Park but treated separately in this book, GFSP has more than 100 miles of trails. The park also includes three developed areas: Hereford, Central (including Sweet Air, which is popular for equestrian use; Sweathouse Branch Wildlands, popular with birdwatchers and wildflower enthusiasts; and Jerusalem Village, a restored historic town), and Hammerman, plus the NCRR and Dundee Creek Marina. With all of these areas to choose from, you can enjoy boat launches, swimming beaches, picnic areas, historic

PREFACE

sites, trails galore, and numerous tubing, paddling, and fishing opportunities. You can even stay at the well-appointed but pricey Mill Pond Cottage and have park staff arrange itineraries for you. The four GFSP hikes in this book take in the differing areas of the park and, as a result, provide a fantastic mix of scenery.

THE RESERVOIRS: LIBERTY, LOCH RAVEN, AND PRETTYBOY

Loch Raven Reservoir, built in 1881 and holding more than 23 billion gallons, provides the drinking water for most of Baltimore County. Its popularity with joggers, hikers, bicyclists, and fishermen means that parking areas are often at a premium and the chances for solitude are slim. But once you've hiked here, the reasons for its popularity become obvious: it's an absolute gem and a mere 6 miles north of the city line. The three Loch Raven hikes in this book attempt to bring together the best of what the reservoir watershed has to offer, including one hike where you may find otherwise elusive solitude.

Every bit as beautiful as Loch Raven (many would argue more so), Prettyboy Reservoir in upper Baltimore County lies in what is still a relatively rural area and offers the isolation that is difficult to experience at Loch Raven.

Fishermen routinely catch record-sized bass and trout at Liberty Reservoir, which straddles Baltimore and Carroll counties. People also enjoy bird-watching and horseback riding here, as well as hiking, as the two Liberty treks in this book show. Each of these reservoir watershed areas has many more trails and hiking opportunities beyond what this book describes, and I've tried to present the "best of the best." Of course this is a highly subjective choice, and I encourage you to investigate and discover many more of the trails, which are usually marked with orange cables strung between wooden posts, making them easy to spot.

▶ GREENWAYS

The 60 hikes listed in this book do not begin to exhaust the hiking possibilities in and around Baltimore. Plans are under way, and some of them have already been implemented, to increase and/or develop additional greenways in Baltimore City and Baltimore County. As of June 2005, the 14-mile Gwynns Falls Trail had been completed, with plans for an additional 1-mile trail linking to the Park and Ride at the eastern terminus of I-70. The trail runs from the western edge of the city all the way to the Inner Harbor, connecting some 30 neighborhoods with 2,000 acres of parkland. I incorporated the most scenic sections of the trail under the hikes at Leakin Park and Gwynns Falls Park. I chose to include the rest of the Gwynns Falls Trail as a separate hike as Gwynns Falls Trail (from Leon Day Park to Cherry Hill Park) because this section is much more urban than the Gwynns Falls Park and Leakin Park portions. The two hikes in these two parks also include trails that radiate from the Gwynns Falls Trail. I have included the entire greenway trail in this book, in one form or another.

PREFACE

The Jones Falls Trail, which will run about 10 miles from Robert E. Lee Park to the Inner Harbor, will follow the Jones Falls stream valley and connect 20 neighborhoods and also link with Druid Hill Park. Stoney Run Trail will connect to the Jones Falls Trail near Druid Hill Park where the two waterways intersect. While this book features major portions of these greenways as separate hikes, hikers, bikers, and walkers can look forward to one day incorporating the greenery of Robert E. Lee, Druid Hill Park, and Stoney Run with pathways through urban neighborhoods, such as Mount Vernon. I have included a significant portion of the planned Baltimore Waterfront Promenade, an urban walkway designed on the order of Boston's Freedom Trail, in this book. The completed promenade will extend 7.5 miles from Canton to Federal Hill through the Inner Harbor along the Patapsco River. Educational signage and plantings of tidewater trees and plants will further enhance the walk. Indeed, Baltimore residents and visitors have much to look forward to in the coming years.

HIKING RECOMMENDATIONS

▶ HIKES 1-3 MILES IN LENGTH

Cylburn Arboretum
Double Rock Park
Druid Hill Park Lake Loop
Eastern Regional Park
Fort Howard Park
Fort McHenry
Gillis Falls
Hashawha Environmental Appreciation Area

Irvine Nature Center
Kinder Farm Park
Lake Kittamaqundi
Loch Raven Reservoir–Deadman's Cove Trail
Patterson Park
Prettyboy Reservoir–Hemlock Trail
Rockburn Branch Park
Rocks State Park–Falling Branch Area

▶ HIKES 3-6 MILES IN LENGTH

Baltimore Inner Harbor–Waterfront
   Promenade
Banneker Historical Park–No. 9 Trolley Line
Centennial Park
Downs Memorial Park
Gunpowder Falls State Park–Jerusalem Village Trail with Jericho Covered Bridge Trail
Gunpowder Falls State Park (Hereford Area)–Lost Pond Trail
Gunpowder Falls State Park–Sweet Air Area
Gwynns Falls Park
Lake Montebello–Herring Run Park
Leakin Park
Liberty Reservoir–Middle Run Trail
Middle Patuxent Environmental Area

Morgan Run Natural Environmental Area
North Point State Park
Oregon Ridge Park
Patapsco Valley State Park–Glen Artney Area
Patapsco Valley State Park–Hilton Area
Patapsco Valley State Park–Hollofield Area
   with Pickall Area Add-on
Patapsco Valley State Park–Orange Grove—
   Avalon Areas
Piney Run Park
Prettyboy Reservoir–CCC Trail
Prettyboy Reservoir–Gunpowder River
Rocks State Park
Savage Park
Wyman Park–Stoney Run Trail

▶ HIKES 6-9 MILES IN LENGTH

Cromwell Valley Park with Loch Raven
   Add-on
Elk Neck State Forest
Liberty Reservoir–Liberty West–Morgan Runs
Loch Raven Reservoir–Glen Ellen–Seminary
   Trail
Patapsco Valley State Park–Hollofield Area
   with Pickall Add-on
Patapsco Valley State Park–McKeldin Area

Patapsco Valley State Park–Unmaintained
   Area–Granite–Woodstock
Robert E. Lee Park–Lake Roland
Soldiers Delight Natural Environmental Area
Susquehanna State Park–River Trails
Susquehanna State Park–Woodland–Farm
   Trails
Union Mills

▶ HIKES 9-PLUS MILES IN LENGTH

Baltimore and Annapolis (B&A) Trail
BWI Trail

Elk Neck State Park

HIKING RECOMMENDATIONS

▶ HIKES 9-PLUS MILES IN LENGTH (CONTINUED)

Gunpowder Falls State Park (Hereford Area)–Gunpowder North–South Circuit

Gwynns Falls Trail from Leon Day Park to Cherry Hill Park

Loch Raven Reservoir–Merryman Trail

NCRR (North Central Railroad) Trail

Patuxent Branch Trail

▶ HIKES FEATURING HISTORIC SITES

Baltimore and Annapolis (B&A) Trail

Baltimore Inner Harbor–Waterfront Promenade

Banneker Historical Park–No. 9 Trolley Line

Cylburn Arboretum

Downs Memorial Park

Druid Hill Park

Fort Howard Park

Fort McHenry

Gunpowder Falls State Park–Jerusalem Village Trail with Jericho Covered Bridge Trail

Gwynns Falls Trail from Leon Day Park to Cherry Hill Park

Leakin Park

North Point State Park

Oregon Ridge Park

Patapsco Valley State Park–Glen Artney Area

Patapsco Valley State Park–Hilton Area

Patapsco Valley State Park–Orange Grove– Avalon Areas

Patapsco Valley State Park–Unmaintained Area–Granite–Woodstock

Patterson Park

Patuxent Branch Trail

Robert E. Lee Park–Lake Roland

Savage Park

Soldiers Delight Natural Environmental Area

Susquehanna State Park–River Trails

Susquehanna State Park–Woodland—Farm Trails

▶ HIKES FEATURING RIVERS OR LAKES

Banneker Historical Park–No. 9 Trolley Line

Centennial Park

Double Rock Park

Eastern Regional Park

Gillis Falls

Gunpowder Falls State Park (Hereford Area)—Gunpowder North–South Circuit

Gunpowder Falls State Park—Jerusalem Village Trail with Jericho Covered Bridge Trail

Gunpowder Falls State Park (Hereford Area)—Lost Pond Trail

Gunpowder Falls State Park—Sweet Air Area

Gwynns Falls Park

Lake Kittamaqundi

Lake Montebello–Herring Run Park

Leakin Park

Liberty Reservoir—Middle Run Trail

Middle Patuxent Environmental Area

Patapsco Valley State Park—Glen Artney Area

Patapsco Valley State Park—Hilton Area

Patapsco Valley State Park—McKeldin Area

Patapsco Valley State Park—Orange Grove– Avalon Areas

Patapsco Valley State Park—Unmaintained Area—Granite–Woodstock

Patuxent Branch Trail

Piney Run Park

Prettyboy Reservoir–Gunpowder River

Prettyboy Reservoir–Hemlock Trail

Robert E. Lee Park–Lake Roland

Savage Park

Susquehanna State Park–River Trails

Susquehanna State Park–Woodland–Farm Trails

Wyman Park–Stoney Run Trail

HIKING RECOMMENDATIONS

▶ HIKES FEATURING RESERVOIRS, WATERFALLS, OR CHESAPEAKE BAY

Baltimore Inner Harbor–Waterfront
  Promenade
Downs Memorial Park
Elk Neck State Park
Fort Howard Park
Fort McHenry
Liberty Reservoir–Liberty West–Morgan Runs

Loch Raven Reservoir–Deadman's Cove Trail
Loch Raven Reservoir–Glen Ellen–Seminary
  Trail
Loch Raven Reservoir–Merryman Trail
North Point State Park
Prettyboy Reservoir–CCC Trail
Rocks State Park–Falling Branch Area

▶ HIKES GOOD FOR CHILDREN

Baltimore and Annapolis (B&A) Trail
  (Portions)
Banneker Historical Park–No. 9 Trolley Line
BWI Trail (Portions)
Double Rock Park
Downs Memorial Park
Druid Hill Park Lake Loop
Eastern Regional Park
Elk Neck State Park

Fort Howard Park
Fort McHenry
Irvine Nature Center
Kinder Farm Park
Patterson Park
Patuxent Branch Trail (Portions)
Rockburn Branch Park
Rocks State Park–Falling Branch Area

▶ HIKES GOOD FOR SOLITUDE

Elk Neck State Forest
Gillis Falls
Liberty Reservoir–Middle Run Trail
Loch Raven Reservoir–Deadman's Cove Trail
Morgan Run Natural Environmental Area
Patapsco Valley State Park–Hollofield Area
  with Pickall Area Add-on
Patapsco Valley State Park–McKeldin Area

Patapsco Valley State Park–Unmaintained
  Area–Granite–Woodstock
Prettyboy Reservoir–CCC Trail
Prettyboy Reservoir–Hemlock Trail
Susquehanna State Park–Woodland–Farm
  Trails
Union Mills

▶ HIKES GOOD FOR SPOTTING WILDLIFE

Cromwell Valley Park with Loch Raven
  Add-on
Elk Neck State Forest
Elk Neck State Park
Liberty Reservoir–Liberty West–Morgan Runs
Loch Raven Reservoir–Deadman's Cove Trail
Loch Raven Reservoir–Glen Ellen–
  Seminary Trail

Loch Raven Reservoir–Merryman Trail
Middle Patuxent Environmental Area
Morgan Run Natural Environmental Area
NCRR Trail
Oregon Ridge Park
Patapsco Valley State Park–Glen Artney Area
Patapsco Valley State Park–Hilton Area
Patapsco Valley State Park–McKeldin Area

HIKING RECOMMENDATIONS

▶ HIKES GOOD FOR SPOTTING WILDLIFE (CONTINUED)

Patapsco Valley State Park–Unmaintained Area–Granite–Woodstock

Prettyboy Reservoir–CCC Trail

Prettyboy Reservoir–Hemlock Trail

Robert E. Lee Park–Lake Roland

Rocks State Park

Soldiers Delight Natural Environmental Area

Susquehanna State Park–River Trails

Susquehanna State Park–Woodland–Farm Trails

Union Mills

▶ HIKES INSIDE THE BELTWAY

Baltimore Inner Harbor–Waterfront Promenade

Cylburn Arboretum

Double Rock Park

Druid Hill Park

Fort McHenry

Gwynns Falls Park

Gwynns Falls Trail from Leon Day Park to Cherry Hill Park

Lake Montebello–Herring Run Park

Leakin Park

Patterson Park

Robert E. Lee Park–Lake Roland

Wyman Park–Stoney Run Trail

▶ HIKES OUTSIDE THE BELTWAY

Baltimore and Annapolis (B&A) Trail

Banneker Historical Park–No. 9 Trolley Line

BWI Trail

Centennial Park

Cromwell Valley Park with Loch Raven Add-on

Downs Memorial Park

Eastern Regional Park

Elk Neck State Forest

Elk Neck State Park

Fort Howard Park

Gillis Falls

Gunpowder Falls State Park (Hereford Area)–Gunpowder North–South Circuit

Gunpowder Falls State Park–Jerusalem Village Trail with Jericho Covered Bridge Trail

Gunpowder Falls State Park–Lost Pond Trail

Gunpowder Falls State Park–Sweet Air Area

Hashawha Environmental Appreciation Area

Irvine Nature Center

Kinder Farm Park

Lake Kittamaqundi

Liberty Reservoir–Liberty West–Morgan Runs

Liberty Reservoir–Middle Run Trail

Loch Raven Reservoir–Deadman's Cove Trail

Loch Raven Reservoir–Glen Ellen–Seminary Trail

Loch Raven Reservoir–Merryman Trail

Middle Patuxent Environmental Area

Morgan Run Natural Environmental Area

NCRR Trail

North Point State Park

Oregon Ridge Park

Patapsco Valley State Park–Glen Artney Area

Patapsco Valley State Park–Hilton Area

Patapsco Valley State Park–Hollofield Area with Pickall Add-on

Patapsco Valley State Park–McKeldin Area

Patapsco Valley State Park–Orange Grove–Avalon Areas

Patapsco Valley State Park–Unmaintained Area–Granite–Woodstock

Patuxent Branch Trail

Piney Run Park

Prettyboy Reservoir–CCC Trail

HIKING RECOMMENDATIONS

▶ HIKES OUTSIDE THE BELTWAY (CONTINUED)

Prettyboy Reservoir–Hemlock TrailPrettyboy
  Reservoir–Gunpowder River
Robert E. Lee Park–Lake Roland
Rockburn Branch Park
Rocks State Park
Rocks State Park–Falling Branch Area
Savage Park
Soldiers Delight Natural Environmental Area
Susquehanna State Park–River Trails
Susquehanna State Park–Woodland–Farm
  Trails
Union Mills

▶ HIKES ACCESSIBLE BY PUBLIC TRANSPORTATION

Baltimore and Annapolis (B&A) Trail
Baltimore Inner Harbor–Waterfront
  Promenade
BWI Trail
Cylburn Arboretum
Druid Hill Park Lake Loop
Fort McHenry
Gwynns Falls Park
Gwynns Falls Trail from Leon Day Park to
  Cherry Hill Park
Lake Kittamaqundi
Lake Montebello–Herring Run Park
Leakin Park
Loch Raven Reservoir–Glen Ellen–Seminary
  Trail
Patterson Park
Robert E. Lee Park–Lake Roland
Wyman Park–Stoney Run Trail

▶ HIKES GOOD FOR BIRD-WATCHING

Banneker Historical Park–No. 9 Trolley Line
Centennial Park
Cromwell Valley Park with Loch Raven
  Add-on
Cylburn Arboretum
Downs Memorial Park
Eastern Regional Park
Elk Neck State Forest
Elk Neck State Park
Gunpowder Falls State Park–Sweet Air Area
Hashawha Environmental Appreciation Area
Irvine Nature Center
Kinder Farm Park
Lake Kittamaqundi
Lake Montebello–Herring Run Park
Liberty Reservoir–Liberty West—Morgan
  Runs
Middle Patuxent Environmental Area
Morgan Run Natural Environmental Area
NCRR Trail
North Point State Park
Oregon Ridge Park
Patapsco Valley State Park–Glen Artney Area
Patapsco Valley State Park–Hilton Area
Patapsco Valley State Park–Unmaintained
  Area–Granite–Woodstock
Patterson Park
Patuxent Branch Trail
Robert E. Lee Park—Lake Roland
Soldiers Delight Natural Environmental Area
Susquehanna State Park–River Trails
Susquehanna State Park–Woodland–Farm
  Trails

60 HIKES within 60 MILES
BALTIMORE

INCLUDING ANNE ARUNDEL, CARROLL, CECIL, HARFORD, AND HOWARD COUNTIES

INTRODUCTION

Welcome to *60 Hikes within 60 Miles: Baltimore.* If you're new to hiking or even if you're a seasoned trail-smith, take a few minutes to read the following introduction. We explain how this book is organized and how to use it.

▶ HIKE DESCRIPTIONS

Each hike contains eight key items: a locator map, an "In Brief" description of the trail, a "Key At-a-Glance Information" box, directions to the trail, a trail map, an elevation profile, a trail description, and a description of any notable nearby activities. Combined, the maps and information provide a clear method to assess each trail from the comfort of your favorite reading chair.

IN BRIEF

A "taste of the trail." Think of this section as a snapshot focused on the historical landmarks, beautiful vistas, and other sights you may encounter on the trail.

KEY AT-A-GLANCE INFORMATION

The information in the Key At-a-Glance boxes gives you a quick idea of the specifics of each hike. The information covers the following basic elements.

LENGTH   The length of the trail from start to finish. There may be options to shorten or extend the hikes, but the mileage corresponds to the described hike. Consult the hike description to help you decide how to customize the hike for your ability or time constraints.

CONFIGURATION   A description of what the trail might look like from overhead. Trails can be loops, out-and-backs (trails on which you enter and leave along the same path), figure eights, or balloons.

DIFFICULTY   The degree of effort an "average" hiker should expect on a given hike. For simplicity, difficulty is described as "easy," "moderate," or "difficult."

SCENERY   A rating of the overall environs of the hike and what to expect in terms of plant life, wildlife, streams, and historic buildings.

EXPOSURE   A quick check of how much sun you can expect on your shoulders during the hike. Descriptors used include terms such as "shady," "exposed," and "sunny."

TRAFFIC   Indicators of how busy the trail might be on an average day, and if you might be able to find solitude here. Trail traffic, of course, varies from day to day and season to season.

TRAIL SURFACE   A description of the trail surface, be it paved, rocky, dirt, or a mixture of elements.

HIKING TIME   The length of time it takes to hike the trail. A slow but steady hiker will

1

INTRODUCTION

average 2 to 3 miles an hour, depending on the terrain. Most of the estimates in this book reflect a speed of about 2.3 miles per hour.

ACCESS A notation of any fees or permits needed to access the trail (if any) and whether pets and other forms of trail use are permitted.

FACILITIES What to expect in terms of restrooms, phones, water, and other amenities available at the trailhead or nearby.

MAPS Which maps are the best, or easiest, for this hike and where to get them.

SPECIAL COMMENTS These comments cover little extra details that don't fit into any of the above categories. Here you'll find information on trail-hiking options and facts, or tips on how to get the most out of your hike.

DIRECTIONS TO THE TRAIL

The detailed directions will lead you to each trailhead. If you use GPS (Global Positioning System) technology, the provided UTM (Universal Transverse Mercator) coordinates allow you to navigate directly to the trailhead.

TRAIL DESCRIPTIONS

The trail description is the heart of each hike. Here, the author provides a summary of the trail's essence and highlights any special traits the hike offers. Ultimately, the hike description will help you choose which hikes are best for you.

NEARBY ACTIVITIES

Look here for information on nearby activities or points of interest.

▶ WEATHER

Hiking can be done pretty much year-round in Baltimore. But as any resident knows, there can be uncomfortable extremes during both summer and winter. While it's not that unusual to get a balmy 60-degree day in December or even January, it's also not unusual to have temperatures with wind-chill readings below zero. A snowfall for an entire winter can sometimes measure a paltry few inches, while several feet of accumulated snow isn't terribly rare either. Likewise, summer days are usually fine for hiking provided you take plenty of water with you. But the sometimes-oppressive humidity that is part of living in the mid-Atlantic region can make some summer days quite unbearable. With the temperature approaching 100 °F with 90% humidity, it's best to leave the hiking for another day. But generally speaking, these extremes are rare, and you can hike in all seasons. Since the Baltimore area is blessed with pleasant springs and absolutely gorgeous autumns, you may find hiking during these months the most enjoyable, although you may also enjoy the extended light of summer as well as the increased views the leafless winter trees offer.

INTRODUCTION

AVERAGE DAILY TEMPERATURES BY MONTH

	JAN	FEB	MAR	APR	MAY	JUN
HIGH	40°	43°	54°	64°	74°	83°
LOW	23°	25°	34°	42°	52°	61°

	JUL	AUG	SEP	OCT	NOV	DEC
HIGH	87°	85°	78°	67°	56°	45°
LOW	66°	65°	58°	45°	37°	26°

▶ ALLOCATING TIME

I found that the shorter the hike, the more I lingered in one place. Something about staring at the front end of a 10-mile trek naturally pushes you to speed up. That said, take close notice of the elevation maps that accompany each hike. If you see many ups and downs over large altitude changes, you'll obviously need more time. Inevitably you'll finish some of the "hike times" long before or after what I have suggested. Nevertheless, use my suggestions as a guide and leave yourself plenty of time for those moments when you simply feel like stopping and taking it all in.

▶ MAPS

The maps in this book have been produced with great care and, used with the hiking directions, will direct you to the trail and help you stay on course. However, you will find superior detail and valuable information in the United States Geological Survey's 7.5-minute series topographic maps. Topo maps are available online in many locations. The easiest single Web resource is located at **terraserver.microsoft.com.** You can view and print topos of the entire United States there and view aerial photographs of the same area. The downside to topos is that most of them are outdated, having been created 20 to 30 years ago, but they still provide excellent topographic detail.

If you're new to hiking, you might be wondering, "What's a topographic map?" In short, a topo indicates not only linear distance but elevation as well, using contour lines. Contour lines spread across the map like dozens of intricate spiderwebs. Each line represents a particular elevation, and at the base of each topo, a contour's interval designation is given. If the contour interval is 200 feet, then the distance between each contour line is 200 feet. Follow five contour lines up on the same map, and the elevation has increased by 1,000 feet.

Let's assume that the 7.5-minute series topo reads "Contour Interval 40 feet," that the short trail we'll be hiking is 2 inches in length on the map, and that it crosses five contour lines from beginning to end. What do we know? Well, because the linear scale

INTRODUCTION

of this series is 2,000 feet to the inch (roughly 2-3/4 inches representing 1 mile), we know our trail is approximately four-fifths of a mile long (2 inches represent 2,000 feet), but we also know we'll be climbing or descending 200 vertical feet (five contour lines represent 40 feet each) over that distance. And the elevation designations written on occasional contour lines will tell us if we're heading up or down.

In addition to outdoor shops and bike shops, you'll find topos at major universities and some public libraries, where you might try photocopying the ones you need to avoid the cost of buying them. But if you want your own and can't find them locally, visit the United States Geological Survey (USGS) Web site at **topomaps.usgs.gov.** I also recommend **topozone.com** as a resource for topographic maps and software.

GPS TRAILHEAD COORDINATES

To collect accurate map data, each trail was hiked with a handheld GPS unit (Garmin Etrex Venture and/or Garmin Etrex Legend). Data collected was then downloaded and plotted onto a digital USGS topo map. In addition to rendering a highly specific trail outline, this book also includes the GPS coordinates for each trailhead. More accurately known as UTM coordinates, the numbers index a specific point using a grid method. The survey datum used to arrive at the coordinates is NAD27. For readers who own a GPS unit, whether handheld or onboard a vehicle, the Universal Transverse Mercator (UTM) coordinates provided on the first page of each hike may be entered into the GPS unit. Just make sure your GPS unit is set to navigate using the UTM system in conjunction with NAD27 datum. Now you can navigate directly to the trailhead.

Most trailheads, which begin in parking areas, can be reached by car, but some hikes still require a short walk to reach the trailhead from a parking area. In those cases a handheld unit would be necessary to continue the GPS navigation process. That said, however, readers can easily access all trailheads in this book by using the directions given, the overview map, and the trail map, which shows at least one major road leading into the area. But for those who enjoy using the latest GPS technology to navigate, the necessary data has been provided. A brief explanation of the UTM coordinates follows.

UTM COORDINATES—ZONE, EASTING, AND NORTHING

Within the UTM coordinates box on the first page of each hike, there are three numbers labeled zone, easting, and northing. Here is an example from Lake Montebello–Herring Run Park on page 55:

> **UTM Zone (WSG84)   18S**
>
> **Easting   363869**
>
> **Northing   4354855**

The zone number (18) refers to one of the 60 longitudinal zones (vertical) of a

Orange Trail beach

map using the UTM projection. Each zone is 6° wide. The zone letter (S) refers to one of the 20 latitudinal zones (horizontal) that span from 80° South to 84° North.

The easting number (363869) references in meters how far east the point is from the zero value for eastings, which runs north-south through Greenwich, England. Increasing easting coordinates on a topo map or on your GPS screen indicate you are moving east; decreasing easting coordinates indicate you are moving west. Since lines of longitude converge at the poles, they are not parallel as lines of latitude are. This means that the distance between Full Easting Coordinates is 1,000 meters near the equator but becomes smaller as you travel farther north or south; the difference is small enough to be ignored, but only until you reach the polar regions.

In the Northern Hemisphere, the northing number (4354855) references in meters how far you are from the equator. Above the equator, northing coordinates increase by 1,000 meters between each parallel line of latitude (east-west lines). On a topo map or GPS receiver, increasing northing numbers indicate you are traveling north.

In the Southern Hemisphere, the northing number references how far you are from a latitude line that is 10 million meters south of the equator. Below the equator, northing coordinates decrease by 1,000 meters between each line of latitude. On a topo map, decreasing northing coordinates indicate you are traveling south.

▶ TRAIL ETIQUETTE

Whether you're on a city, county, state, or national-park trail, always remember that great care and resources (from nature as well as from your tax dollars) have gone into creating these trails. Treat the trail, wildlife, and fellow hikers with respect.

1. Hike on open trails only. Respect trail and road closures (ask if you're not sure), avoid possible trespassing on private land, and obtain all permits and authorization as required. Also, leave gates as you found them or as marked.

INTRODUCTION

2. Leave only footprints. Be sensitive to the ground beneath you. This also means staying on the existing trail and not blazing any new trails. Be sure to pack out what you pack in. No one likes to see the trash someone else has left behind.

3. Never spook animals. An unannounced approach, a sudden movement, or a loud noise startles most animals. A surprised snake or skunk can be dangerous for you, for others, and to themselves. Give animals extra room and time to adjust to your presence.

4. Plan ahead. Know your equipment, your ability, and the area in which you are hiking—and prepare accordingly. Be self-sufficient at all times; carry necessary supplies for changes in weather or other conditions. A well-executed trip is a satisfaction to you and others.

5. Be courteous to other hikers, bikers, or equestrians you meet on the trails.

▶ WATER

"How much is enough? One bottle? Two? Three?! But think of all that extra weight!" Well, one simple physiological fact should convince you to err on the side of excess when it comes to deciding how much water to pack: A hiker working hard in 90-degree heat needs approximately ten quarts of fluid every day. That's 2.5 gallons—12 large water bottles or 16 small ones. In other words, pack along one or two bottles even for short hikes.

Serious backpackers hit the trail prepared to purify water found along the route. This method, while less dangerous than drinking it untreated, comes with risks. Purifiers with ceramic filters are the safest but also the most expensive. Many hikers pack along the slightly distasteful tetraglycine-hydroperiodide tablets (sold under the names Potable Aqua, Coughlan's, and others).

Probably the most common waterborne "bug" that hikers face is giardia which may not hit until one to four weeks after ingestion. It will have you passing noxious rotten-egg gas, vomiting, shivering with chills, and living in the bathroom. Other parasites to worry about include *E. coli* and *Cryptosporidium,* both of which are harder to kill than giardia.

For most people, the pleasures of hiking make carrying water a relatively minor price to pay to remain healthy. If you're tempted to drink "found water," do so only if you understand the risks involved. Better yet, hydrate prior to your hike, carry (and drink) 6 ounces of water for every mile you plan to hike, and hydrate after the hike.

▶ FIRST-AID KIT

A typical first-aid kit may contain more items than you might think necessary. These are just the basics:

INTRODUCTION

Ace bandages or Spenco joint wraps

Antibiotic ointment (Neosporin or the generic equivalent)

Aspirin or acetaminophen

Band-Aids

Benadryl or the generic antihistamine equivalent diphenhydramine (in case of allergic reactions)

Butterfly-closure bandages

Epinephrine in a prefilled syringe (for people known to have severe allergic reactions to such things as bee stings)

Gauze (one roll)

Gauze compress pads (a half dozen 4 × 4-inch pads)

Hydrogen peroxide or iodine

Insect repellent

Matches or pocket lighter

Moleskin/Spenco "Second Skin"

Snakebite kit

Sunscreen

Water-purification tablets or water filter (for longer hikes)

Whistle (it's more effective in signaling rescuers than your voice)

▶ SNAKES

Generally speaking, snakes are not a concern in Baltimore, and the prospect of being bitten should never deter a hiker in this area. Maryland has only two native poisonous snakes: northern copperheads, which you may see in Baltimore, and timber rattlers, which live in the western, mountainous part of the state. Although the chances of being bitten by a snake on one of the hikes described in this book are slim to none, take proper caution. If you see a snake and it has an hour glass-shaped head, give it a wide berth.

▶ TICKS

All hikers should be concerned about ticks, especially when hiking along trails that traverse areas of brush and high grass, the insect's favorite hangouts. Your best protection (aside from applying a repellent that contains Deet, which is fairly toxic stuff) is to be vigilant: Check yourself frequently, and look hard. Often the smaller the tick, the greater the chance for subsequent serious health problems. Tiny deer ticks (black-legged ticks), for example, carry Lyme disease; if you find a tick attached to your skin, gently remove it with tweezers, taking care to pull it off gently so the mouth part does not break off and remain attached. Always shower after a hike to wash off any ticks you might not have caught earlier, and check your hair thoroughly with your fingers. (It's a good idea to wear a hat while hiking to prevent ticks from falling from above and burrowing into your scalp.)

In general, ticks pose a major threat only during the warmest months of summer, but an unseasonably mild spring and/or warm autumn can mean a solid six or seven months of "tick season." So do take precautionary measures, but don't let ticks keep you inside. On all of the many hikes and many hours I spent on the trail compiling this book, no tick managed to pierce my skin.

7

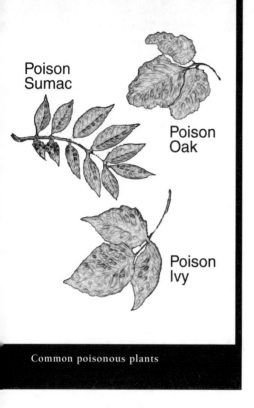

Poison Sumac

Poison Oak

Poison Ivy

Common poisonous plants

I want to note that Lyme disease tends to be overdiagnosed, but if you see a bull's-eye rash radiating from a tender red spot, see a doctor right away. If you experience flu-like symptoms (intense malaise, fever, chills, and a headache) a day or two after hiking, look very hard for the telltale bull's-eye rash, and see a doctor to alleviate any concerns.

▶ POISON IVY

The old maxim for poison ivy holds true: "Leaves of three, let it be." Poison sumac, however, can contain anywhere from 7 to 13 leaves. Since I am extremely allergic to poison ivy, I always take the following precautions: I do not scratch anything under any circumstances; if poison ivy is sitting on the skin, scratching and then touching skin anywhere else is the surest way of spreading it. Also, in summer I pull up my socks as far as they will go; no, this doesn't look cool, but it's worth it! Third, I always carry alcohol-based moist towelettes, and at the end of the hike, I rub my legs gently with the towelettes to stave off infection until I can get home and shower. (Note: It is very important that these moist towelettes contain alcohol. If they contain just soap, wiping with them will only move the poison ivy oil, urushiol, around, increasing the risk of infection.) Always shower to get rid of any clinging poison ivy oils.

▶ MOSQUITOES

The Asian Tiger mosquito, which spreads the West Nile virus, has been seen in Maryland, especially in places with lots of water, including urban areas. Unfortunately, Baltimore has both (part of its charm, after all).

Protect yourself against mosquito bites by applying an effective repellent. Since many repellents contain toxins, I prefer to use Avon Skin-So-Soft. It has a pleasing smell, and the sweet fragrance repels mosquitoes pretty effectively. Even though West Nile has understandably grabbed headlines in the last few years, your chances of contracting it are extraordinarily slim, and even if you do contract it, a reasonably healthy person who receives medical treatment would be able to stave off the disease's most damaging effects.

▶ HIKING WITH CHILDREN

No one is too young for a hike in the woods or through a city park. Be careful, though. Flat, short trails are best with an infant. Toddlers who have not quite mastered walking can still tag along, riding on an adult's back in a child carrier. Use common sense to judge a child's

INTRODUCTION

capacity to hike a particular trail, and always rely on the possibility that the child will tire quickly and need to be carried.

When packing for the hike, remember the child's needs as well as your own. Make sure children are adequately clothed for the weather, have proper shoes, and are protected from the sun with sunscreen. Kids dehydrate quickly, so make sure you have plenty of fluid for everyone.

A list of Hikes Good for Children is provided in the "Hiking Recommendations" section on page XVIII. Finally, when hiking with children, remember that the trip will be a compromise—a child's energy and enthusiasm alternate between bursts of speed and long stops to examine snails, sticks, dirt, and other attractions.

ANNE ARUNDEL COUNTY

BALTIMORE AND ANNAPOLIS (B&A) TRAIL

KEY AT-A-GLANCE INFORMATION

LENGTH: 12.7 miles (13.3 miles for the complete trail)

CONFIGURATION: One way

DIFFICULTY: Moderate to strenuous only because of length

SCENERY: Mixed hardwoods, railroading structures, pocket wetlands

EXPOSURE: Mostly sunny

TRAFFIC: Heavy

TRAIL SURFACE: Asphalt

HIKING TIME: 4–4.5 hours

ACCESS: Sunrise to sunset

MAPS: USGS Relay, Curtis Bay, Round Bay, Gibson Island. A printable map with directions to each of the parking areas can be found online at **dnr.state.md.us/ greenways/b&a_trail.html.**

FACILITIES: Found all along the trail in nearby businesses

SPECIAL COMMENTS: The hike described here begins at the Glen Burnie Parking Area and moves south, totaling 12.7 miles. An additional 0.6 miles of trail heads north, terminating at Baltimore-Annapolis Boulevard. Several parking areas along the way make shortening the hike easy. Additionally, hikers coming from the south would find it most logical to begin in Annapolis, arguably the more pleasant portion of the trail.

Baltimore and Annapolis (B&A) Trail

UTM Zone (WGS84)   18S

Easting   359698

Northing   4336083

IN BRIEF

The B&A Trail serves as Anne Arundel's linear island in the most congested part of the county. This park provides a haven for bikers, strollers, and hikers.

DESCRIPTION

The B&A Trail, a rails-to-trails park that is part of the East Coast Greenway, follows the old Baltimore and Annapolis Railroad from Glen Burnie in the north (not quite Baltimore) to Annapolis in the south. The 115-acre park runs as a 10-foot-wide paved path that follows a more or less straight line along Ritchie Highway and the more twisty Baltimore-Annapolis Boulevard to MD 50 heading into Annapolis. It's interesting to note that the boulevard and the highway, built to accommodate the increased automobile traffic, hastened the end of the short line railroad. Nowadays, Baltimore-Annapolis Boulevard has been increasingly displaced by Interstate 97, the Baltimore–Annapolis Expressway, built to connect Maryland's capital with its largest city. So the railroad corridor, once rendered obsolete, has now become popular again, despite the presence of the boulevard, the highway, and the interstate.

Beginning in the north at Glen Burnie, the trail remains fairly urban, with businesses, residences, roads, and parking lots never too far away. From this vantage, it's easy to believe an oft-quoted statistic about the trail: one third of

DIRECTIONS

Take I-695 to I-97 south to Exit 15, Aviation Boulevard/Dorsey Road east to Dorsey Road. Take the first right onto MD 648, Baltimore-Annapolis Boulevard. Cross Crain Highway, and take a right at the "Free Parking" sign in the Glen Burnie Town Center. The trail starts just north of the parking garage.

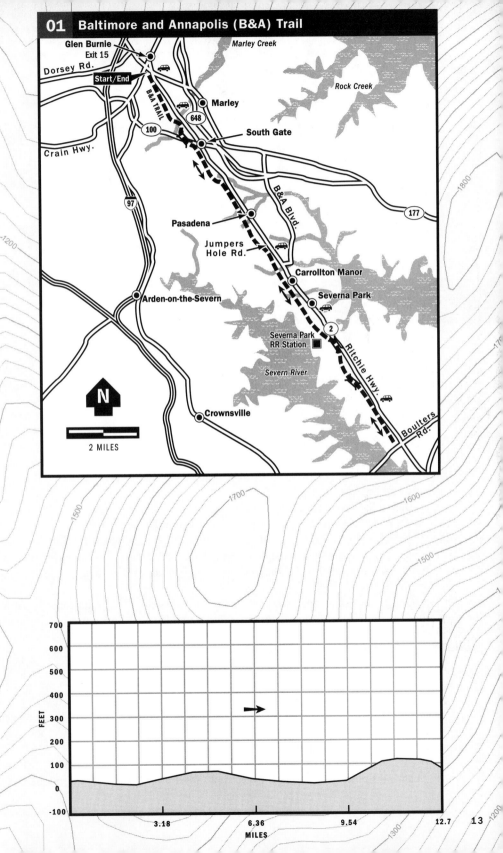

Glen Burnie
Exit 15
Dorsey Rd.
Start/End

Marley Creek

Rock Creek

Marley

648

100

B&A Trail

South Gate

Crain Hwy.

97

B&A Blvd.

177

Pasadena

Jumpers
Hole Rd.

Carrollton Manor

Severna Park

Arden-on-the-Severn

2

Severna Park
RR Station

Ritchie Hwy.

Severn River

N

Crownsville

2 MILES

Boulters
Rd.

1800

1200

1300

1500

1700

1600

1500

1500

1300

1200

700

600

500

400

300

200

100

0

-100

FEET

3.18

6.36

9.54

12.7

MILES

13

Trailside ducks

Anne Arundel County's more than 400,000 residents live within a mile of it. The hike begins behind the parking garage at the swing set and benches. You will also find a water fountain here.

At 1 mile, you'll see an interesting solar sculpture with explanatory signs about the sun. Signs for each of the planets, spaced out proportionately along the trail, correspond to their location and comparative distance from the sun. Beyond the solar sculpture, a wooded buffer turns a bit marshy, with some cattails, a reminder of the area's dominant ecozone; the nearby Severn and Magothy rivers meander their separate ways to the Chesapeake.

After 1.4 miles you'll see a nice wooded stream valley full of honeysuckle to the left. You will come to the first of several old railroad bridges soon after, this one crossing Marley Creek in a forest full of maple, hickory, and oak. Wildflowers line the edge of the trail. Marley Station Mall soon appears on the left, very convenient if you need to make a quick pit stop. (The abundant parking here also makes it a popular access point for the B&A.)

At 2.2 miles cross over MD 100. Once you cross the bridge, the trail becomes more pleasant and wooded, heading to another parking area on Jumpers Hole Road at 3 miles. A gazebo with benches, just beyond Jumpers Hole, begins a nice stretch with flower plantings on both sides of the trail, which leads to a marsh full of ducks and sunning turtles, clearly the nicest spot thus far.

At 4.2 miles cross East-West Boulevard on a railroad bridge and enter a wooded residential neighborhood. A third parking area at Earleigh Heights, at 5 miles, provides a good area to rest; you'll see several places to eat just off the trail. You'll come to a pond and a Ranger Station just on the other side of Earleigh Heights. You can check your position on the trail map at the station.

This area feels a bit more aquatic, and in summer you'll see dragonflies shuttling back and forth over the trail. Every now and again, you'll cross a tiny one-lane road, but for the next few miles the trail is nicely wooded and semi-isolated. You will pass another series of wildflower plantings—lilies, daffodils, petunias, peonies, coneflowers—at 7 miles. You'll also see the old Severna Park Railroad Station, one of the few intact structures left from the railroad. You will have probably noticed several switch boxes and a powerhouse along the trail as well, but the Severna Park Station (aside from the Ranger Station at Earleigh Heights) is the most stark reminder of this corridor's earlier incarnation. Most stations along the route amounted to nothing more than small platforms, which are indicated along the trail by rectangular outlines in stone along with a small sign giving the station's name.

You will cross another wooden railroad bridge at 7.6 miles, and you'll come to a trails maintenance shop at 8.4 miles. Just beyond, to the left, is the only spot along the trail where you can still see railroad tracks (about 20 feet). By 9 miles, you can hear Baltimore-Annapolis Boulevard to the left, but a big wooded gully sits between you and the road. To the right lies a thickly wooded forest of oak, poplar, and maple, and dense stands of bamboo soon line the trail.

As you cross the steel railroad bridge at 9.5 miles, look to the left for a series of wire-contained rocks that form a drainage system. A nice rural scene of rolling hills with horses, a short distance on the right, provides a quick view of what the area looked like when the trains still came through. The Arnold Parking Area, at 10.9 miles, marks the beginning of a very pleasant couple of miles with nice buffers (some extended a couple hundred feet) between the road to the left and neighborhoods to the right. The trail ends at Boulters Road; a sign points to MD 50 to the left, where you'll find the Annapolis parking area. (If you've hiked the trail in reverse, beginning at Annapolis, head up Boulters Road east from the parking area and you'll very quickly reach the trail).

▶ NEARBY ACTIVITIES

Take your pick! The location and configuration of the B&A Trail offer you a variety of choices: a historic capital (Annapolis, just across the bridge on MD 50 east), a big city (Baltimore's Inner Harbor just a few miles north of the trail's end in Glen Burnie), town centers (Glen Burnie, Severna Park, Pasadena, and Arnold), more hiking (BWI Trail, see page 16), and shopping (Marley Station Mall as well as numerous establishments along the trail).

BWI TRAIL

KEY AT-A-GLANCE INFORMATION

LENGTH: 11.6 miles

CONFIGURATION: Loop

DIFFICULTY: Moderate because of length

SCENERY: BWI airport, pines, wetlands

EXPOSURE: Mostly sunny

TRAFFIC: Moderate to heavy (mostly bike, but lots of walkers too)

TRAIL SURFACE: Asphalt, wooden boardwalk

HIKING TIME: 3.5–4 hours

ACCESS: Open; use caution crossing roads after dark

MAPS: USGS Relay; maps online at **dnr. state.md.us/greenways/bwi_trail.html** and **www.bwiairport.com/7arndtwn/ in_trl.shtml**

FACILITIES: None on the trail, but food is available at BWI Plaza and bathrooms and water at various airport and transportation buildings along route.

SPECIAL COMMENTS: As suggested below, the hike distance and configuration can be altered by taking the light rail. Directions for the hike described here are to the Linthicum Light Rail station. To go to the BWI station, take I-195 toward the airport, and exit at Aviation Boulevard (MD 170, Exit 1) east and follow the signs to Light Rail. Light Rail operation hours: Monday–Friday, 6 a.m.–11 p.m.; Saturday, 7 a.m.–11 p.m.; Sundays and holidays, 11 a.m.–7 p.m.

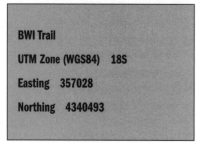

BWI Trail

UTM Zone (WGS84)   18S

Easting   357028

Northing   4340493

▶ IN BRIEF

Hiking at an airport? It's a lot more pleasant than it sounds. Marvel at the woods and wetlands that still coexist with the airport and be awed by jets flying just above your head.

▶ DESCRIPTION

One caveat: the BWI Trail is an absolute must for aviation aficionados, but it's not for those who crave the solitude of a walk in the woods. Even if you count yourself in that latter group, the BWI Trail is worth a go; it's not hard to find something to like along its well-used route.

Starting across from the Linthicum Light Rail station, take the asphalt path adjacent to the tracks as it parallels a small buffer of woods to the right with a residential neighborhood beyond. You'll quickly come to two small streets: Shipley Road at 900 feet and Music Lane at 0.2 miles. Beyond that the trail is simply the sidewalk that runs along Hammonds Ferry Road. Cross over Andover Road, and pick up the asphalt path on the other side at just under half a mile. Go left and continue to Camp Meade Road. Ignore the signs pointing to the airport to the right, and follow the "bike route" signs straight ahead over Camp Meade. At just under 0.7 miles, cross over the light rail tracks and swing around into a little wooded section. There's a parking area for the airport beyond a small pond with cattails and (usually) Canada geese. It's a fairly nice stretch of woods here, and it makes up for the initial "sub-urbanity."

▶ DIRECTIONS

Take I-695 to Exit 6 (Camp Meade Road south); take the second right (Maple Road), and follow Maple to the first light. Turn left onto Hammonds Ferry Road, and then turn left onto Oakdale Road. The trail begins at the end of Oakdale Road across from the Linthicum Light Rail station.

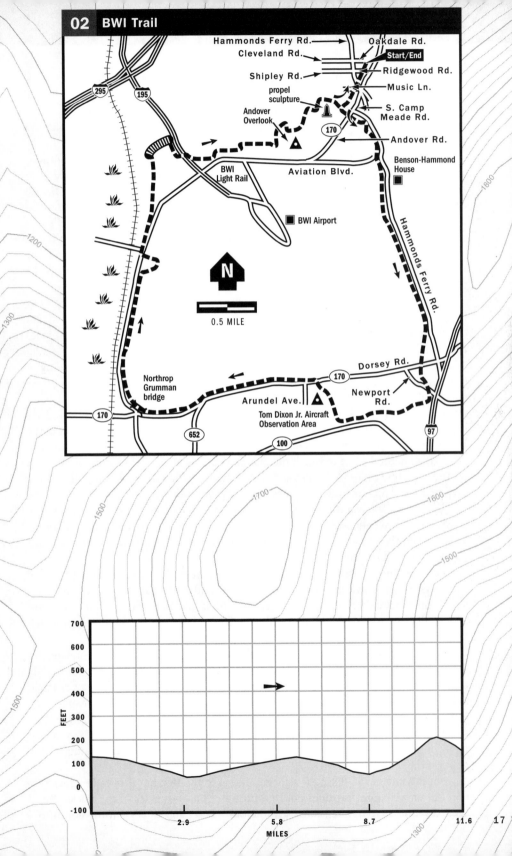

Hammonds Ferry Rd.
Oakdale Rd.
Cleveland Rd.
Start/End
Shipley Rd.
Ridgewood Rd.
Music Ln.
propel sculpture
S. Camp Meade Rd.
Andover Overlook
170
Andover Rd.
Benson-Hammond House
BWI Light Rail
Aviation Blvd.
Hammonds Ferry Rd.
BWI Airport
295
195

N

0.5 MILE

Northrop Grumman bridge
Dorsey Rd.
170
Newport Rd.
170
Arundel Ave.
Tom Dixon Jr. Aircraft Observation Area
652
100
97

FEET
700
600
500
400
300
200
100
0
-100

2.9   5.8   8.7   11.6

MILES

About 1 mile later, cross Aviation Boulevard, and continue to the Benson-Hammond House, home of the Anne Arundel County Historical Society. Built in the 1830s and the only structure left from the farming period of a post-colonial settlement, the house now serves as a farm museum. A short post in front of the museum reads "East Coast Greenway."

At 1.25 miles stands a grove of pines, the dominant trees around the airport. You will also see cattails, a reminder that this is marshy Chesapeake watershed area. At 1.3 miles, cross a little driveway that parallels Aviation Boulevard and heads into the BWI General Aviation Facility, and continue to the Maryland Aviation Administration at 1.8 miles. The area becomes very boggy, and you'll see more cattails and marshland. You'll come to Dorsey Road at 2.9 miles and Newport Road at just under 3.3 miles. Going straight here takes you to the B&A Trail (see page 12); to stay on the BWI, go right toward the sign reading "BWI Overlook." You'll soon enter arguably the nicest stretch of the trail.

Immediately to the left is busy Aviation Boulevard, but you'll quickly turn away from the road and head into the woods, where you'll see red oaks, tulip poplars, and of course the dominant pines. Even though you're deep within the woods, planes roar overhead, maybe only a couple hundred feet or so above the ground. It's an amazing dichotomy—serene woods shattered by screaming jet engines, retreating to serenity again, and on and on. In all, this wooded stretch lasts 0.7 miles. On the other end of it, at 4.2 miles, a field opens to the right; this makes a great spot to sit and watch the planes—if you're awed by jets, don't pass up this opportunity. They come roaring over the tree line in descent and zoom past, barely a hundred feet in the air. Only air traffic controllers and runway directors get a better view. In addition to this perfect natural place to watch the planes, you may want to stop at the Tom Dixon Jr. Aircraft Observation Area just ahead at 4.2 miles; the trail runs to the left of the parking area, which includes benches and a playground.

At 4.4 miles you'll reach Dorsey Road, which parallels the trail. When you reach Arundel Avenue at 4.7 miles, cross over Dorsey Road and go left. You'll pass a VFW hall on the left at 5.25 miles. Just beyond is the BWI Plaza if you need a quick pit stop for food or drink.

Continuing on, the trail turns into one of many boardwalks; these wooden walkways denote environmentally sensitive wetland sections. At just past 6 miles, you'll come to another nice wooded area away from the roads where again you'll have a good view of planes taking off, but they're fairly high at this point. Pass through a large pine grove, and then cross a 900-foot boardwalk at 6.7 miles.

At 7.2 miles you'll come to the metal "Car Rental Return" sign; if you hang out for a moment, a plane will come roaring over the hill to your right—you'll be directly under it and can see its belly from a pretty close distance. At the top of the hill at 7.6 miles, head left at the Rental Car Return and Maryland Department of Transportation (MDOT) headquarters sign. On the bridge, as you go over MD 170, look for the bicycle icon to the right; when you see it, head down the ramp, passing thick woods—again, mostly pine—to the left. You'll see the Northrop Grumman building to the right on the other side of MD 170.

At 8.2 miles, you'll see the light rail tracks to the left, but they're in a nice section full of sycamore and tulip poplar with water on both sides of the tracks. You'll soon see a big marsh, often filled with herons, geese, and ducks, on the left. At 8.7

miles, you'll come to a sign pointing to Amtrak/MARC parking in front of the Maryland Aviation Administration Kauffman Building; go right across the street to a long wooden boardwalk. Stop for a moment on the boardwalk—this is one of the nicest spots on the trail. Herons often wade here, the vegetation is abundant and aquatic, and the marsh itself is ringed with pines.

When you climb the big ramp over I-195 at 9 miles, you'll have a decent view of the entire airport to the right; but the view is not all mechanical—a wildflower meadow sits to the right at 9.2 miles. The trail splits at 9.4 miles; head left in the direction of the sign pointing toward Andover Park (heading right will take you on a half-mile spur that includes a pedestrian bridge over MD 170, but it ends at the MDOT headquarters). At Andover Park you'll find a pasture observation area and an equestrian park, as well as the continuation of the loop that will take you back to the Linthicum Light Rail station.

At 9.7 miles, cross over two small sections of roadway (Elm and Elkridge Landing roads). Once on the other side, you'll see the BWI Light Rail station. There's parking here too, and you can alter the hike length and configuration by parking here instead of at the Linthicum station. Or you can park at one station, walk to the other, and ride the light rail back.

Continuing on the trail, at 10 miles you'll come to an open area that runs up a hill and into a field, where you'll see some old farm equipment, a reminder of what the area looked like before the airport was built. From the late 18th century until 1947, when construction began on BWI (née "Friendship International Airport"), farmers cultivated the land for tobacco and grains as well as fruits and vegetables. At the Andover Overlook at the top of the hill, you can see the layout of the entire airport—runways, arriving and departing planes, and control towers. Take time to rest on the benches here; sitting in this pastoral setting and looking off into the distance gives a nice feeling of being removed from the hectic everyday world.

Just beyond you'll come to the Andover equestrian area—not surprisingly, you'll see horses all over the field in front of a farmhouse. Just off the trail you'll see another jarring juxtaposition—the "propel" sculpture, which is part of the Maryland Millennium Legacy Trail Art Project. The sculpture, made of stainless steel, weighs more than a ton, and its curves reflect the uniqueness of the area. Within the sculpture you can see shapes reminiscent of rolling fields, clouds, waterways, and industry (such as a plane propeller).

Follow the asphalt path until it turns into a sidewalk in front of Lindale Middle School at 10.8 miles; at 11 miles you'll reach Hammonds Ferry Road. Take a left; you've now made a complete loop back to the sidewalk where you entered the trail.

▶ NEARBY ACTIVITIES

The 1830s Benson-Hammond House, on the first part of the BWI Trail, is open Thursday through Saturday from 11 a.m. to 3 p.m.; phone (410) 768-9518.

For a more nature-oriented hike that will take you through habitat varying from marsh to mature forest, head to the Severn Run Environmental Area. Follow I-97 south to Benfield Boulevard west (Exit 10), and take the first left onto Najoles Drive and then the first right onto Dicus Mill Road. A well-defined trail heads out from Dicus Mill, where it crosses over the Severn Run. You can fish for perch, bass, and trout from this point. The trail is open year-round from dawn to dusk.

DOWNS MEMORIAL PARK

ℹ️ KEY AT-A-GLANCE INFORMATION

LENGTH: 3.8 miles

CONFIGURATION: Jagged loop

DIFFICULTY: Easy

SCENERY: Chesapeake Bay, beach, pond, mature trees

EXPOSURE: Slightly more shade than not

TRAFFIC: Light on trails, moderate to heavy at overlooks and pavilions

TRAIL SURFACE: Mostly asphalt, some dirt, some beach

HIKING TIME: 2 hours with linger time on the beach

ACCESS: Cost is $5 per vehicle; annual and senior citizen lifetime passes can be purchased. Park hours are 9 a.m.–dusk year-round. The visitor center is open Monday and Wednesday–Friday, 9 a.m.–4 p.m.; 11 a.m.–3 p.m. on weekends. The park and all of its facilities are closed on Tuesday; holiday hours vary.

MAPS: USGS Gibson Island; trail maps at Gate House and Information Center

FACILITIES: Restrooms, water, playground, gazebos, picnic, ball fields

SPECIAL COMMENTS: No alcohol, no swimming, and dogs must be leashed except in designated areas. For more information call (410) 222-6230 or visit www.aacpl.net/rp.

Downs Memorial Park

UTM Zone (WGS84)   18S

Easting   375547

Northing   4329815

▶ IN BRIEF

Enjoy a heady combination of mature forest, boggy marshland, self-guided nature trails, golden sand beach, and stunning water views.

▶ DESCRIPTION

This land, now owned by the Anne Arundel County Department of Parks and Recreation, comes well stocked not only in natural beauty but also in human history. Downs Memorial stands on Bodkin Neck, a peninsula at the confluence of the Patapsco River and Chesapeake Bay. Deeds to its earliest settlement date back to 1670 and include Charles Carroll, a signer of the Declaration of Independence, among its initial landowners.

After paying the entrance fee (which is well worth it when you see how incredibly well maintained this park is), immediately turn right into the first parking area. You'll find two trailheads, one closest to where you've pulled in and the other on the far end of the parking area; take the one closest to the entrance. It begins in the woods under the overhanging sign that reads ECO TRAIL–SELF GUIDED NATURE TRAIL.

This stand of hardwoods contains oak, poplar, beech, birch, sycamore, holly, gum, and sassafras. The trail, which is packed dirt and wide, has no blazes, but you'll find it very easy to follow. At 180 feet, you'll see a bench and little sign suggesting that hikers stop and listen to the sounds of the forest. You'll find interpretive signs

▶ DIRECTIONS

Take I-695 to I-97 south. Leave I-97 at Exit 14, and take MD 100 east to Mountain Road East. When Mountain Road veers off to the right, stay straight on Pinehurst Road, and take a right into the park entrance at Chesapeake Bay Drive. The gatehouse will be straight ahead.

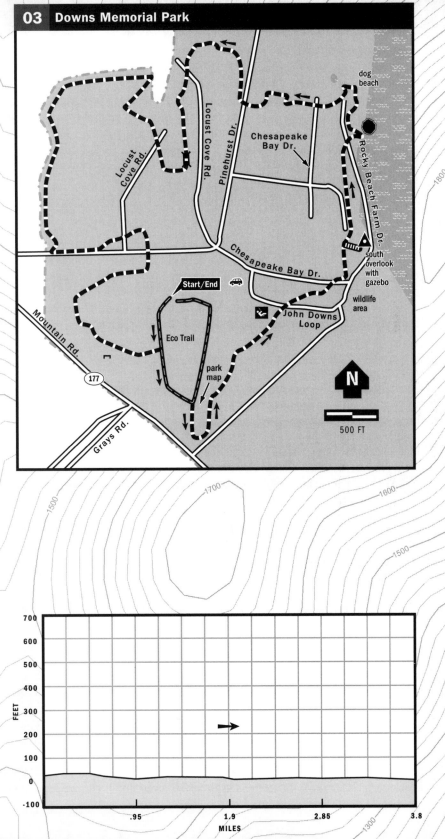

such as this one all along the Eco Trail; they describe the bark, trees, moss, leaves, insects, and animals you'll see as you hike.

At 440 feet, you'll come to a map that, like all others in the park, has a "you are here" marker to help you keep your bearings. The trail splits here; go to the right. You're still on the Eco Trail, and accordingly you'll see more signs; the next one gives a rundown of Maryland's official state tree (white oak), flower (black-eyed Susan), dog (Chesapeake Bay retriever), bird (Baltimore oriole), insect (Baltimore checker spot butterfly), and fish (rockfish).

You'll soon reach an unpaved sand trail; follow it to the asphalt perimeter trail, and take a left. You're now off the Eco Trail, but you'll finish the portion you've skipped toward the end of the hike. On the perimeter trail, which is close to Pine-hurst Drive, the traffic can be loud; but very soon you'll leave the road behind and follow the trail deeper into the thick woods. Look closely through the dense tree cover to see a chain-link fence that delineates the park boundary. The woods beyond the fence give the trail a remote, woodsy feel.

In a half mile, the perimeter trail links with the senior trail, which is paved and leads to the left; keep going straight, and you'll soon pass an open play area with a basketball court on the left. The trail opens up as you pass a soccer field. To the left is a wildlife area and to the right an exercise pavilion and bulletin board with illus-trations depicting proper stretching techniques.

You'll pass through another stand of trees before the view opens up again and the south overlook appears. Walk up the wooden boardwalk toward a gazebo that once belonged to H. R. Mayo Thom, a wealthy Baltimorean; his family's estate included this area from 1913 through 1937. The gazebo provides a quintessential Maryland view: open waters as far as the eye can see (Chesapeake Bay is the largest estuary in the United States and boasts the world's largest crop of clams and oysters). If you have some quarters with you, operate the binoculars and view the osprey plat-form out in the water; you'll also see an oyster nursery below and an aviary and rap-tor pen inside the buildings behind you. Next to the raptor pen you'll find "mother's garden," where there's a stone bench built in 1915. If you sit on it and make a wish, the wish supposedly comes true.

When you've had your fill of the expansive vista and inhaled deeply, head down from the overlook and continue toward the beach, where you'll walk among aquatic plants, skimmers, kingfishers, and gulls. You're not allowed to swim, but feel free to kick off your hiking boots and feel the soft golden sand under your feet while you delight in the soothing scene: birds wheeling in the air, water lapping against the rocks, smooth stone and bleached driftwood on the beach. The seemingly endless view gives you every reason to believe you're at the ocean. Dry off your feet and put on your boots while sitting on a large rock before you continue the hike.

At the big jumble of rocks, head left toward the paved trail on the other side. Cut in on the dirt path, and follow it to a tiny spit of sand and a series of rocks where you can walk out into the water a few feet so that there's nothing in front of you but the waters of the bay lapping on both sides of the rocks. You can go even farther, but I don't recommend it—these rocks are exposed only occasionally, and they're slippery.

At 1.1 mile, you'll see a volleyball net to your left. Head right toward the wood blocks, which are set up as seats, and the north overlook. If you were standing here in 1822, you'd see workmen building Bodkin Island Lighthouse, which stayed in use until 1855. The tower has since crumbled and remains only as a "navigational hazard" on present day maps.

Just beyond the north overlook you'll find a beach where dogs can roam off leash. Heading back to the paved path from the dog beach, you'll see an unpaved trail immediately to the right; it heads through the woods and takes you to a big, scummy, stagnant pond. Walk under the wooden boardwalk, and then go up for a view of the entire pond. You'll most likely see a few frogs and snakes, none of them poisonous. Next, head back up the wooden ramp to the paved perimeter trail, where you'll see picnic benches to the left. Stay to the right, and at 1.25 miles, you'll come to bathroom facilities and a water fountain with pavilions and volleyball nets just beyond.

At 1.4 miles, head uphill to a wide footbridge, where you'll cross over Pinehurst Drive; pick up the trail on the other side. Side trails to the left will take you to tennis, basketball, and handball courts, but keep going straight, cutting back into the woods away from all the facilities. On either side of the trail, you'll see tall, straight oaks as well as holly trees. You'll come to one more stand of picnic benches and open play areas before you hit a valley of marshy aquatic plants to the right. Here, at 1.8 miles, you'll cross over the southern tip of Locust Cove and head into a Natural Area. Head right toward the trail split; this puts you deep into the Natural Area and parallels Locust Cove on the right. Thick woods, mostly pines and oaks, dominate this area, and spongy, green moss lines both sides of the trail. Moss also fills the occasional cracks where roots have broken through the pavement.

At 2.1 miles, take a little gravel path off the main trail. It takes you close to the water and then loops back to the paved perimeter trail. You'll soon come to the park boundary and see a few private houses pop into view through the woods on the right. In this increasingly boggy and marshy area, clumps of moss and trees with lichen-covered trunks attest to how low the elevation is here; you're barely above sea level. Invariably, both sides of the trail will be muddy, and you'll appreciate the fact that the trail is a bit raised in this section.

At 2.7 miles, the trail crosses over Pinehurst Drive. If you're tired, you can go to your car just ahead, but to continue the hike, head right when you see the gatehouse. The perimeter trail parallels first Pinehurst Drive and then Mountain Road. Cut along an unnamed, unpaved trail at 2.9 miles to stay deeper in the woods and lose the sound of the occasional car going by (though it's not terribly busy). You'll see three separate unpaved trails; take the one in the middle. It can be easy to lose, but as long as you continue in more or less a straight line, you'll link back up with the perimeter trail soon enough; even if you do stray off the path, you won't need to bushwhack—the vegetation is relatively sparse.

Head left on the perimeter trail, and at 3 miles, you'll see a bench on the left and an unpaved trail behind it immediately to the right; follow it to a V. Take the right side; it will allow you to link up with the Eco Trail where you first began. Even though you've already been on this section, you're now heading in the opposite direction, and you'll soon link up with the section you skipped originally. At 3.2 miles, take a left where the trail splits, and finish hiking the Eco Trail. About midway down this section, you'll be walking on an old farm road once traversed by horses and carriages and later used by farmers and lumberjacks.

You'll see rare chestnut trees as well as the ubiquitous oaks and hickories on this section of the trail. At 3.4 miles, you'll come to Chesapeake Bay Drive; take a left to return to the other side of the parking area from where you began the hike.

▶ NEARBY ACTIVITIES

Plenty of opportunities exist for fishing or picnicking with the whole family at one of the many pavilions inside the park. Check out the Victorian-style garden behind the south overlook as well as the nearby raptor pen and aviary. Children may be interested in the Rocky Beach Farm Youth Group Camping Area; pick up a brochure at the visitor center. If you haven't had your fill of bay view parks, visit nearby Fort Smallwood Park; take Mountain Road west to Hog Neck Road north to Fort Smallwood Road east.

KINDER FARM PARK

▶ **IN BRIEF**

You can view varied birdlife in the meadows and trees that sit between the paved perimeter trail and the many dirt and sand connector trails.

▶ **DESCRIPTION**

The perimeter trail, which is mostly paved asphalt, offers a few opportunities for "off-road" hiking, but it begins with asphalt bordered by vegetable and flower gardens planted and maintained by apprentice gardeners. Butterflies shuttle busily over the 20-by-30-foot garden plots, which are rented to the public and are open from mid-March to late November.

The trail splits just after 200 feet, at the playground; go to the right. You will see goldenrod and sassafras off the path on the right, and you can watch hawks wheel overhead. You will come to stables and horses on the right at 0.3 miles as well as a large marsh full of cattails, milkweed, poppy, frogs, crickets, and grasshoppers. I was lucky enough to spot a gray heron there as well. At just under 0.4 miles, turn right onto the East-West Boulevard Trail. You'll find a group camping area and horse trail to the right and a wooded area thick with oak and tulip poplar on the left. Pines also abound at 0.5 miles.

Just ahead, the trail swings around to the left and heads toward the north entrance of the

▶ **DIRECTIONS**

Take I-695 to I-97 south (Annapolis–Bay Bridge) to Exit 14A (MD 100 east to Gibson Island). Take Exit 16A, MD 2 south toward Pasadena; stay in the far right lane, and take a right at the first light—Jumpers Hole Road. Proceed 2.1 miles to the park entrance on the right at Kinder Farm Park Road; drive past the gatehouse to the parking, which is straight ahead. The trail starts to the right of the parking area between the community garden and the disc golf course.

▶ **KEY AT-A-GLANCE INFORMATION**

LENGTH: 2.9 miles

CONFIGURATION: Loop

DIFFICULTY: Easy

SCENERY: Pond, mixed hardwoods, meadow

EXPOSURE: More sun than shade

TRAFFIC: Moderate

TRAIL SURFACE: Asphalt, sand, grass, rock, and packed dirt

HIKING TIME: 1 hour

ACCESS: Open every day but Tuesday, 7 a.m. to dusk

MAPS: USGS Round Bay, trail maps at gatehouse, printable map online at **www.kinderfarmpark.org/directions/kinderdis.pdf**

FACILITIES: Bathrooms and concessions at park office, open Monday, Wednesday, Thursday, and Friday, 9 a.m.–4 p.m., and Saturday and Sunday, 10 a.m..–3 p.m.; ball fields, tot lot

SPECIAL COMMENTS: Kinder Farm Park charges a $5 per day use fee, but you can park free at the tot lot. To reach the tot lot, go past the park entrance on Jumpers Hole Road, and turn right at Kinder Road; the parking area is 0.3 miles on the right.

Kinder Farm Park

UTM Zone (WGS84)   18S

Easting   363311

Northing   4329103

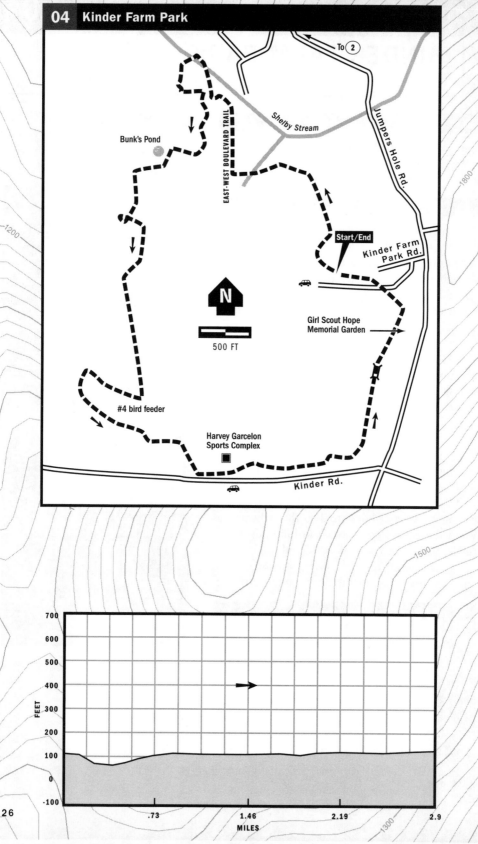

To (2)

Shelby Stream

Jumpers Hole Rd.

EAST-WEST BOULEVARD TRAIL

Bunk's Pond

Start/End

Kinder Farm
Park Rd.

N

500 FT

Girl Scout Hope
Memorial Garden

#4 bird feeder

Harvey Garcelon
Sports Complex

Kinder Rd.

FEET

700
600
500
400
300
200
100
0
-100

.73   1.46   2.19   2.9
MILES

Bunk's Pond

park and East-West Boulevard; instead of following it, take a left into the cut where the foliage is cleared. You'll pass a birdhouse with a #42 on it. This section is full of thickets of greenbrier, recognizable by their bluish-black berries. When you come to another birdhouse and paved asphalt again, take a quick right into the woods on the sand-and-cedar chip trail. Birch trees dominate this thickly wooded, shaded section of the trail. You'll find serviceberry, holly, and walnut trees here.

At just under a mile, you'll come to a T-intersection. Take a right; the trail becomes fine white sand and leads to a stand of evergreens—pines and red cedars— with the catch-and-release Bunk's Pond beyond. Go left to circle the pond, and you'll be in the middle of a stand of bamboo, some of it reaching well over 100 feet. Expect to send dozens of little frogs hopping off the trail and into the pond. On the far end of the pond, as you emerge from the bamboo, you'll see a magnificent pine to the left that is at least 12 feet in circumference.

When you hit the sand trail on the other side of the pond, take a left; this is the park boundary. At 1.25 miles, the trail splits; go to the left. At 1.4 miles, where a bench sits on the right, take a left off the asphalt onto the rock and sand Blackberry Trail. You'll pass a barn and silos through an open field to the left. Here you'll see lots of scrub brush, nubby trees, and loads of bird feeders, where red-winged blackbirds, cardinals, and jays congregate.

You'll come to another T-intersection at 1.7 miles; take a right at the big field of goldenrod and buttercups. You should see a bird feeder with a #4 on it; take a left on the paved trail just past the feeder. Unfortunately, you'll lose solitude here since many private homes crowd the park boundary, but the field to the left, which has been allowed to revert to its original ecology, is a bustle of winged activity. Look for bluebirds, indigo buntings, and blue jays. As for flora, you'll see purple coneflower, primrose, lance-leaved coreopsis, Indian grass, big bluestem, and little bluestem.

At 2.1 miles, you'll pass a soccer field and parking area; the tot lot is just beyond. Continuing on the perimeter trail on the outside of the baseball fields and playgrounds, you'll pass lots of pines that stand between you and Kinder Road. You'll see a large field of milkweed to the left, and just after, at 2.6 miles, you'll cross over a wooden footbridge; bluebirds congregate in the little wooded area to the right. Cross over Kinder Farm Park Road at 2.8 miles, and head left on the other side. You'll soon come to the Girl Scout Hope Memorial Garden, a redbird grove dedicated to the 86 countries that lost citizens during the attacks of September 11, 2001. The parking area is just ahead.

▶ NEARBY ACTIVITIES

You can reach the 13.3-mile-long Baltimore and Annapolis (B&A) Trail (see page 12) by returning to MD 100 and taking Exit 13B to Ritchie Highway (MD 2) north; park at Marley Station Mall.

Annapolis, the country's oldest (and arguably prettiest) continuous capital city, with its bevy of attractions (colonial-era waterfront and U.S. Naval Academy, to name just two), is a short drive down MD 2 to MD 450 west over the Severn River (or take I-97 south to MD 450 east).

CITY OF BALTIMORE

BALTIMORE INNER HARBOR–WATERFRONT PROMENADE

KEY AT-A-GLANCE INFORMATION

LENGTH: 3.6 miles

CONFIGURATION: Out-and-back

DIFFICULTY: Easy

SCENERY: Downtown Baltimore, Inner Harbor, Federal Hill, monuments, historic sites

EXPOSURE: Sunny

TRAFFIC: Extremely heavy

TRAIL SURFACE: Asphalt, brick, concrete

HIKING TIME: 1.5 hours

ACCESS: MTA bus #10 runs along Eastern Avenue, past Caroline Street, three blocks north of Lancaster.

MAPS: USGS Baltimore East

FACILITIES: Food, water, bathrooms in restaurants and shops along route

SPECIAL COMMENTS: Use normal caution when walking downtown; the Inner Harbor is so populated that even night walks are generally safe.

Baltimore Inner Harbor–Waterfront Promenade

UTM Zone (WGS84) 18S

Easting 362292

Northing 362292

IN BRIEF

Join the throngs strolling around Baltimore's tourist mecca, but end up where few tourists venture.

DESCRIPTION

At the Living Classroom Foundation, you'll see a sign pointing you to the "pedestrian walkway" (the "Baltimore Waterfront Promenade" sign is 0.1 mile away on Lancaster Street). You'll see the water right in front of you; head left on the brick walkway toward the Inner Harbor. Initially you'll see lots of construction to the right, and even though this isn't always the most pleasant view, it indicates a growing, vibrant city. The small skiffs in the water to the left make a more pleasing backdrop.

Invariably on nice days people will be sitting on the benches to the right under the shade trees. Despite the heavy boat traffic here, the water is cleaned frequently, and it's a pleasant spot to sit and read, eat, or people-watch. Across the street on Lancaster you'll see new hotels and restaurants, including the fantastic Charleston Restaurant.

At 0.2 miles, across the harbor, you'll see the Domino's sugar sign, a Baltimore icon; its red glow can be seen at night from anywhere in the harbor. To the right stands the striking memorial

DIRECTIONS

Take I-83 south until it ends at President Street; go 0.6 miles to Fleet Street at the big curve to the left. Take a quick right onto Central Avenue, and continue 100 yards on Lancaster Street; turn left and drive another 0.1 mile to Caroline Street, where there is usually abundant parking using the EZ parking machines. You can pay with a credit card in 25-cent increments; it's $1 per hour with a maximum of four hours. The Caroline Street Garage is another option. The trail starts at the corner of Caroline and Lancaster, in front of the Living Classrooms Foundation campus.

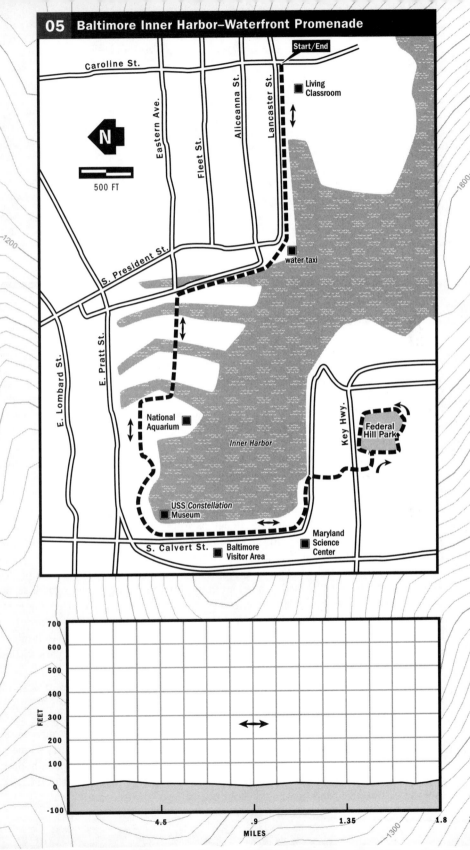

Caroline St.

Start/End

Living Classroom

Eastern Ave.

Fleet St.

Aliceanna St.

Lancaster St.

N

500 FT

S. President St.

water taxi

E. Lombard St.

E. Pratt St.

National Aquarium

Inner Harbor

Key Hwy.

Federal Hill Park

USS Constellation Museum

Maryland Science Center

S. Calvert St.

Baltimore Visitor Area

700

600

500

400

300

200

100

0

-100

FEET

4.5

.9

1.35

1.8

MILES

31

Harbor view from Federal Hill

to the 1940 massacre in Katyn, Poland; the three-story sculpture is in the shape of a golden flame with bronze figures intertwined. Behind the monument is the Civil War Museum (1850 President Street Station, open 10 a.m. to 5 p.m. daily); history students will know that it was here, not Fort Sumter, where the Civil War actually began when, on this very spot, a Confederate-sympathizing mob attacked Union soldiers on their way to Washington, D.C.

At just under 0.3 miles, head right to stay on the brick; if you go straight on the wooden boardwalk in front of you, you'll end up on the patio of Victor's Café. Now the downtown financial district and Inner Harbor come into view. The National Aquarium is straight ahead, and to the left, you'll see Federal Hill, your ultimate destination. Pass the water-taxi stand on the left as you parallel President Street. Mature shade trees border the water, and ducks congregate in this area; it gives them access to people throwing bread and keeps them clear of water traffic.

The Baltimore Public Works Museum (open Tuesday to Sunday, 10 a.m. to 4 p.m.) is on the right, housed in a beautiful old brick building. Nearby you'll see a series of Italian flags; you're on the edge of Little Italy, one of the best on the East Coast (conceded as true even by my New York friends and family). Go left over the bridge at 0.5 miles, and you'll see the sail-dominated architecture of the Columbus Center to the right and the National Aquarium straight ahead. As you pass it, the Hard Rock Café and ESPN Zone, the country's first, will come into view.

For a taste of history, visit the USCG Cutter *Taney* sitting in the water to the right. It's the only remaining survivor of the attack on Pearl Harbor; you can go on board and check it out. Walk to the second bridge over the water, and follow that to the left. Cross over the pedestrian bridge at the Hard Rock Café at three quarters of a mile. You'll come straight to the World Trade Center, which is the country's tallest pentagonal building; the 27th floor offers an unmatched view of Baltimore's harbor and skyline (open Wednesday to Sunday, 10 a.m. to 6 p.m.). If you want to ride out into the harbor, you can rent a paddleboat just below the World Trade Center.

Continuing on the trail, at just under 1 mile you'll come to the Pratt Street Pavilion, a popular place for shopping and dining—here you can find almost anything you might want to eat or purchase in either the Pratt Street Pavilion or the adjacent Light Street Pavilion. The open space between the two provides an outdoor stage for a variety of performances—music, juggling, dancing, and magic shows. The performers are often quite good, making it worth a stop to check out whatever's going on. But use common sense; obviously a large, stationary crowd offers lots of opportunities for pickpockets.

The USS *Constellation* Museum, in the water at 1 mile, comes next. The crowds begin to thin out a bit after the Light Street Pavilion, and you'll have fantastic views of the aquarium to the left across the harbor. To the right you'll see the visually striking brand-new Baltimore Area Visitor Center (BAVC), which complements the nautical theme built into the architecture of the Columbus Center and the Aquarium. About a half mile straight up Conway Street to the right of the BAVC stands Oriole Park at Camden Yards, still widely regarded as the nicest stadium in Major League Baseball.

The popular Maryland Science Center, with its massive tyrannosaurus in the window, looms straight ahead. When you reach the Science Center at 1.3 miles, head left, keeping the water on your left; the crowds thin even more here. When you see the merry-go-round to the right, exactly across the harbor from the World Trade Center, turn right and go through Rash Field, where ice-skating is a popular wintertime activity; you'll know it by its surrounding wooden amphitheater. Head up the concrete steps, and cross over Battery Avenue and Key Highway. You'll see a stone wall on your left; climb the stairs to the top of Federal Hill, which has been a popular spot ever since the founding of Baltimore in 1729. About 4,000 people crammed in here for a feast in 1788 to celebrate the ratification of the U.S. Constitution by the State of Maryland. During the Civil War, Union troops fortified Federal Hill and trained their guns on the city. The site officially became a park in 1880, and has continued to grow in popularity as a place for relaxation and recreation.

Head right, and marvel at the wonderful views all around you. First up is the historic neighborhood of Federal Hill; bear witness to the craze of building rooftop decks on these narrow row homes, many built in the 1700s. M & T Bank Stadium, home of the Ravens, sits about a mile in the distance. Keep circling around on the sidewalk, past the playground, shade trees, and benches until, eventually, you catch a glimpse of where you've just walked. Standing next to the antique cannons, the 15-star American flag, and the monuments to Colonel George Armistead and Major General Samuel Smith, gives you an unparalleled view of the harbor. Lots of people hang out at Federal Hill, but they're mostly locals, and you'll probably feel decidedly removed from the crush of humanity below—you're literally above it all.

▶ NEARBY ACTIVITIES

Since this is the epicenter of Baltimore tourism, "nearby activities" are simply too numerous to list. Your best bet is to stop at the Baltimore Area Visitor Center, which is open daily from 9 a.m. to 6 p.m., just off the harbor south of Conway Street. There you can get any information you need and also see "The Baltimore Experience," an 11-minute film that captures the highlights of the city. Call (877) BALTIMORE or visit **www.baltimore.org/visitors/v_vc.html**.

CYLBURN ARBORETUM

Cylburn Arboretum

UTM Zone (WGS84) 18S

Easting   357386

Northing 4357108

IN BRIEF

Take in a stunning array of flowers and trees on the grounds of a beautiful 19th-century mansion.

DESCRIPTION

Construction on the Italianate Cylburn Mansion began in 1863, but it wasn't completed until 1888, when Jesse Tyson, a wealthy Baltimore businessman, moved in with his much younger bride, Edyth Johns. After Jesse died in 1906, Edyth remarried, and she and her husband lived in Cylburn until 1942, when the house became property of the Baltimore City Department of Public Welfare. By 1954, the Board of Parks and Recreation created the Cylburn Wildflower Preserve and Garden, which was later renamed Cylburn Arboretum. A circular driveway ringed by marigolds and black-eyed Susans, with a centuries-old black walnut tree in the middle, fronts the mansion.

The surrounding gardens appear just as beautiful as the mansion. There are no less than 13 separate gardens that range from Victorian-designed formal spaces to backyard vegetable gardens and a plot devoted to alpine plants. All of this flora goes a long way toward attracting birds.

DIRECTIONS

Take I-83 to Exit 10, Northern Parkway west. Take the first left onto Cylburn Avenue, and continue until it ends at Greenspring Avenue. Take a left onto Greenspring Avenue and then another immediate left into Cylburn Arboretum. Follow the road to the parking area on the left. Once you've parked, walk back toward the arboretum entrance. When you see the brown Cylburn Arboretum rules sign, about 100 yards from the parking area, turn left and head toward the woods. The trail starts straight ahead at the edge of the woods.

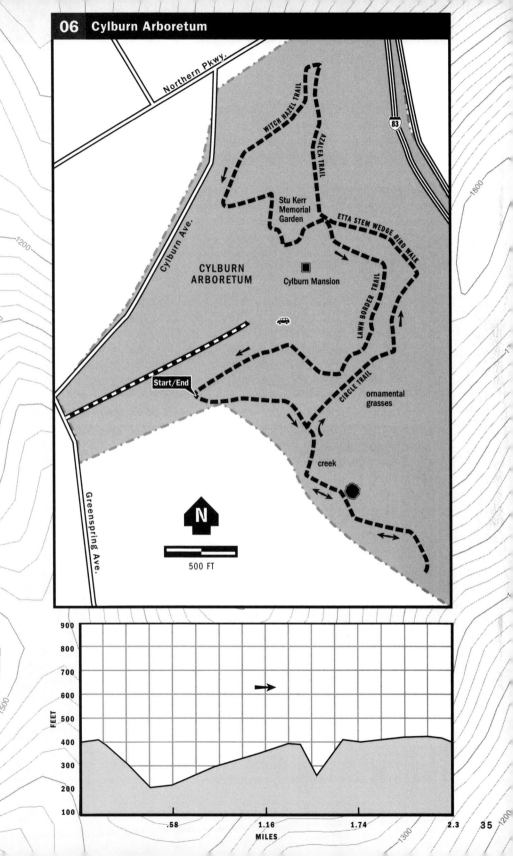

Some would be surprised to learn that bald eagles have been spotted here, but the eagle is only one of the 161 birds seen at Cylburn.

The thin tree trunks placed on the ground on both sides of the path make the trailhead easy to spot. Initially cedar chips cover the trail in this section, but at 250 feet, the trail emerges from the woods. Follow the tree line back into the woods to where the trail slopes precipitously downward at 0.15 miles; be aware that this section can be treacherous when it is covered with ice, snow, or wet leaves. Also watch for the many rocks and exposed roots on the trail.

Soon you'll come to a small creek bed; expect water only after snowmelts and heavy rains; the trail begins to parallel a valley that may hold a trickle of water. A huge fallen oak sits over the trail and reaches all the way down into the valley, some 50 feet below. While negotiating your way over the massive trunk, consider the situation: here you are, in the middle of the city, and you can't see any man-made structure at all. It's unlikely you'll see any hikers either; people generally contain themselves to the wide and well-maintained Circle Trail up the hill. This section is extremely underused, as the many beech trees that remain free of graffiti attest.

Just before 0.4 miles, a series of low-lying vines hangs over the trail, giving the hike a Tolkienesque feel. The trail heads down to the water to the right in the valley, where it ends; you'll have to backtrack to return to the main Circle Trail, but you gain a nice stretch of solitude by taking this spur. Just be aware that the spur, due to many rocks and roots and up-and-down nature, can be moderate to strenuous.

When you reach the Circle Trail on your backtrack, head right. A series of stone benches lines the Circle Trail, and the trail runs through the woods, but not very deep. Occasionally you'll see cuts out to the open areas, as well as the mansion beyond. Ornamental grasses, diverse trees, and stands of bamboo make these cuts quite pleasant.

At 0.8 miles, you'll see a sign for the Etta Stem Wedge Bird Walk, a pleasant little diversionary trail that runs parallel to the Circle Trail but deeper in the woods. When you rejoin the Circle Trail from the Etta Stem Wedge Bird Walk, you'll most likely scatter unsuspecting squirrels and birds at the feeder at the intersection of these two trails. When you see a stand of bamboo and signs for the Lawn Border and Circle Trail, take a quick right detour onto the Azalea Trail, which is blazed in white. Like the Etta Stem Wedge Trail, this too runs parallel to the Circle Trail but also deeper in the woods. You'll see lots of beech trees and, of course, azaleas. Railroad ties will ease your way when this path begins its gradual descent down the hill. When you reach a sign pointing to the left to stay on the Azalea Trail, you'll also see a wide path cut to the right. From this spot, it's easy to gaze longingly down the hill, but be aware that it starts out as an easy descent, soon tightens, and then stops abruptly in a thick stand of vegetation, which has been allowed to overtake the path. Unless you want to attempt a near-impossible bushwhack (which would be environmentally destructive in any case), it's best not to bother taking this spur. That said, you can take comfort in knowing that the initial spur you took at the beginning of the hike gives you a very good idea of what it is you're missing down there.

So, head left, back toward the Circle Trail. Before you reach it, however, you'll see signs for the Witch Hazel Trail, a nice little detour worth taking. The very mossy trail has lichen-covered granite all around it. You will come to two wooden foot-bridges at 1.6 miles, and soon after, you'll be back on the Azalea Trail. Take a right, and end up yet again on the Circle Trail. Almost immediately, you'll come out onto the garden grounds; to the left is a stone building and composting demonstration site, and ahead lies the Stu Kerr Memorial Garden with its little red schoolhouse. Nearby you'll see lots of stone and metal sculptures. On Saturday mornings in June and July, children age 3 to 6 can enjoy a nature story hour here. Passing the garden takes you back onto Circle Trail. Along the trail you'll see poplars, Japanese maple, oak, gum, and birch, among others. Heading back toward the parking area, you'll pass the Garden of the Senses, where you'll see shooting star, celandine poppy, white trillium, blue phlox, pawpaw, weeping cherry, and several different types of magno-lias. Both the Circle Trail and the Lawn Border Trail, which are about 10 feet apart, head back to the parking area. Don't miss the little footbridge straddling the bog at 1.9 miles before you reach your car.

▶ **NEARBY ACTIVITIES**

Just down I-83 is Druid Hill Park, where you'll find tennis and basketball courts, a public swimming pool, a disc golf course, the Baltimore Conservatory (thousands of plants and flowers in a lovely glass pavilion), and, of course, the Baltimore Zoo, the country's third oldest. Go south on I-83 to Exit 7 and head west on Druid Hill Park Drive to the park entrance off Swann Drive.

DRUID HILL PARK LAKE LOOP

KEY AT-A-GLANCE INFORMATION

LENGTH: 1.5 miles

CONFIGURATION: Loop

DIFFICULTY: Easy

SCENERY: Lake, mature trees

EXPOSURE: Mostly open to the sun

TRAFFIC: Moderate–heavy

TRAIL SURFACE: Asphalt

HIKING TIME: 45 minutes

ACCESS: Always open; Maryland Transit Administration (MTA) M–Line bus #1 runs to Druid Hill Park; for a complete schedule, visit **www.mtamaryland.com** or call (866) RIDE-MTA.

MAPS: Baltimore City Parks and Recreation Map

FACILITIES: Restrooms, water, playground, gazebos, picnic, pool, and tennis and basketball courts

SPECIAL COMMENTS: No alcohol, no swimming in lake, and dogs must be leashed

Druid Hill Park Lake Loop

UTM Zone (WGS84)   18S

Easting   358892

Northing   4353464

IN BRIEF

With plenty of opportunity to relax, enjoy a loop around Druid Lake and everything else that historic Druid Hill Park has to offer. Most traffic will be folks trying to get into (or stay in) shape.

DESCRIPTION

If you had to dream up the perfect "urban hike," Druid Hill Park Lake Loop might very well be it. It's long enough and configured in such a way to give people a serious workout if they choose to circle several times, but easy enough for those who just want a leisurely stroll. Along the way, your choice of views includes the busy downtown, serene woodlands, and the mix-and-match character of north Baltimore.

Druid Lake lies within Druid Hill Park, a 674-acre park listed on the National Register of Historic Places that was created from revenue collected from a penny tax on nickel horsecar fares. Druid Hill was once Victorian Baltimore's fashionable playground. Couples in love would head out onto the lake in rowboats, and the women shielded themselves from the sun with fancy umbrellas while the men rowed. A lot has changed since those days, but the lake remains just as lovely. Still used for city drinking, the water looks clean and fresh. The fountain that sat dormant for more than ten years was restored to working order in June 2004, and multicolored lights below the surface now accompany its sprays at night.

DIRECTIONS

From I-83 (Jones Falls Expressway), take Exit 7 (28th Street–Druid Park Lake Drive). Bear west on Druid Park Lake Drive, and continue for 1 mile to Swann Drive (opposite a massive arch and an American flag); take a right into the park. Turn right onto Hanlon Drive where you see the sign for the Baltimore Zoo; park when you see the tennis and basketball courts.

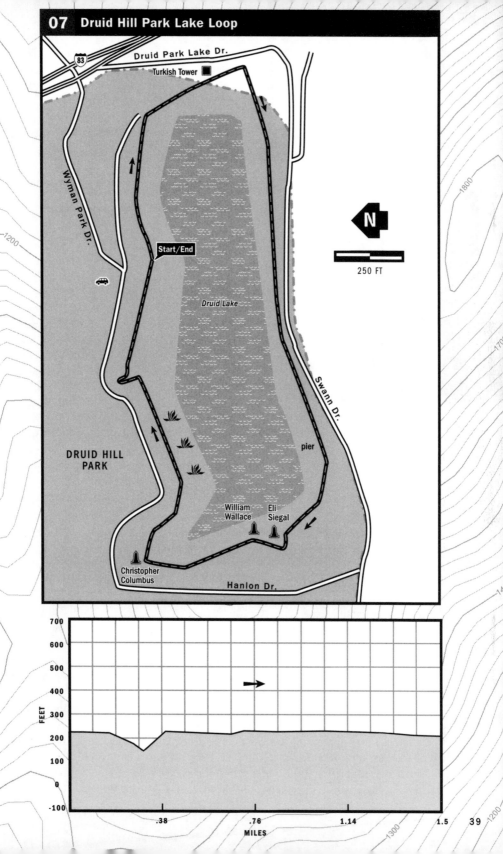

07 Druid Hill Park Lake Loop

Druid Park Lake Dr.

83

Turkish Tower

Wyman Park Dr.

Start/End

Druid Lake

N

250 FT

DRUID HILL PARK

pier

Swann Dr.

William Wallace

Eli Siegal

Christopher Columbus

Hanlon Dr.

1200

1300

1500

1800

1700

1300

1200

39

Moorish Tower

The trail around the lake, which is maintained in excellent condition, has become a favorite of walkers who live in the city. Park anywhere along Hanlon Drive across from the tennis and basketball courts. Walk to the lake, and head left. The lake, which is ringed with aquatic plants, is home to a multitude of ducks. They glide confidently along the shore, free of human disruption. Please obey the "No Trespassing" signs; if they are not enough to dissuade you from making a go at the lake, the metal, spike-tipped bars along the path should do it.

Head southeast around the lake; at 0.15 miles you'll reach an overlook above I-83 (Jones Falls Expressway, or JFX) and a nice, sweeping view beyond it. From here you'll see Wyman Park, the bell tower of Gilman Hall on the Johns Hopkins University campus, and the old brick Stieff Silver building, among other notable landmarks. Being in this spot in late March and early April yields a special treat: the hill below is completely covered in yellow tulips.

Continuing south, you'll see the tall buildings of downtown (the harbor is obscured from view) with an interesting tower just ahead at 0.2 miles. This is the "Moorish" or "Turkish" Tower, a squat, white marble structure with club-shaped windows. It will invariably be locked, but it's worth walking around and peeking inside; you can see the white-and-black tile floor inside.

Continuing west you'll begin to head down until you reach street level and walk alongside Druid Park Lake Drive. It can get quite noisy here, which breaks the idyllic mood for a while, but don't despair—you'll soon lose the street and head back into the greenery of the park. Along the way, at 0.6 miles, you'll pass a small pier with a boat tied to it; municipal workers use the boat when they need to get out on the lake. The big box you'll see on your left, opposite the pier, houses the controls for the restored fountain.

Baltimore has had many nicknames over the years, including Mobtown for the population's penchant for fomenting . . . well, mobs; Charm City, the current nickname; and Monument City, a popular name in the 19th and early 20th centuries for the city's profusion of monuments. Name the person, and there is probably a monument somewhere to him or her in Baltimore.

As you begin to head west past the pier, you'll see three of these monuments in quick succession, starting at 0.85 miles, and their eclectic nature truly is a testament to Baltimore's love of monuments. First is Eli Siegel, founder of aesthetic realism. His likeness is cast onto a bronze plate that has been set into a large rock.

Just beyond Siegel, you'll see a very impressive statue of a man in chain mail, shield by his side, sword raised above his head; this is William Wallace, "Guardian of

Scotland." He stands atop five massive granite boulders. The statue was presented originally by William Wallace Spence on November 30, 1893, and was rededicated on August 22, 1993, by Baltimore's Society of St. Andrew. The inscription below the statue reads: "It is in truth, not for glory, nor riches, nor honors that we are fighting, but for freedom. For that alone, which no honest man gives up but with life itself— Declaration of Arbroath 1320."

A few hundred feet farther stands the small marble monument to Christopher Columbus. The simple inscription etched in the marble reads: "Cristoforo Columbo. The Italians of Baltimore, 1832."

As you continue around the lake and approach where you began, enter the one shady section of this walk, at 1.25 miles. Beautiful old oaks and tulip poplars spread their branches over the asphalt. Beyond them sit benches and picnic tables. This is where one of the fireworks scenes was filmed in Barry Levinson's movie *Avalon*. Your car is just up ahead, but why not linger in this lovely spot a while?

▶ NEARBY ACTIVITIES

Loads to choose from in this very park! You'll find tennis and basketball courts, a public swimming pool, a disc golf course, the Baltimore Conservatory (thousands of plants and flowers in a lovely glass pavilion), and of course the Baltimore Zoo, the country's third oldest.

FORT McHENRY

KEY AT-A-GLANCE INFORMATION

LENGTH: 1 mile

CONFIGURATION: Loop

DIFFICULTY: Easy

SCENERY: Fort McHenry, Northwest Harbor

EXPOSURE: Sunny

TRAFFIC: Moderate to heavy

TRAIL SURFACE: Asphalt

HIKING TIME: 0.5 hours (but add time to visit the fort and its grounds)

ACCESS: Grounds open daily 8 a.m.– 5 p.m (8 p.m. in summer); fort and visitor center open daily 8 a.m.–4:45 p.m. (7:45 p.m. in summer); closed Thanksgiving Day, December 25, and January 1.

MAPS: USGS Baltimore East

FACILITIES: Bathrooms and water in visitor center; concessions and bathroom at trailhead

SPECIAL COMMENTS: No climbing on cannons or earthworks. Pets must be leashed. Fort McHenry is served by public transportation; Maryland Transit Administration (MTA) bus #1 stops at the park main gate; call (866) RIDE-MTA for schedules. Fort McHenry is also served by water taxi; schedules and locations vary; call Ed Kane's Water Taxi at (410) 563-3901 or the National Historic Seaport Taxi at (410) 675-2900.

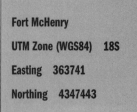

Fort McHenry

UTM Zone (WGS84)   18S

Easting   363741

Northing   4347443

IN BRIEF

Feel the stirrings of patriotism as you circle the most prominent symbol of the indomitable will of the fledgling United States. Walk along the seawall of the harbor where Francis Scott Key wrote our national anthem.

DESCRIPTION

From where you can see the water taxi stand, about 150 feet to the left, head right until you reach the seawall, and then keep it on your left. You'll see many signs telling you not to walk on the seawall itself; people have fallen in here, and as you'll notice, getting back out of the water is no easy task. The water is pretty choppy and slams against the big rocks several feet below the wall. Despite people having fallen in, it's refreshing to see that no obtrusive walls have been erected and your view of busy Northwest Harbor is unobstructed. Just be especially careful here with children.

When you first reach the seawall, you'll see Broadway Pier, once home of NBC's long-running series *Homicide: Life on the Street*, and the distinctive gold-tipped dome of St. Michael's Ukrainian

DIRECTIONS

Take I-83 to Exit 4 and head south on St. Paul Street. Continue on St. Paul Street to Light Street and then take Light Street until it intersects with Key Highway behind the Maryland Science Center. When Key Highway splits after Lawrence Street, turn left onto Fort Avenue and continue until it ends at Fort McHenry. Drive through the main gates and park at the far end of the lot to the left of the visitor center (assuming you didn't take public transportation here—see "Special Comments" above). You'll see concessions and bathrooms to your left. Begin the hike on the paved asphalt path.

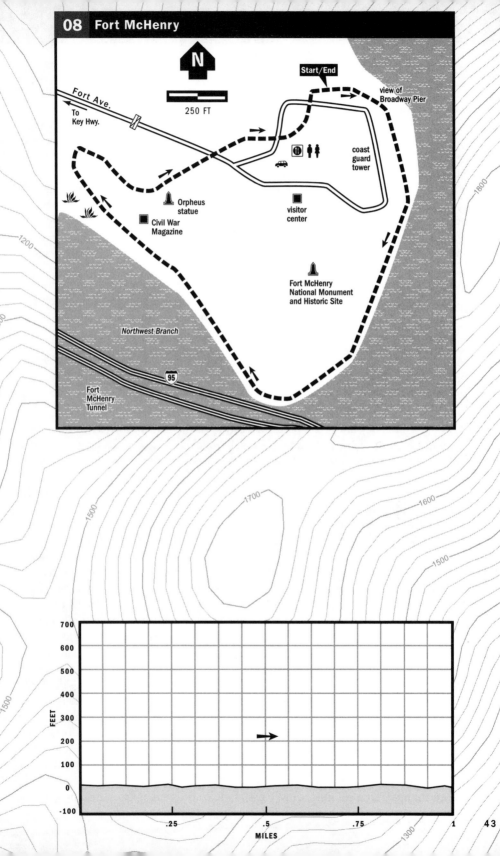

N

250 FT

Start/End

view of
Broadway Pier

Fort Ave.

To
Key Hwy.

coast
guard
tower

Orpheus
statue

visitor
center

Civil War
Magazine

Fort McHenry
National Monument
and Historic Site

Northwest Branch

95

Fort
McHenry
Tunnel

1200

1300

1500

1700

1600

1500

1800

FEET

700
600
500
400
300
200
100
0
-100

.25   .5   .75   1

MILES

1300

1200

Church behind that to the far left on the other side of the harbor. Within that working Northwest Harbor itself, away from the glitz of the Inner Harbor, you'll get a sense of what makes the port of Baltimore so important. This view by no means affords a look at the entire port of Baltimore, but you can see the busy Canton industrial area ahead. On the water, you're likely to see folks out for a pleasure cruise in their sailboats as well as the much larger bulk cargo ships, general cargo ships, British frigates, cruise ships, and container ships.

As you continue walking, keeping the water on your left, close your eyes and inhale; it's easy to imagine that you're at the ocean. You can smell salt on the breeze and hear the gulls wheeling above. Depending on the strength of the wind, you may even get a spray on your cheeks. (You should note that because of the stiff and steady wind coming off the water, the temperature can be a good 10 to 20 degrees cooler than just about anywhere else in the city).

On the right you'll see Fort McHenry, site of the famous battle of the War of 1812. During nice weather, you'll see picnickers in the nicely maintained grassy area between the fort and the water; mature trees provide welcome shade. At 0.08 miles, you'll see an informational sign about the Port of Baltimore that explains the leading imports (petroleum, iron ore, bananas, raw sugar, and automobiles), as well as the exports, which include coal, food products, and grain from the Midwest. The Coast Guard tower behind you stands directly in line with Fort McHenry Channel and blinks its green beacon every two seconds to help pilots follow a straight course into the harbor.

You'll see Key Bridge a short distance away to the left. Fortunately you won't see I-895, otherwise known as Harbor Tunnel, which is below you under the water. Ducks frequent this area, and I once saw a pelican here in the summer, no doubt quite confused and most probably blown way off its intended course.

At 0.5 miles, you'll pass some enormous old sycamores and pines in front of the fort. Soon the trail splits—to the right you'll see a gargantuan statue. Stay left, closest to the water, and you'll soon be able to check out the statue, which stands 24 feet from head to toe on a large frescoed base. The breeze dies out here as the seawall wraps around to the left and then gets lost in the nearby industrial zone. Just before that, though, you'll pass a tidal salt marsh to the left; the marsh serves as a nursery for fish and blue crabs, a resting spot for migratory birds, and a feeding area for ducks, great blue herons, redwing blackbirds, and ospreys. The red brick building to your right is the Civil War Magazine, built in 1864; during WWI it served as a rifle range.

As you approach the park entrance, you'll pass a grove of evergreens to the left, and the scenery turns industrial just beyond. You can walk out to the paved road where you drove in, but I recommend cutting across the field (at 0.75 miles) to your right toward the massive statue you saw earlier; you're now on the other side of the Civil War Magazine. Walk toward the statue on the paved path, and just ahead to the left you will see a series of commemorative plaques explaining that the nearby trees were planted in honor of the soldiers who died defending the fort in 1814. These simple and poignant remembrances, such as one that reads "Dedicated to Charles Messenger, gunner in Barney's marine artillery, killed in action during bombardment of Fort McHenry September 13, 1814," preserve the memory of those brave soldiers who defended our young country. Sadly, most of the corresponding trees are long gone.

Take a few minutes to marvel at the statue in front of you. Unveiled on June 14, 1922, to belatedly mark the centennial of the writing of "The Star-Spangled Banner", it depicts Orpheus—not Francis Scott Key, as many people mistakenly think. A medallion on the statue's base commemorates Key as the writer of the words of our national anthem. The speech President Warren Harding gave at the unveiling ceremony was the first presidential speech to be broadcast by radio from coast to coast.

Head left on the paved trail toward the visitor center. Your car is just ahead to the left, but don't leave without exploring the fort grounds. Admission is $5 for adults 17 and older.

▶ NEARBY ACTIVITIES

Cross Street Market, a city institution since 1846 and chock-full of great food, is in nearby Federal Hill. From Fort McHenry, take Fort Avenue to its intersection with Charles Street and turn right; the market sits at the intersection of Charles and Cross streets. Inner Harbor, with its myriad attractions, is nearby as well, but if you want to keep a patriotic theme going, you can head to Francis Scott Key's once-burial place, before he was moved to Frederick County, at Mt. Vernon Methodist Church (across from the country's first monument to George Washington in beautiful Mt. Vernon square—Charles and Centre streets) or the Star-Spangled Banner Flag House at 844 East Pratt Street; it's open Tuesday–Saturday, 10 a.m.–4 p.m.; (410) 837-1793.

GWYNNS FALLS PARK

▶ IN BRIEF

Adjacent to and connected with Leakin Park, this section of the Gwynns Falls Trail runs through the largest unbroken urban forest in the United States. Follow the falls several miles through its most scenic sections to Leon Day Park and back.

▶ DESCRIPTION

Walk away from Clifton Avenue and head straight into the woods. Initially very tall oaks completely covered in kudzu flank the wide trail, but after 300 feet the trail turns to cedar chips; you're now deep in the woods. Ignore the cut to the right and continue down the hill straight ahead until you can see Gwynns Falls; be careful—this downhill section of the trail is very rocky and it's easy to trip and twist an ankle. When you reach the falls, head left and walk downstream.

You'll see hundreds of spiderwebs across this little-used narrow section of the trail. At 0.35 miles, the trail rises above the falls and gets much wider. Enormous beech trees abound, along with lots of sassafras, holly, oak, and walnut. You'll reach Windsor Mill Road at 0.5 miles. Take care crossing the road and head left on the other side; take a quick right into the Windsor Mill parking area.

You'll see an informational sign about the Gwynns Falls Trail, as well as a trail map with a "you are here" indicator. The trail surface becomes

▶ DIRECTIONS

Take I-83 to Exit 6, North Avenue west. Go 3.5 miles and turn right onto North Hilton Street. Go two blocks and turn left onto Bloomingdale, which soon becomes Clifton Avenue. Continue 1.3 miles where Clifton swings around abruptly to the right at a guardrail; park here. You'll see a sign to the left marking the trailhead, "Windsor Hills Conservation Trail."

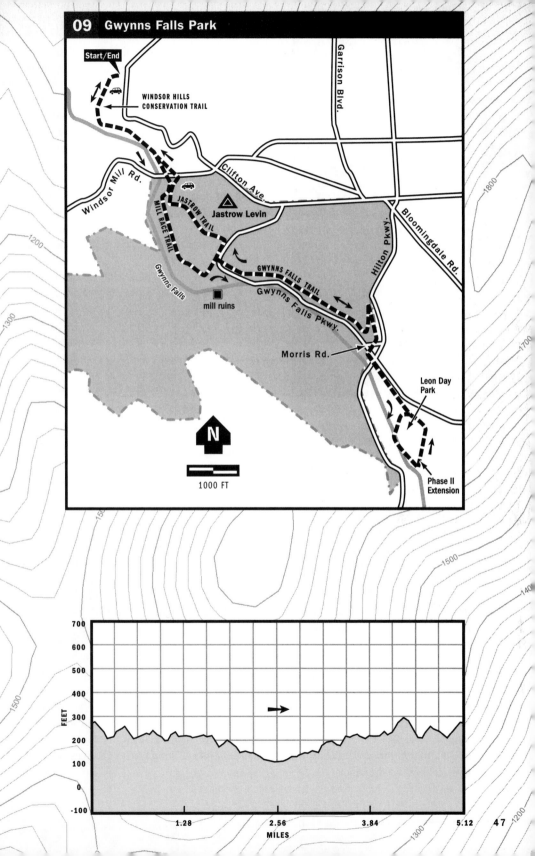

Start/End

WINDSOR HILLS
CONSERVATION TRAIL

Garrison Blvd.

Clifton Ave.

Windsor Mill Rd.

MILL RACE TRAIL

JASTROW TRAIL

Jastrow Levin

Gwynns Falls

mill ruins

GWYNNS FALLS TRAIL

Gwynns Falls Pkwy.

Hilton Pkwy.

Bloomingdale Rd.

Morris Rd.

Leon Day
Park

Phase II
Extension

N

1000 FT

FEET

700
600
500
400
300
200
100
0
-100

1.28   2.56   3.84   5.12

MILES

Gwynns Falls

crushed stone on the Mill Race Trail section named for the waterwheels that once conveyed water five mills downstream to Calverton (present-day Rosemount). You'll see the Jastrow Trail immediately to the left, but stay straight—you'll return on the Jastrow Trail. An informational sign points out the three distinct tree levels along the trail: oak, hickory, tulip poplar, beech, and black walnut form the canopy; redbud, dogwood, serviceberry, and spicebush form the mid-level; and laurel, rhododendron, azalea, multiflora rose, jack-in-the-pulpit, may apple, and fern fill the understory.

This is a pleasant section. Even though Windsor Mill Road is not far away, the falls below easily drowns out the noise of the traffic. To the left, the thickly wooded hill rises precipitously; here the beech and walnut are especially enormous, somewhat amazing considering the lumber needs of the growing city over the last few centuries. Some of these trees have clearly been here since Baltimore was but a notion.

At 0.8 miles, cross over a little footbridge that is covered alternately with rock, metal, and plastic. Just beyond lie pure, thick woods. Occasionally views open up on the right and all you can see are the tops of trees—no roads and no buildings, despite being right in the middle of the city. You'll see mill ruins to the right at 1 mile. You have several options here: Jastrow Trail to the left, Stream Trail to the right, and the Gwynns Falls Trail straight ahead. The out-and-back Stream Trail is little different from the Windsor Hills Conservation Trail you took originally, and since you'll take Jastrow coming back, head straight.

For almost the next mile, the scenery doesn't change much, but it's consistently stunning; every time it opens up you'll have phenomenal views of the stream valley below, especially in winter. In summer, you'll see nothing but a riot of green, and in autumn, yellow, orange, and red dominate. At 1.8 miles, you'll hit asphalt as the trail parallels Morris Road and Hilton Parkway. Unfortunately you'll lose the solitude here, but it's not an unpleasant walk by any stretch.

At just under 2 miles, you'll reach Franklintown Road. Take a left and go under the Hilton Parkway bridge. Follow the signs to Leon Day Park. You'll see a Gwynns Falls Trail sign to the left just before you go under the bridge. Cross Franklintown Road and pick up the asphalt on the other side; Gwynns Falls sits in a buffer of trees to the right. At 2.2 miles, cross over a wooden footbridge and come to Leon Day Park, named in honor of the West Baltimore resident and Negro League baseball star who was inducted into the Baseball Hall of Fame in 1995. A loop circles the park so you can go in either direction.

On the far side of the park, at 2.5 miles, you'll see a railroad bridge and a small truss bridge. The path continues there and marks the beginning point of the Phase II Extension of the Gwynns Falls Trail; in its completion it ranks as one of the largest urban greenway trails in the United States. Just beyond the bridge lies Western Cemetery. For more information about the trail, visit **www.gwynnsfallstrail.org** or call the Baltimore City Department of Parks and Recreation at (410) 396-0440; to participate in the Gwynns Falls Trail Council, call the Parks and People Foundation at (410) 448-5663.

Loop the park; on your return trip you'll reach the three-way trail intersection at 3.7 miles. This time, take the Jastrow Trail to the right. (The short connector trail between the Gwynns Falls Trail and the Jastrow Trail is indicated as the Girl Scouts Trail on the Phase I Trail Guide, but there are no signs on the trail to indicate that). When you see Chesholm Road straight ahead, take a left up the hill on the asphalt, which soon crumbles into dirt and grass; this is the Jastrow Trail (250 feet after turning up the Girl Scouts Trail).

The Jastrow Trail rises uphill above the stream valley to the left. At just over 4 miles, you'll pass the Jastrow Levin campsite, a youth group campground and picnic area, on the left. The trail here is much tighter and wilder than the major sections of the Gwynns Falls Trail. You'll see lots of mid-level growth, and you'll have to duck under vines a few times. At 4.3 miles, Windsor Mill Road reappears; railroad ties on the trail will ease the steep descent. As soon as you reach the bottom of the hill, you'll rejoin the Mill Race Trail at the Windsor Mill parking area. Head right, cross over Windsor Mill back to the Windsor Hills Conservation Trail, and back to your car.

Note: This hike travels along the Phase I section of the Gwynns Falls Trail, which includes 14 miles of trails from Gwynns Falls–Leakin Park, following the falls to the Middle Branch of the Patapsco and the Inner Harbor. The hike described here turns around at Leon Day Park, where it starts to become decidedly urban as it heads toward the harbor (but not before running along scenic Western Cemetery, with some 18th-century tombstones), even incorporating sidewalks at some points. For a continuation of the Gwynns Falls Trail starting at Leon Day Park, see the hike description on the following page.

The Gwynns Falls Trail intersects with the Leakin Park Trail (see page 60) at Hutton Street. Within 10 miles, plenty of other hiking and recreation opportunities abound. Head south on Hilton Parkway from Gwynns Falls Park to MD 40 west and continue to Patapsco Valley State Park (see pages 131, 135, and 139). Go east on Hilton Parkway to Liberty Heights to Druid Hill Park (see page 38), home of the Baltimore Zoo, among other attractions. Also on Hilton Parkway, just before Liberty Heights, is Hanlon Park and Lake Ashburton; although not a hiking destination, the view of downtown over the lake is fantastic—and something of a local secret.

GWYNNS FALLS TRAIL FROM LEON DAY PARK TO CHERRY HILL PARK

(i) KEY AT-A-GLANCE INFORMATION

LENGTH: > 11.1 miles

CONFIGURATION: One way

DIFFICULTY: Moderate because of length

SCENERY: Gwynns Falls, historic sites, city neighborhoods, waterfront parks

EXPOSURE: More sun than shade

TRAFFIC: Moderate to heavy

TRAIL SURFACE: Asphalt, cement

HIKING TIME: 4 hours

ACCESS: Many of the parks along the route are open dusk to dawn; however, because much of the trail is on public sidewalks, it's always open but best avoided after dark. The Light Rail stops at Westport and Cherry Hill and Maryland Transit Administration (MTA) bus stops at many points along the route; for a schedule call (410) 539-5000 or (866) RIDE-MTA or visit **www.mtamaryland.com/services/lightrail/schedule/map.cfm.**

MAPS: USGS Baltimore West, Baltimore East, Curtis Bay; a printable trail map is available at **www.gwynnsfallstrail.org.**

FACILITIES: Many establishments along the route provide opportunities for food, shelter, phone, and bathrooms.

SPECIAL COMMENTS: This is a hike for the urban adventurer, often running along city sidewalks through neighborhoods, substations, and even industrial parks. If you prefer green spaces, stay on the portions of the trail within Gwynns Falls Park and Leakin Park as well as the southern end of the trail at Middle Branch and Cherry Hill Parks.

Gwynns Falls Trail from Leon Day Park to Cherry Hill Park

UTM Zone (WGS84) 18S

Easting 355860

Northing 4351425

IN BRIEF

Follow the city's newest greenway trail through West Baltimore. Bracketed by wooded and waterfront parks on both ends, the middle section is entirely urbanized, running through some of Baltimore's less known and more interesting neighborhoods.

DESCRIPTION

John Smith mapped Gwynns Falls in 1608, but the Susquehannock and Algonquian Indians had lived nearby for centuries. Smith said the stream tumbled over "felles," or falls, which explains the sometimes confusing local practice of naming streams and rivers as "falls" (Jones Falls and Gunpowder Falls, for example). If you're looking for actual waterfalls, you might be disappointed. The stream itself is named for Richard Gwinn, who established a trading post here in 1669.

Beginning at Leon Day Park, go 0.3 miles to the other end of Leon Day where you'll cross under a steel bridge and enter CSXT property, which for the next 1.5 miles is very nicely wooded with large rock outcroppings up the hill to the left and Gwynns Falls to the right down the hill. Cross under a bridge at 0.6 miles and look for the informational sign and benches at 0.8 miles. The sign will tell you that this section was once known as "Baltimore's Niagara Falls." You'll be tempted to laugh at the hyperbole, but the water pouring over the rocks is nice nonetheless. With this pleasing scene, there's no mistaking the

DIRECTIONS

Take I-83 to Exit 6, North Avenue west. Go 3.5 miles, cross North Hilton Street, and take the very next left, the detour to Franklintown Road. Follow the detour to the end of the road and turn left. Take the first right, under the bridge, to the parking lot for Leon Day Park.

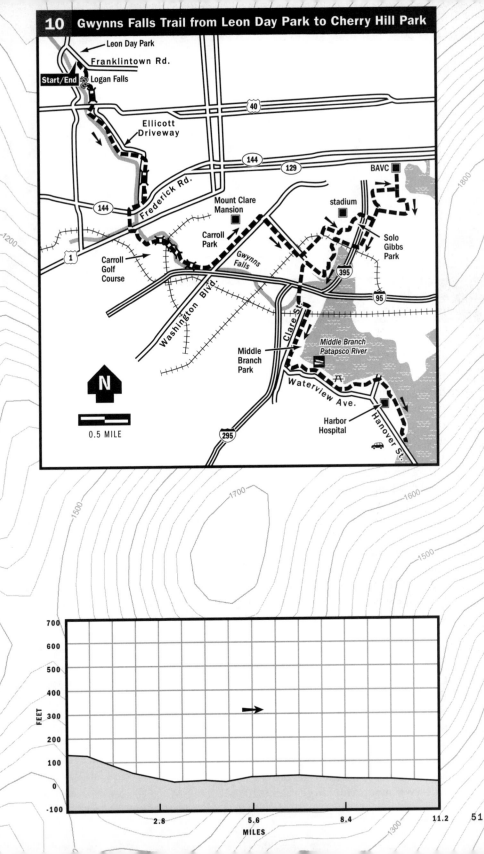

Leon Day Park

Franklintown Rd.

Start/End Logan Falls

Ellicott
Driveway

40

144

129

BAVC

Mount Clare
Mansion

stadium

Solo
Gibbs
Park

Carroll
Park

Gwynns
Falls

395

144

Carroll
Golf
Course

1

95

Washington Blvd.

Clare St.

Middle Branch
Patapsco River

Middle
Branch
Park

Waterview Ave.

N

Harbor
Hospital

Hanover St.

0.5 MILE

295

1200

1300

1500

1700

1600

1800

1700

1500

1500

1400

1300

1200

700

600

500

400

300

200

100

0

-100

FEET

2.8   5.6   8.4   11.2

MILES

Cherry Hill Park

strange dichotomy around you: rocks in Gwynns Falls and thick woods full of beautiful sweet gum, hickory, and maple—but then you pass a dumped furnace or plastic tubing. Things are on the upswing though, and the more people use the trail, the better things will become.

The informational signage along the Gwynns Falls Trail (GFT) enhances the natural charm. The signs usually contain images of what the place looked like 100 or 150 years ago—it's interesting to look at the very spot and see the changes (or, better yet, that very little has changed). One such spot is at 1.2 miles, at the triple-arched Baltimore Street Bridge, constructed in 1932.

Cross over Baltimore Street, and follow the Ellicott Driveway, once a millrace and later a vehicular road, but now closed to traffic and crowded with thick woods. At 1.8 miles, turn right at Frederick Road (you'll see GFT signs at all the sections where it's not abundantly clear which way to go). Cross over the CSX line and Gwynns Falls on a bridge and head left at Dukeland. Cross Hurley at 2.2 miles and take a left, crossing the falls once again. Initially you'll see a dead-car graveyard to the left, but the landscape soon becomes quite wooded again, and just ahead you'll come to one of the most interesting and scenic sections of the entire trail: a series of three steel bridges crisscrossing old stone abutments of the former Brunswick Street Bridge.

Long before the bridges, this is where Native Americans crossed the stream. You'll come to a fourth bridge soon after, and you'll head under the wagon pass of the old Carrolton Aqueduct, the B&O's first bridge, constructed in 1829. The trail soon skirts the outer edge of Carroll Golf Course and quickly becomes very urban as it passes the renovated Montgomery Business Park to the left (not like the other green parks you've passed, but a very impressive building), paralleling Washington Boulevard.

Enter Carroll Park at 3.7 miles; aside from many recreational opportunities, the park is most famous for being the home of the circa 1760 Mount Clare Mansion, Maryland's first house museum and one of the oldest colonial Georgian houses in Baltimore; visit **www.mountclare.org** or call (410) 837-3262. When you see three wooden poles in the path, take a right and cross Washington to Bush Street. The trail is delineated as a well-marked bike route in the street; obviously if you're walking, use the sidewalk. Warning: this will no longer feel like a hike, but rather a city stroll. Further warning: if you follow the length of the GFT, it will remain urbanized for quite a while.

Nevertheless, you'll pass through some historic and interesting city neighborhoods. First up is the Camden-Carroll Industrial Area. Follow the Bike Route signs to a left onto and then straight up Ridgely Road. Cross the railroad tracks and take a right onto West Ostend Street, again following the Bike Route and GFT signs; you're on the edge of downtown, passing M&T Bank Stadium, home of the Ravens, on the left. Take a right onto Warner Street across from the stadium. Once you cross the railroad tracks, you'll see signs for the GFT pointing straight as well as left. If you've had enough urbanity and want a return to green, go straight; if you want to do the whole trail, head left. Assuming you've headed left, pass under I-395 and through Solo Gibbs Park, a small community park in Sharp-Leadenhall, a neighborhood that is more than 200 years old and home to the city's first African-American enclave.

Take a right on Henrietta Street and then a left on Williams Street to Light Street. Follow Light Street to the Baltimore Area Visitor Center (BAVC) at the Inner Harbor at 6.4 miles, where you can find out anything and everything about what to see and do. (If you're really up for a vigorous day, ask about the guided Heritage Walk, which leaves from the BAVC and connects 20 historic sites and museums near the Inner Harbor.)

Coming back to the GFT, take a right on Lee Street and then a left on Sharp Street, going through Otterbein. This mid-19th-century neighborhood of orderly row houses and flower boxes is a true success story. Locals might remember Otterbein as the site of the $1 houses, sold to those willing to settle and revitalize. These days, those same houses fetch six figures.

Continue on Sharp Street to Stockholm Street; turn right, once again go under I-395, and turn left back onto Warner Street. Turn left onto Ridgeman Street and then another quick left into a little wooded area, still following the Bike Route signs. You'll immediately go over a steel bridge that crosses short tentacles of the Middle Branch of the Patapsco River. After you cross another bridge you'll see the Greyhound Bus Terminal nearby, but you're waterside, sort of "underneath" the city. If you've done any downtown driving and entered the city from I-95 on the I-395 ramp, you'll be familiar with this view; it's interesting to be far below it now, somewhat removed. On one hike while I was marveling at the swirl of interstate ramps above, I turned to the left and saw a large great white heron lope off in the Patapsco, bounded by a grove of wildflowers.

When you pass under I-95, you'll be crossing water—Gwynns Falls again close to where the falls empty into the Middle Branch. Take a left onto Clare Street and pass through the Westport Electric Substation. Take a right onto Kloman Street when you hit the railroad tracks. Pass a Light Rail stop and take a left when you reach Waterview Avenue. If you've had enough urban adventuring, you'll feel relieved when you enter Middle Branch Park. You'll come to a wooden boardwalk to the left that ends at a wildlife viewing observation deck at 9.5 miles. Surrounded by milkweed, cattails, goldenrod, and wildflowers, you'll see many water birds here—herons, gulls, ducks, and geese, a somewhat incongruous but pleasing sight against the backdrop of the city skyline.

Go left onto the asphalt from the wooden boardwalk and pass another observation deck and then the Cherry Hill Marina. Follow the path as it winds along the water, passing picnic benches and shade trees, and go under the Vietnam Veterans Memorial Bridge, where you'll see people fishing. The Broening Boat Ramp is just ahead, yielding to a lovely little section that winds along the edge of the Patapsco. Unfortunately you're likely to see garbage in the water along with algae blooms because of too much nitrogen runoff. Amazingly the birdlife seems undaunted; a recent Baltimore Bird Club outing spotted common snipes, ring-necked pheasant, Savannah sparrows, and tree sparrows, along with the ubiquitous water birds.

You'll see Harbor Hospital on the right, buffered by a hill of wildflowers. The trail ends at the fishing piers near Hanover Street. There's actually a little path that leads under the road; it's overgrown and full of trash, but plans are afoot to clean and continue this trail, linking it with the BWI and B&A trails to the south, part of the East Coast Greenway. There's parking available at Harbor Hospital for the shuttle to make the GFT one way; take I-95 to Exit 54, Hanover Street. Cross the Hanover Street Bridge and turn left at Cherry Hill Road or Reedbird Avenue; the parking lot is at 3001 South Hanover Street.

▶ NEARBY ACTIVITIES

Too numerous to list here—ask for help at the Baltimore Area Visitor Center on Light Street at the Inner Harbor. You'll find enough nearby activities to keep you occupied for a long, long time.

LAKE MONTEBELLO–HERRING RUN PARK

▶ IN BRIEF

Stroll around the busy urban retreat of Lake Montebello and then plunge into the thick woods surrounding Herring Run, a forested marvel surrounded by a mass of humanity.

▶ DESCRIPTION

Since I was heading left in my car, by natural inclination I headed left on foot as well, but I soon realized this was incorrect. Several signs along the route make the traffic pattern clear: automobiles on the farthest left, heading clockwise; bikers and in-line skaters in the next circle toward the lake heading clockwise as well; and then walkers in the innermost circle, closest to the lake, heading counterclockwise. I also soon realized that it didn't much matter as there's plenty of room in any case, and no one shot me dirty looks for heading in the wrong direction. But if you're a stickler for order, head right, not left, after you park. That said, be aware that the mileage markers around the lake are clockwise.

Either direction you go, you'll be flanking a 15- to 20-foot well-maintained buffer of grass between the asphalt and aquatic plants at the lake; I saw several people picking up a stray bottle or two from the grass, and I got in on the act (penance for my rogue direction). The bad news is that you're initially accompanied by the heavy vehicle traffic around you, but that will change as vehicles can only go so far—and you won't have

▶ KEY AT-A-GLANCE INFORMATION

LENGTH: 3.7 miles

CONFIGURATION: 2 loops connected by an out-and-back

DIFFICULTY: Easy

SCENERY: Lake Montebello, Herring Run

EXPOSURE: Half and half

TRAFFIC: Heavy around lake, light to moderate at Herring Run

TRAIL SURFACE: Asphalt

HIKING TIME: 1.5 hours

ACCESS: Dawn to dusk

MAPS: USGS Baltimore East

FACILITIES: Bathrooms, water

SPECIAL COMMENTS: A $20 million restoration to Lake Montebello, removing sludge buildup from the chemically treated water, as well as landscaping and road improvements, begun in early 2005, is expected to take three years to complete; expect periodic road closures and limited lake access during this time. In addition, the water of Herring Run has been deemed dangerous by the Baltimore City Department of Health; walking near the water poses no threats, but stay out of the water itself. On a happier and more obscure note, the country's first monument to Christopher Columbus sits in Herring Run Park, on Harford Road between Walther Boulevard and Argonne Drive.

▶ DIRECTIONS

Take I-83 to Exit 9 to Cold Spring Lane east. Follow Cold Spring Lane to Harford Road (0.5 miles after Morgan State University) and turn right; after you enter Herring Run Park turn right onto Lake Montebello. Once you've entered the park, you can only head left; there's plenty of parking on the side of the street.

Lake Montebello–Herring Run Park

UTM Zone (WGS84) 18S

Easting 363869

Northing 4354855

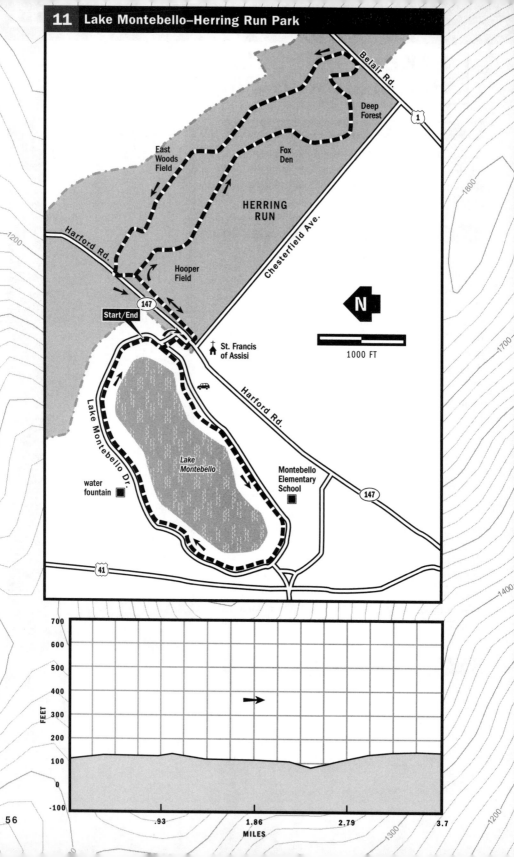

Belair Rd.

1

Deep Forest

East Woods Field

Fox Den

HERRING RUN

Harford Rd.

Chesterfield Ave.

Hooper Field

147

Start/End

St. Francis of Assisi

N

1000 FT

Harford Rd.

Lake Montebello Dr.

Lake Montebello

water fountain

Montebello Elementary School

147

41

1800

1200

1300

1700

1400

1500

1300

1200

700
600
500
400
300
200
100
0
-100

FEET

.93   1.86   2.79   3.7
MILES

Lake Montebello

to jump out of the way because of the configuration described above. Straight across the lake you'll see the green-roofed, brick Montebello State Hospital looming on the hill. The lake itself is partially shielded from view by tall aquatic plants, including cattails, but in return, you'll get a nice view of the birds that perch on the tops of them. I also saw lots of red-winged blackbirds as I walked the trail.

You'll see the nice and tidy (and ubiquitous) Baltimore row houses to the left, but at 375 feet you will pass a hill covered in beautiful old evergreens, and the houses and traffic will begin to fade in the distance. A chain-link fence circles the lake, but it is covered in greenery, which makes it difficult to see. In summer, it's covered in honeysuckle vines and morning glories. As part of the renovation (see "Special Comments," page 55), this fence will be replaced with an iron-barred one.

You'll pass a grove of beautiful mature evergreens and Montebello Elementary School at just under 0.5 miles. There are no official facilities around the lake, but you'll see a water fountain at 0.8 miles. Just beyond you'll see the beautiful stone reservoir works building with the sign "Lake Montebello—1880." More evergreens dot the field just beyond. At 1 mile, a series of evergreens planted in nice neat rows appears on the left, while the cattails continue to dominate the lakefront on the right. Loads of birds and butterflies shuttle between these two oases.

When you return to where you've parked, head down the hill and cross Harford Road at the light at the intersection of Montebello Terrace, Harford Road, and Chesterfield Avenue (you'll see St. Francis of Assisi Church across the street). Once you've crossed, head left down the hill on the paved trail. Hooper Field, ringed by mature trees, opens up to your right. This path continues to descend until Harford Road is high above you to the left. At 1.6 miles, you'll come to a T intersection with the Harford Road Bridge to the left; take a right. Herring Run is on your left inside a stand of woods; it's difficult to see, especially in summer. You'll immediately pass the posted warning from the Baltimore City Health Department: DANGEROUS. POLLUTED WATER—KEEP OUT.

At 1.7 miles, the water comes into better view, but unfortunately trash spoils it, especially after a heavy rain, which speaks to the fragile nature of such urban runs as Herring. Even so, the water sounds wonderful. Also, the path where you're walking is generally tidy, which seems to suggest that the problem isn't necessarily people throwing their garbage here, but rather rainwater picking up city trash and carrying it into the river.

After reading the previous paragraph, you're probably wondering why I've even suggested this hike. As you continue to walk, you'll understand. At 1.9 miles, you'll enter the woods, well away from the city traffic. Hearing swiftly moving water to the left and seeing thick woods on either side is heavenly. You'll soon come to a little stone bridge. To the right are some beautiful rock formations, creating natural cave-like shelters. Just beyond to the left you'll see a sign informing you that you are in "Fox Den." Old oaks and maples dominate this truly magnificent, isolated, idyllic, stretch of forest. The trail remains wide and paved, with lots of underbrush and trees towering above on either side—a perfect example of how truly beautiful this entire area was, is, and can be.

At 2 miles, you'll enter the section appropriately called "Deep Forest." At 2.2 miles, the trail begins to head left. You'll see woods in front of you. Row houses come into view behind as you enter "Orlinksy Grove." Here the trail follows the natural curve of the run itself and then opens up as a field comes into view on the right. Straight ahead is Belair Road; if you head left, you'll see a little dirt path to the water. This is a good place to stand—the water flows clear and absolutely free of trash. On either side, the water moves quickly over a series of rocks, while straight ahead it runs smoothly past a nice rock outcrop on the other side.

Head back to Belair Road; head left and cross over the bridge. The trail picks up again on the other side to the left, down the hill, and back into the woods. It's worth stopping a moment on the bridge to gaze out over the run, a view that people speeding by in their cars can't have.

Back in the woods on the other side of the run, at 2.6 miles, you'll cross a raised bridge over a small tributary. To the left you'll see a yellow pump house. There are sporadic arrows painted on trees, but disregard these and stay on the path, which is easy to follow. Along the way, you'll see cut dirt paths on either side; these either lead to the water or serve as paths to the surrounding neighborhoods. It's worth taking one of the neighborhood paths out and back; they're all less than half a mile or so, but it's nice to see how thick the woods are in some of these places.

At 2.9 miles, you'll pass a sign that reads "WILDLIFE HABITAT. This brush pile provides protection from weather and predators for many small birds and mammals." This section is called "Second Tributary," and the path opens up as the trail swings around to the right, passing ball fields to the left. A series of brick duplexes to the right pops up in the clearing up the hill. At a sign telling you this area is called "East Woods Field," take the small dirt path into the woods, paralleling the paved path below. This dirt path rises up the hill and soon links again with the paved path at 3.2 miles; taking this path allows you to stay in the woods, which is nice if it's a hot day. When you come back onto the paved trail, Herring Run will be straight ahead. Head to the right on the paved trail and cross over "First Tributary." The path runs much closer to the water on this side than it did on the outbound side. Despite the warnings described above, a series of rocks in the water gives off a pleasing sound, almost enough to drown out the sound of traffic, which you'll hear again as soon as you head back toward Harford Road. When you reach the bridge, walk under it; you'll see bathrooms and a water fountain to the right. This is a popular area for dog walkers. Loop around and walk under the next arch of the bridge back to the path you took into the park.

▶ NEARBY ACTIVITIES

A city-owned public golf course is in Clifton Park, just a half-mile south from Lake Montebello on Harford Road, and a half-mile north is Morgan State University. If you have the opportunity, try to catch a performance by the university's world-famous choir, which has earned international acclaim over the years; for information call (443) 885-3333. For good eats and a bit of shopping, head to the revitalized Belvedere Square; from Lake Montebello, go south on Harford, take an immediate right on 32nd Street, and another quick right on Hillen Road. When it turns into Perring Parkway, take a left onto East Belvedere Avenue and you'll reach Belvedere Square in 3 miles; on Friday nights in the summer, enjoy live music outside from 6 to 9 p.m. If it's not too packed, try the Irish restaurant Ryan's Daughter—if you consider yourself a beer connoisseur, try Smitchwick's on draft, long one of my favorite beers and only recently available in the United States.

LEAKIN PARK

IN BRIEF

Have several "I can't possibly be anywhere near a city" moments along this amazingly wild and isolated trail through the largest unbroken urban forest in the United States.

DESCRIPTION

The directions below might seem a little confusing. Here's the reasoning: Turning onto Franklintown Road from Forest Park Avenue will indeed eventually bring you to the Winans Meadow parking area; however, you have to swerve around a confusing "Road Closed" sign at Franklintown that actually refers to Winans Way, a few miles away. In addition, once you're on Franklintown Road, if you proceed past the Winans Meadow parking area, you find yourself on an obstacle course of debris that is Franklintown Road just beyond the park entrance. Some of the roads are closed to traffic, and others are not—and it's often difficult to tell which is which. To avoid all of this, I choose to park at Winans and Briarclift (see directions below) and walk from there; the hike described below corresponds to where I parked.

At the intersection of Briarclift and Winans,

DIRECTIONS

To reach the Winans Meadow parking area, take I-695 to Exit 16, I-70 East/Park and Ride; bear right onto the Security Boulevard exit and then turn right onto Forest Park Avenue. Turn right onto Franklintown Road; Winans Meadow is 1.4 miles on the left.

To reach the trailhead, take I-695 to Exit 16, I-70 East/Park and Ride; bear left onto Cooks Lane at the Security Boulevard exit and then turn left on Briarclift Road. Park at the intersection of Briarclift and Winans Way at the "Road Closed" sign; the trailhead is Winans Way beyond the road closure sign.

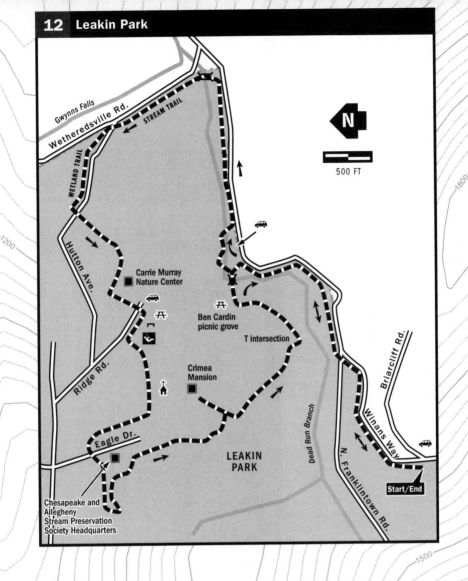

Gwynns Falls

Wetheredsville Rd.

STREAM TRAIL

WETLAND TRAIL

Hutton Ave.

N

500 FT

Carrie Murray
Nature Center

Ben Cardin
picnic grove

T intersection

Ridge Rd.

Crimea
Mansion

Eagle Dr.

Chesapeake and
Allegheny
Stream Preservation
Society Headquarters

LEAKIN
PARK

Dead Run Branch

Briarcliff Rd.

Winans Way

N. Franklintown Rd.

Start/End

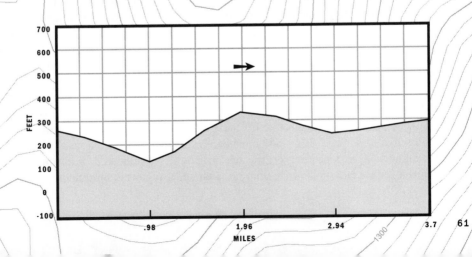

Dead Run at Leakin Park

you'll see a wooden sign with a waterwheel labeled "Gwynns Falls Leakin Park." Walking down Winans, you're pretty well in the woods, but since this was once a vehicle passage, the trail is wide and exposed in some sections. As you begin to gradually descend, the lovely houses on the hill at Briarclift slowly fall out of view. At 0.3 miles, you'll come to Franklintown Road; head right. This road also is theoretically closed to vehicular traffic, but unlike Winans, you're likely to see cars slowly zigzagging through logs, rocks, and other debris. Inevitably several people will stop and ask you just what the heck is going on with the road. If you're like me, you'll also have difficulty answering. It is confusing, and that's why I prefer to walk this section.

At 0.6 miles, you'll reach the Winans Meadow parking area. (If you prefer to eliminate 1.2 miles from this hike, park here and brave the perplexing road patterns.) In colonial times Gwynns Falls marked the boundary between the Iroquoian-and Algonquian-speaking tribes. At this time, around 1800, Baltimore was the nation's third-largest city, and growth and industrialization came quickly. This swath of natural beauty miraculously managed to survive. Unfortunately this park eventually became synonymous with crime, but it has been restored, is vigorously maintained, and is heavily policed—it has ironically become a safe haven.

Despite this, you might initially have a sour taste in your mouth as you head right on the paved path at the parking area since you're likely to see a lot of trash on either side of the trail as well as in Dead Run to your left. You might find this depressing and have some desire to give up. Don't—pleasures await you farther down the trail.

At three-quarters of a mile, you'll see a footbridge over Dead Run to the left, but head straight. Despite the trash in the river, Dead Run actually sounds nice because it is swift and full of rocks. At 1 mile, you'll cross over a pretty steel bridge; immediately merge left onto Wetheredsville Road, which is closed to traffic. Grass and weeds have begun their job of reclaiming the road. Immediately head uphill into the woods and turn right on the dirt "Stream Trail." Over the road below is the broad and lovely Gwynns Falls; your view will be mostly unimpeded in winter.

When you come out of the woods at the intersection of two paved roads, head left toward the sign for the Carrie Murray Nature Center—you're now on Hutton Road, which is also closed to traffic. Straight ahead you'll see a sign for the Gwynns Falls Trail (see page 50), and immediately to your left, you'll pass a greenway meadow, where, depending on the season, you'll see milkweed, fiddlebug nymph, Queen Anne's lace, goldenrod, and monarch and swallowtail butterflies.

Walking up Hutton Road, you'll be mostly in the shade and see lots of rocks and moss on either side of the cracked asphalt. At 1.4 miles, you'll see signs for the Wetland Trail and Nature Center. Head into the woods and walk along the boardwalk through a stand of smaller, newer trees—mostly oaks, birches, and beeches. You'll be thankful you're on a raised boardwalk as you cross over small streams, marshy aquatic plants, mud, and poison ivy.

At 1.5 miles, the boardwalk ends and the trail becomes dirt and moss. Here comes one of those moments that if you were dropped here from a plane, you would never guess you were in the middle of an industrialized city. All you can see are sky and trees. Portions of the hit movie The *Blair Witch Project* were shot here.

The trail leads uphill and becomes a loose collection of exposed roots and rocks. You begin to zigzag up and down—mostly up—until you come to a clearing and the Carrie Murray Nature Center. If it's open, it's worth going inside. Most interesting is the rehabilitation center for injured birds of prey; the center also provides a nice display of reptiles.

Moving away from the nature center, turn right at the paved trail and go up and over the hill. You'll see a small parking area to the right and a dirt footpath across from it on the left; follow the path into the woods. You'll see white blazes on this trail, which is very dense and well shaded, mostly by tall oaks, and again you'll feel as if you can't possibly be anywhere near Baltimore. The blazes soon turn red, and at 1.9 miles you'll see a sign pointing to the Ridge Trail, but go straight under the canopy of a fallen pine tree. To the left you'll see pavilions, picnic benches, a parking area, playground, volleyball net, and tennis courts. This part of the trail is called the Norman Van Allen Reeves Memorial Trail. You'll see a boarded-up chapel to the left; colorful wildflowers surround it in spring and summer.

When the trail emerges from the woods onto a paved road and parking lot, turn left and cross over the train tracks through the open field; head left, and follow the tracks to the Chesapeake and Allegheny Steam Preservation Society Headquarters, which was constructed to look like an old train depot. (On the second Sunday of each month from April to October, the society runs trains for passenger pleasure rides from 11 a.m. to 3:30 p.m.) Circle around the tracks, keeping the woods on your right. This area is exposed, but to your right you'll see a wildflower meadow loaded with milkweed.

At 2.5 miles, follow the dirt road into the woods, which will bring you to a clearing. Follow the tree line until you come to a paved road, and take a right; stone buildings appear on your right. Keep walking and soon on your left you'll see the carriage house, chapel (which you passed earlier), caretaker's house, and honeymoon cottage of the Crimea Mansion, now the headquarters of Outward Bound.

Crimea was built in the mid-1800s by Thomas Winans, who made a fortune in Russia overseeing construction of the transcontinental railroad for Czar Nicholas I. He called the estate Crimea after the Russian peninsula of the same name. The owners, who were known Southern sympathizers, tried to discourage Union troops from entering their estate by constructing a faux fort with fake cannons. It didn't work; the troops of General Benjamin Butler cut up the orchard for firewood, arrested Winans' father, Ross, and locked him away in Fort McHenry (see page 42).

With the mansion in front of you, backtrack and turn left on the gravel road at the little parking area at 2.8 miles. Head downhill in the woods; to the right you'll see some absolutely magnificent huge old white oaks. Be careful—the trail is rocky here, and it's easy to twist a knee. After about a hundred yards, you'll see a foot trail to the right; take it and it will lead you to that magnificent stand of white oaks.

The trail gets a little tighter here, and a few sections are washed away from erosion. Get ready for the next "I can't believe . . ." moment. When you come to a T intersection, head left. You'll soon arrive in a big clearing with picnic benches and a pavilion, the Ben Cardin picnic grove, named after the Baltimore congressman. Walk downhill toward the patch of wetlands next to the pavilion. You might see mudflat dragonflies, red-winged blackbirds, and periwinkle. Walk along the paved path and cross over Dead Run on the bridge to the parking area at Winans Meadow.

▶ NEARBY ACTIVITIES

The Gwynns Falls Trail, 14 miles of hiking and biking trails, follows the falls to the Middle Branch of the Patapsco River all the way to the Inner Harbor. It intersects with Leakin Park trails at Hutton Street. Within 10 miles, plenty of other hiking and recreation opportunities abound. Head west on MD 40 to get to Patapsco Valley State Park (see pages 131, 135, and 139). Head east on Hilton Parkway to Liberty Heights to reach Druid Hill Park (see page 38), home of the Baltimore Zoo among other attractions. Also on Hilton, just before Liberty Heights, is Hanlon Park and Lake Ashburton; although these are not hiking destinations, the view of downtown over the lake is a fantastic one that's something of a local secret.

PATTERSON PARK

Enjoy a renewed urban oasis, 137 acres in Baltimore's oldest park, created in 1827.

▶ DESCRIPTION

Often referred to as "Baltimore's Backyard," Patterson Park ran into some hard times during the 1980s and early 1990s and became synonymous with drug activity. Recent neighborhood revitalizations and booms in the housing markets of nearby Highlandtown and Canton, however, have renewed interest in the park as a place of recreation, and a true urban oasis has been created. The "Friends of Patterson Park" gets the primary credit for the park's renaissance. You'll pass the organization's white brick headquarters as you head left from the trailhead.

You'll see a fountain straight ahead; take a left where the giant shade trees tower over the benches. Baltimore's ubiquitous row houses ring the park, and you will have views of East Baltimore from several points in the park, especially the higher ground near the trailhead. Open, well-maintained, trash-free fields border the first part of the trail. At a quarter mile, take a left when you see the Virginia S. Baker Recreation Center, and then take a quick right onto the narrow paved path, which runs alongside mature maple and white oak.

At just under 0.4 miles, take a left and another quick left 50 feet later, heading down a sycamore-studded hill. You'll see ball fields to the

▶ DIRECTIONS

Take I-83 south until it ends at President Street. Continue straight on President Street and then left onto Eastern Avenue and go approximately 25 blocks to Patterson Park Avenue; turn left and park on the side of the road. The trail starts between the two concrete pillars where Lombard Street ends at Patterson Park Avenue.

ⓘ KEY AT-A-GLANCE INFORMATION

LENGTH: 2 miles

CONFIGURATION: Loop

DIFFICULTY: Easy

SCENERY: East Baltimore, historic structures, duck pond

EXPOSURE: Sunny

TRAFFIC: Moderate to heavy

TRAIL SURFACE: Asphalt

HIKING TIME: 45 minutes

ACCESS: Open 24 hours a day year-round; take due caution after dark. Maryland Transit Administration (MTA) bus #20 runs north, bus #13 runs east, bus #7 runs west, and bus #10 runs south, bordering the park on all four sides; for a complete schedule visit **www.mtamaryland.com** or call (866) RIDE-MTA.

MAPS: USGS Baltimore East; non-portable park map just beyond trailhead

FACILITIES: Water fountains throughout park; the park also has ball fields, tennis and basketball courts, playgrounds, and a swimming pool.

SPECIAL COMMENTS: The Chinese Pagoda is open Sundays from May–October, 12 p.m.–6 p.m., with free music Sunday nights from May–August. The park makes arrangements for private appointments and special group tours; for information call the Friends of Patterson Park at (410) 276-3676. For more information on Patterson Park, visit **www.pattersonpark.com**.

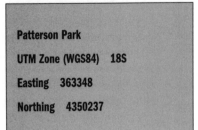

Patterson Park

UTM Zone (WGS84) 18S

Easting 363348

Northing 4350237

Pond popular with birds

right farther down the hill. Take the next right onto a narrower path, which descends slowly until it is level with the fields. You'll see a bench here, surrounded by more shade trees, and at 0.5 miles you'll come to tennis courts, on the left. Stay on the paved inner path, passing the water fountain to the left. When you see the red Tudor-style building straight ahead, take a left; you'll pass by playgrounds, swing sets, and an Olympic-sized pool (it's a bargain to swim here—just $25 to join for the whole summer and day passes only $1.50). You'll come to the Mimi DiPietro Family Skiing Center (a blue building) next; take a left here. When you reach the grass buffer near the street, across from the tennis courts, take a right; you'll pass the Butz Twardow-icz Field to the right and a portable bathroom to the left.

At 0.8 miles, you'll come to a ring of iron bars protecting an impressive concrete monument to the "Father of the American Cavalry," General Casimir Pulaski, fronted by an enormous American flag and flanked by tall evergreens; go right. At 0.9 miles, you'll come to another water fountain. On the next pretty, serene stretch you'll walk uphill past lots of mature trees. At 1 mile, you'll see a laminated map of the park on a bulletin board. Head up three concrete steps to the black asphalt that winds through trees and heads toward the interior of the park.

You'll soon reach a catch-and-release duck pond; it requires a fishing license. Take a right to circle the pond. While many ducks and geese congregate here, more than 100 bird species have been spotted in Patterson Park, mostly members of the thrush, warbler, and sparrow families but also some very rare birds, such as the gad-wall, blue-winged teal, and merlin.

Cross over the pond on a wooden boardwalk, winding through a large concentration of cattails and lily pads, which produce attractive white and yellow blooms in the summer. The boardwalk, which is just under a tenth of a mile long, ends at the stone wall that encircles the pond. At 1.3 miles, when you've made a full circuit of

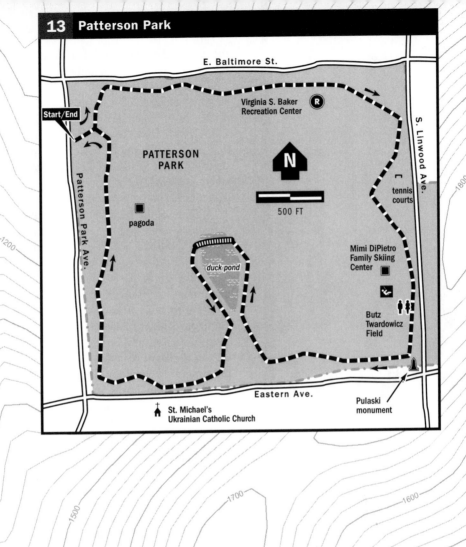

E. Baltimore St.

Virginia S. Baker
Recreation Center ®

Start/End

PATTERSON
PARK

N

500 FT

Patterson Park Ave.

pagoda

duck pond

S. Linwood Ave.

tennis
courts

Mimi DiPietro
Family Skiing
Center

Butz
Twardowicz
Field

Eastern Ave.

Pulaski
monument

St. Michael's
Ukrainian Catholic Church

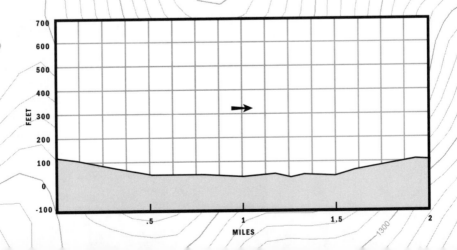

700

600

500

400

300

200

100

0

-100

FEET

.5

1

1.5

2

MILES

St. Michael's Ukrainian Catholic Church

the pond, take a right and then head straight toward the white asphalt and row houses. At 1.4 miles, turn right and you'll soon be standing in front of the gold-tipped onion-domes of St. Michael's Ukrainian Catholic Church, which would look far more at home in Kiev than Baltimore. Follow the path to the right as it heads uphill and take a left when you reach the wider path. You will see playgrounds and a pavilion to the right.

Some of the park signs in this area are in Spanish, reflecting the changing nature of the neighborhood, which is seeing an influx of Latino residents from Upper Fells Point, just to the south. At 1.7 miles, you'll pass a monument to German composer Conrad Kreutzer to the left and see the octagonal, four-story Chinese Pagoda, Patterson Park's main attraction and iconic symbol, up the hill on the right. Charles Latrobe designed the structure, which was originally known as the Observation Tower, in 1890. This striking hybrid of Oriental and Victorian design, graced by beautiful stained glass, sits on Hampstead Hill and provides scenic views of downtown and the harbor. These views help explain the line of cannons, marked 1814, in front of the pagoda. These cannons delineate the chain of fortifications that once ran from the harbor all the way to Johns Hopkins Hospital. The one directly in front of the pagoda, erected in 1914, marks the centennial commemoration of the cannon's original placement. Next to this cannon stands a bronze statue of two small children, also erected in 1914, to commemorate the centennial of the writing of "The Star-Spangled Banner"; the public schools of Baltimore paid for and erected the statue. After walking around the pagoda, head left and you will see the concrete pillars where you began your hike straight ahead. Note the lovely fountain to the right and the water fountain just off the path.

▶ NEARBY ACTIVITIES

The Inner Harbor, with its multitude of things to see and do, is just half a mile to the west via Eastern Avenue or Lombard Street. Take Eastern Avenue to Albemarle Street to taste the great food that can be found in Little Italy and Greektown, which is just east of Patterson Park and Highlandtown; if you're in the area in June, be sure to go to the annual Greek Festival. Just south is Fells Point, a National Register Historic area, first incorporated in 1773; you'll find plenty of shopping, food, history, and people-watching in this fascinating neighborhood.

WYMAN PARK-STONEY RUN TRAIL

▶ IN BRIEF

Escape the city without leaving it as you hike through a wooded riparian buffer in the neighborhoods of Wyman Park and historic Roland Park, part of the vision of famed American urban architect Frederick Law Olmsted.

▶ DESCRIPTION

When you reach the path, head right so you can rightly claim hiking the entire trail end to end since parking is impossible at the southern terminus—but it's only 0.4 mile to the end. Along the way, you'll cross under a stone bridge below Remington Avenue; a second, larger bridge soon appears, and you'll hear the traffic crossing overhead on Keswick Road. Stay on the trail down toward the water, which disappears in a thick stand of exposed vegetation and plunges underground, eventually making its way to the harbor downtown.

Turn around and retrace your steps; continue on the trail past where you parked to an area that is surprisingly well wooded, with dominating, towering oaks. Stoney Run lies below to the right, but you may have some difficulty seeing it in summer and you may want to take one of the many path offshoots that lead to the water's edge. You'll see Johns Hopkins University up the hill on the other side of the river.

▶ DIRECTIONS

Take I-83 to Exit 9, Cold Spring Lane east. After two lights, turn right onto University Parkway; continue until it ends at 33rd Street and turn right onto Keswick Road. Park at the intersection of 33rd Street and Remington Avenue. Once you've parked, walk past the "Do Not Enter" signs and you will see a dirt path immediately to the right at the edge of the woods.

ⓘ KEY AT-A-GLANCE INFORMATION

LENGTH: 5.3 miles

CONFIGURATION: Out-and-back with a short loop

DIFFICULTY: Easy

SCENERY: Mixed mature hardwoods, Stoney Run

EXPOSURE: Mostly shaded

TRAFFIC: Light to moderate on trail, moderate to heavy at Wyman Park and playgrounds

TRAIL SURFACE: Packed dirt, some sections of asphalt, cement

HIKING TIME: 1.5 hours

ACCESS: Trails always open although signs at Wyman Park and the playground near Cold Spring declare the parks open during sunlight hours only. The Maryland Transit Administration (MTA) bus #27 runs along Remington; for a complete schedule, visit **www.mtamaryland.com** or call (866) RIDE-MTA.

MAPS: USGS Baltimore West, Baltimore East

FACILITIES: Playground, ball field

SPECIAL COMMENTS: Hiking the Stoney Run Trail at dusk in the middle of June will yield the largest concentration of fireflies you're likely to ever see.

Wyman Park-Stoney Run Trail

UTM Zone (WGS84)   18S

Easting   359905

Northing   4354340

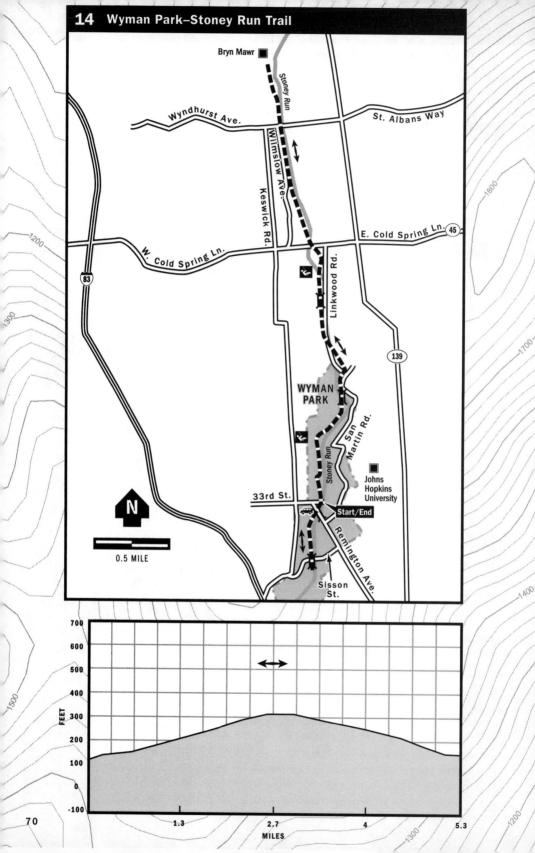

Bryn Mawr

Stoney Run

Wyndhurst Ave.

St. Albans Way

Wilmslow Ave.

Keswick Rd.

83

W. Cold Spring Ln.

E. Cold Spring Ln. 45

Linkwood Rd.

139

WYMAN PARK

San Martin Rd.

Stoney Run

Johns Hopkins University

N

0.5 MILE

33rd St.

Start/End

Remington Ave.

Sisson St.

FEET

700
600
500
400
300
200
100
0
-100

1.3   2.7   4   5.3

MILES

The location of this section of Stoney Run makes it prone to sewage spills and urban runoff after heavy rains, which lower the water quality. It's something of a crapshoot—a hike here one day takes you past clear, swiftly running water, while a follow-up trip the next day can leave you sniffing urban effluvia. Interestingly, the vast quantity of tenacious wildlife that makes its home here doesn't seem to change. Crows, sparrows, blackbirds, and even an oriole or two flitter overhead. Rabbits, squirrels, and chipmunks scurry over the trail, and abundant ducks, frogs, and snakes live at the water's edge. Recently a pair of night herons nesting on Stoney Run became proud parents.

At 1.2 miles, you'll come to Wyman Park, where people come to play football, soccer, or ultimate Frisbee, especially on weekends, while other folks practice their golf swings, and dogs romp unleashed. With all this activity, it's easy to see why this is such a beloved spot and a good reminder of what a treasure an urban green space can be. Neighborhood residents lovingly maintain the area.

Head right toward the water at the bulletin board at the south end of Wyman Park at the woods' edge. Cross the footbridge straight ahead and climb up the steep hill taking either one of the two trails in front of you (they form a loop). Climb over the stone wall and head left, paralleling the wall along wooded San Martin Road. Cross University Parkway and head down Linkwood Road. You may be disappointed when you see that Stoney Run is a small trickle contained within cement in this section of the trail; don't despair—it gets better soon.

You've now entered Roland Park, one of Baltimore's most distinctive neighborhoods. Home to Barry Levinson's *Avalon*, the neighborhood is an eclectic mix of Queen Anne, English Tudor, Georgian, and Shingle architecture. Developed in the 1890s by City Beautiful designer George E. Kessler and Frederick Law Olmsted, the neighborhood continues today as an oft-studied example for urban planners on how to create a neighborhood that naturally conforms to its geological contours. Part of the neighborhood's charm is its vast amount of greenery, with gardens, centuries-old trees, and of course, Stoney Run, which runs through its heart. Stoney Run manages to stay free of trash despite its location in the middle of the city, a testament to very active community involvement all along the trail.

You'll soon see the trail appearing as well-trod packed dirt, with a nice buffer of woods—oak and tulip poplar mostly—shading both sides of the river. Cross Stoney Run on the footbridge and follow the trail as it winds out of the woods and runs through a thick stand of bamboo before crossing a concrete bridge. To the left you'll see a series of private houses and community gardens, all immaculately maintained. Cross Overhill Road and pick up the trail on the other side where it winds along the edge of the tree line, blocking the houses from view. At 2 miles, a group of picnic tables and a well-used playground dominate an open field to the right. Linkwood Road to the east is sufficiently far away, across a green field, and thick trees shield Wickford Road, to the west, entirely from view, making this a pleasant spot for kids to play and for families to picnic.

Passing the playground, you'll soon come to a chain-link fence and Cold Spring Lane beyond it. Cross Cold Spring Lane with care and head left; take a right at the Bank of America sign and pick up the trail as it enters the woods behind the bank parking lot. The trail begins as a bed of cedar chips before reverting to packed dirt. Several varieties of oak and maple, as well as hickory, poplar, sassafras, ash, and the occasional walnut, shade the trail here. You'll also see a thriving understory filled with berry bushes, morning glories and trumpet vines, honeysuckle, and staghorn sumac, among other vegetation. Stoney Run flows to the right over loads of small rocks. Birds, rabbits, and squirrels shuttle between the woods and the water's edge.

The trail emerges into an open field as the surface returns to cedar chips. Just beyond, at a large cut to the left up to Wilmslow Road, you'll see a community bulletin board announcing area happenings and opportunities to help the Stoney Run Association with cleanups and other activities.

At 2.8 miles, cross Wyndhurst Avenue and pick up the trail on the other side as it plunges back into the woods. The trail rises above Stoney Run, and across the water you'll soon see tennis and basketball courts as you pass property owned by the Friends School (the oldest school in Baltimore, founded in 1784), and then Gilman Country School. After another 0.2 miles, the trail ends at the back of a building that is part of the Bryn Mawr campus; you have to turn around here.

When you reach the stone bridge over Stoney Run at Wyman Park on your way back, take a left immediately after crossing instead of the better-established trail straight ahead that you took in the first part of the hike. Follow the obscure footpath down to the water's edge.

The trail gets a bit thick here, and even ceases to be a trail occasionally, becoming a makeshift passageway over rocks and under fallen trees. I love the rough feel of this section—even though you are just below where you hiked before, the trail is decidedly wilder and may even require a bit of bushwhacking. Across the river you'll see granite outcroppings and tree roots clinging to the banks. If the trail becomes impassable, simply head uphill at one of the many path offshoots and rejoin the trail you hiked earlier. If you continue hiking at the water's edge, you'll soon come to a stone wall covered in lichen; you'll have to head back up the riverbank here and follow the well-established trail back to your car.

▶ NEARBY ACTIVITIES

On the campus of Johns Hopkins University, you'll find the Homewood House Museum, the Baltimore Museum of Art, and the National Lacrosse Hall of Fame. You'll also find that a walk through the beautiful Georgian campus can be a treat in itself. The Roland Park Historic District, which is located between Belvedere Avenue, Falls Road, 39th Street, and Stoney Run, includes the country's first shopping center, a Tudor collection of storefronts that is the prettiest strip mall you'll ever see. Here you'll find Petit Louis, an excellent French restaurant owned by famed chef Cindy Wolfe.

BALTIMORE COUNTY

BANNEKER HISTORICAL PARK– NO. 9 TROLLEY LINE TRAIL

ℹ️ KEY AT-A-GLANCE INFORMATION

LENGTH: 3.9 miles

CONFIGURATION: Two-way out-and-back

DIFFICULTY: Easy

SCENERY: Historic homes and towns, Cooper Branch, abundant birdlife.

EXPOSURE: Slightly more sun than shade

TRAFFIC: Moderate

TRAIL SURFACE: packed dirt at Banneker, asphalt on Trolley Line

HIKING TIME: 1–1.5 hours.

ACCESS: Dawn to dusk

MAPS: USGS Ellicott City, trail maps for Banneker property inside the museum (open Tuesday–Saturday, 10–4 p.m.)

FACILITIES: Restrooms, phone, and water at Benjamin Banneker Museum

SPECIAL COMMENTS: The trails around the Banneker property can easily be explored on their own, and the No. 9 Trolley Line Trail can be taken alone too, but combining them and starting in the middle, at Banneker, allows for a number of possible configurations. You can park at both ends of the Trolley Line Trail, as well as at Banneker Museum and Park. The combined itinerary as described in this hike makes for a wonderful afternoon.

Banneker Historical Park–
No. 9 Trolley Line Trail

UTM Zone (WGS84)   18S

Easting   346834

Northing   4348187

▶ IN BRIEF

Take in historic sites with a big dose of nature. Along the way, enjoy a good meal and shopping in Ellicott City.

▶ DESCRIPTION

Benjamin Banneker, the foremost African-American man of science in the early years of the United States, lived his entire life on the land where the museum now sits. Open since 1998, the museum and park continue to grow and develop. Recently the "Molly Bannaky House," a circa 1850 stone farmhouse, has been fully restored and now houses a library and meeting room. Other structures of interest on the property include an archaeological dig area, a nursery, the Banneker "Ice Pond," and the Lee Family Farm Ruin. Banneker was born a free black in 1731 and lived until 1806. His life's accomplishments included constructing a wooden striking clock and a projection of a solar eclipse, helping in the land survey for Washington, D.C., publishing six almanacs, and exchanging correspondence concerning opposition to slavery with Thomas Jefferson. The museum does an excellent job of illuminating the life and contributions of this underappreciated figure in American history, and it is definitely worth a long visit.

About 500 feet beyond the back of the Banneker Museum, you'll reach the edge of the woods. Look there for a barely discernible trail that is alternately cedar chips and packed dirt;

▶ DIRECTIONS

Take I-695 to Exit 13, Frederick Road, toward Catonsville. Go 3 miles and turn right onto Oella Avenue; continue half a mile to the Banneker Historical Park and Museum gates, on the left. Park in front of the museum; the trailhead begins behind the museum, past the botanical conservation area.

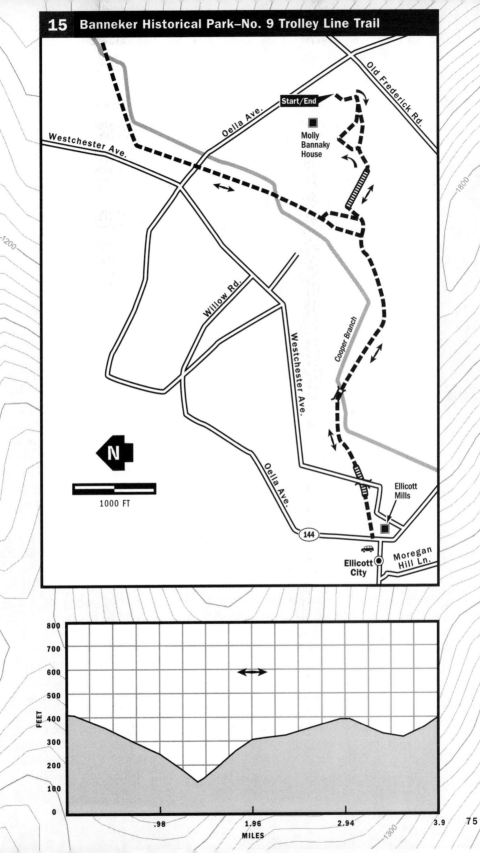

Old Frederick Rd.

Oella Ave.

Start/End

Molly
Bannaky
House

Westchester Ave.

Willow Rd.

Westchester Ave.

Cooper Branch

N

1000 FT

Oella Ave.

144

Ellicott
Mills

Moregan
Hill Ln.

Ellicott
City

1200

1300

1500

1800

1700

1300

1200

FEET

800
700
600
500
400
300
200
100
0

.98   1.96   2.94   3.9

MILES

Cooper Branch

you can see it as a straight line heading away from the museum, but you won't see any blazes or marks on the short, nubbly trees and tall walnuts. At just under 0.2 miles, you'll come to a small section of crushed rock and railroad ties; the path swings around to the right and parallels a small stream to the left. You'll soon come to a better established, packed dirt trail with railroad ties; head left on it.

At 0.25 miles, cross over the stream on a small wooden boardwalk, and then head uphill. The woods are thick with oak, poplar, and maple. You'll reach a hilly rise at just under 0.4 miles, and you'll see a stream valley below. Railroad ties down the hill and a chain-link fence to the right mark the Banneker property boundary. The paved path beyond the fence is the No. 9 Trolley Line Trail; head left on it.

Once on the trolley line, you'll see Cooper Branch to the right as you walk downstream. To the left sits a marshy area, surrounded and protected by a fence. The sound of water spilling over the big rocks in Cooper Branch provides a pleasing accompaniment. To the left rises a big hill studded with beech and Christmas ferns. It's easy to see the natural contours of the valley and the ease with which the trolley ran through here. It looks like no blasting was necessary and judging by the size of nearby oaks, little disturbance was made to the surrounding area.

At 0.75 miles, you'll cross Cooper Branch on an old stone bridge; your path doesn't change since the water runs underneath the trail. The legacy of rock blasting soon becomes clearer; you'll see jagged rocks, covered in fern and moss, jutting toward the trail from the left. At just over 0.8 miles, walk under a power-line cut; be sure to look up for the hawks and turkey vultures that frequently glide above. On my hike here, I saw no fewer than two dozen of them circling around in the sky.

More jagged, moss-covered rocks, decorated here and there with sumac, crowd the trail until it turns into a long wooden boardwalk at 0.9 miles. The boardwalk runs under the Westchester Avenue bridge. Despite the fact that the bridge is a few hundred feet above your head and Westchester Avenue is only a narrow, two-lane road, you might feel a bit unnerved walking under this noisy steel bridge when cars go over.

You will reach Ellicott City at 1 mile, and you'll see a sign that reads, "Historic Ellicott City No. 9 Trolley Line Trail" with a parking area just beyond. The trail soon ends; swing around and go down the wooden stairs lined with a row of Eastern red cedar. You'll see the brick trolley shop to the left, open and serving the public since the mid-1800s. Once down the stairs, you'll come to Ellicott Mills, established in 1772. The rail line that ran from Baltimore, completed in May 1830, ended at this point. Railroading is prominent here, as Ellicott City boasts America's first railroad station; the same building now houses the B&O Railroad Museum, which is open Friday 11 a.m. to 4 p.m., Saturday 11 a.m. to 4 p.m., and Sunday 12 p.m. to 5 p.m.; for information call (410) 461-1944.

Since downtown and Main Street are right in front of you, why not take advantage and eat, shop, or browse? When you're ready to go back, head up the stairs to the trail and retrace your steps. This time, when you reach the Banneker property at 1.7 miles, pass by it. You'll come to a chain-link fence, but the trail goes right through it. The woods here are not as thick or as old as the ones on the part of the trail you took earlier; thin tulip poplar and lots of mid-level growth—vines and briers—dominate here. At 1.8 miles, just beyond the end of the fence, look for a stately and pristine beech tree with its roots spilling over a large rock.

At 2.1 miles, cross Oella Avenue, in the heart of the town of Oella, which can hold its own history-wise with nearby Ellicott City. The town, which was named for the first woman who spun cotton in America, for generations was home to cotton mill workers. The town's first residents built their homes of stone a few years before the War of 1812, while those who settled here in the years leading up to the Civil War used brick. Oella bustled until 1972 when Hurricane Agnes swept through the Patapsco Valley and destroyed much of the town; sadly, it never fully recovered. The trail runs through residential Oella, although not among the oldest houses. A nice wooded buffer flanks the trail, with Cooper Branch running on the right. As the trail becomes more and more residential, Cooper Branch disappears beneath Edmonson Avenue, which is where the trail ends.

At 3.4 miles on your return trip, you'll pass a big white house on the left; head up the hill to take an alternate way back to Banneker. You'll see a little creek to the left and a bunch of bamboo just beyond. The trail naturally continues downhill, but look for a sharp right up the hill; if you see the paved trolley line path again, you've missed it—turn around and head back up.

If you didn't see any white-tailed deer when you came through this section earlier, you're bound to see them now. At 3.8 miles, cut to the right where you came in; keep straight ahead to the field and then cut right into the botanical conservation area. A wildlife habitat checklist, available inside the museum, alerts you to look for spicebush, tulip polar, Christmas fern, eastern bluebird, yellow-bellied sapsucker, warbler, Baltimore oriole, goldfinch, cedar waxwing, blue jay, red-shouldered hawk, box turtle, and owl. The museum also has a "Birds of the Banneker Historical Park Birding Checklist" for more experienced bird-watchers. This brochure lists 60 birds, including four different finches, five sparrows, three owls, and four woodpeckers.

▶ NEARBY ACTIVITIES

Assuming you've already spent significant time in Banneker Museum and checked out Ellicott City's many attractions, you might want to experience the great hiking at nearby Patapsco Valley State Park. The Hollofield Area of the park, with its ball fields, camping playgrounds, equestrian trails, picnic areas, and, of course, hiking trails (page 244), can be reached by taking a right on Rogers Avenue from Frederick Road/Main Street in Ellicott City; turn right on MD 40, Baltimore National Pike. You'll come to the park entrance a couple of miles on the left before you reach the river.

CROMWELL VALLEY PARK WITH LOCH RAVEN ADD-ON

Cromwell Valley Park with
Loch Raven Add-on

UTM Zone (WGS84)   18S

Easting   366753

Northing   4364315

▶ IN BRIEF

An opportunity for pleasant hiking within 371-acre Cromwell Valley Park, as well as adding a more strenuous Loch Raven extension. Keep your eyes open for abundant wildlife.

▶ DESCRIPTION

Cromwell Valley Park (CVP) has a long history; the area was first settled some 300 years ago. Nowadays, thanks to conservation efforts by the county and state as well as the generosity of families that owned the farms that now make up CVP, it exists mostly as an educational park, focusing primarily on farming, history, and nature. Programs demonstrating animal husbandry and organic farming provide educational opportunities year-round. This means that the park is often busy, but the trails remain largely uncrowded.

From the parking area, walk toward Cromwell Bridge Road and take the crossing over Minebank Run, which eventually flows into Loch Raven Reservoir not far to the east. Take a right on the blue-blazed Minebank Trail; recent plantings, part of a 2004-2005 restoration project, flank the wide trail. Also as part of the restoration work, Minebank Run has been stabilized with rock walls.

You'll pass many mature trees, including maple, walnut, tulip poplar, locust, oak, and sassafras. Staghorn sumac, Queen Anne's lace, and goldenrod flank an old property-line fence to the left. These native species compete with the invasive kudzu, porcelain berry, devil's tear thumb, barberry, and multiflora rose, and park volunteers,

▶ DIRECTIONS

Take I-695 to Exit 29A, Cromwell Bridge Road. Go left (west) at the light, and enter the park to the left at 0.9 miles (2002 Cromwell Bridge Road). Follow the road all the way until it ends at a gravel parking area.

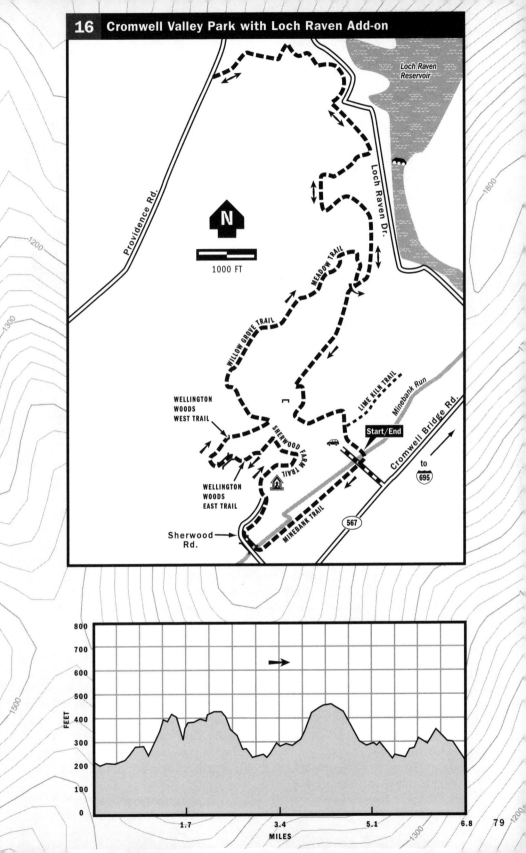

Rock wall restoration on
Minebank Run

in league with the Ecosystem Recovery Institute, continue efforts to rid the park of these damaging plants. As the park is actually made up of three separate farms, you'll see divisions such as the fence as well as a grove of beautiful willow trees. All of the foliage here makes the area a haven for birds. In all, CVP hosts literally hundreds of bird species; for a complete list, visit **www.bcpl.net/~cvpark/wildlifeandbirding/ fullbirdlist.html.**

At 0.5 miles, you'll cross a feeder stream before coming to Sherwood Road. Take the bridge across Minebank Run and then follow the road. Do not take the left turn but stay on the road continuing in the direction indicated by the Sherwood Farm sign. You'll pass the Cromwell Valley Community Supported Agriculture (CSA) site, an organic farm that sells shares to its produce (for more information visit **www. bcpl.net/~cvpark/csa.html**). At 0.8 miles, head left, going the wrong way past a "Do Not Enter" sign and through an alley of stately shade trees. This leads to the park office; stop in for interpretive brochures for the two wooded piedmont trails coming up. When the horseshoe road of the park office begins to slope rightward, cut left toward the woods; you'll see a sign for the orange-marked Sherwood Farm Trail. Take it into the woods.

This area is a riot of mature hardwood with a thriving understory. The trail splits immediately; leave the wide cedar-chip trail and go left onto the narrower packed-dirt Wellington Woods East interpretive trail, marked by green signposts, that heads uphill. You'll come to a rightward cut at 1.1 miles; continue straight. You'll quickly come to a very discernible trail to the right followed immediately by a Y; take a left and you'll see a red #1 signpost—this is the Wellington Woods West Trail. Cross a footbridge and follow the trail along the top of a fairly narrow, very rocky ridge. It soon swings to the right on a bed of moss and reaches the edge of the park property. The trail splits again at a red #11 post; take a left and you'll see a green #1 at the split by an enormous oak.

The path runs over little rippling hills dotted with ferns, a very nice spot. At the next trail split, at the #5 post, go left (or to complete the entire interpretive loop, take a right and then backtrack to this point). You will parallel a little stream to the right and walk uphill along a ridge. You'll hear lots of birds singing as you hike, and you may also see some of the multitude of animals the park hosts. Abundant white-tailed deer live in the park, along with beautiful and elusive red foxes; I saw three during my hike here. Other animal residents include beaver, opossum, raccoons, woodchucks, muskrats, several varieties of squirrels and shrews, voles, chipmunks, and mice—ready meals for red-tailed hawks and kestrels. CVP also hosts many reptiles and amphibians, including frogs, toads, turtles, skinks, and salamanders, as well as more than a dozen different snakes. A word of warning: the northern copperhead, one of Maryland's two venomous snakes, lives in the park; in the unlikely event that you do see one (look for the telltale diamond-shaped head), give it a wide berth.

As you continue on the trail, you'll notice large chunks of Cockeysville marble, remnants of the marble that was heated to produce lime in large kilns in the early 1700s. A couple of the kilns still exist and can be seen near the parking area.

At 1.7 miles, you will see a series of steel cables heading up to a very tall antenna; head right, cross the stream, and go straight up the hill. Cross the intersecting path and continue straight on the wide trail; at the top of the hill, you'll see more offshoot paths—just continue straight on the red-marked Willow Grove Trail. Be on the lookout—this area is especially good for spotting red foxes. Pass through a grove of mountain laurel, and at 2.2, you will connect with the yellow-marked Meadow Trail .

At 2.3 miles, take a right; you'll see the edge of Loch Raven Reservoir through the woods. At 2.7 miles, you'll come to a T intersection on a path that's very wide even though you're still deep in the woods. To stay entirely in Cromwell Valley Park or if you're short on time, take a right; otherwise, take the left to continue hiking within the Loch Raven watershed on a 3.3-mile out-and-back. If you take the out-and-back, you'll soon pass a section of woods filled with pristine beech trees. The trail swings around to the right and then crosses a stream; climb the hill to get a very nice view of the stream valley to the right. When you reach the T intersection near the edge of the reservoir, at 3.1 miles, take a left. Go past a leftward cut and continue straight; at the T intersection at 3.5 miles, take another left and you'll come to Providence Road at 4.3 miles. If you turn around and backtrack, you'll reach the cut where you took a left at 2.7 miles inside the park; you've now completed 6 miles of the total hike.

After another 0.1 mile, take the little cut to the right; you'll come to a trail split in about 1,000 feet. Go right up the hill onto a narrow footpath, which winds through a pretty wild area filled with close vegetation and hanging vines. At the next T intersection, take a left. After you pass a couple of benches on the left, take a right into an open field, a great songbird locale. At the trail split at the edge of the field, go left; when you reach the gravel park road, at 6.7 miles, take a right and your car will be just up ahead, on the other side of the white house. (You'll pass by the white Lime Kiln Trail, an 0.2-mile trail, that runs past the lime kilns, if you want to see them).

▶ NEARBY ACTIVITIES

Take I-695 to Exit 27B to visit Hampton National Historic Site, a stately home that was once the largest mansion in the United States. Built with a fortune amassed during the Revolutionary War and once the northernmost slave-holding plantation in the country, it still boasts extensive gardens.

DOUBLE ROCK PARK

KEY AT-A-GLANCE INFORMATION

LENGTH: 2.25 miles

CONFIGURATION: Loop

DIFFICULTY: Easy; moderate in a few spots

SCENERY: Stemmers Run, mature mixed hardwoods

EXPOSURE: Mostly shaded

TRAFFIC: Light

TRAIL SURFACE: Packed dirt, gravel

HIKING TIME: 1 hour

ACCESS: Dawn to dusk

MAPS: USGS Baltimore East

FACILITIES: Restrooms at the edge of the woods, 0.1 mile from trailhead. Pavilions, ball fields, restrooms, and water at the official park entrance off Glen Road (take Harford Road south, cross Putty Hill Avenue, take a left onto Texas Avenue, go about a mile until Texas Avenue ends at Glen Road, and continue into the park entrance).

SPECIAL COMMENTS: The official park entrance, described above in "Facilities", doesn't provide the best access to the trail; instead, follow the directions below to the park entrance sign, where there is no "official" parking area but street parking is allowed.

Double Rock Park

UTM Zone (WGS84)   18S

Easting   368898

Northing   4359237

IN BRIEF

Enjoy a remarkably isolated spot where Stemmers Run meanders over a slew of rocks in the heart of heavily populated Parkville-Overlea.

DESCRIPTION

The Parkville Recreation Council manages the Double Rock recreational area, which nestles into the urban sprawl of the surrounding neighborhoods and nearby Beltway. You can easily miss it—and you'll just as easily be wowed by the very wild feel of its trails.

Look to your left at the trailhead, and you'll see a large garden that is open to the public. People who want to plant in the garden must obtain a permit; for information call (410) 887-5300.

At 0.1 mile, turn right off the gravel at the wooden bathroom building and head into the woods; two tall white oaks and a wooden marker with yellow blazes mark the footpath here. Take a right, and you'll immediately notice how mature the forest is, with oak, poplar, and maple soaring overhead. These fantastic foliage trees make autumn a wonderful time to hike this trail. Ferns also abound all around the trail. You'll see a little gulley to the right with a hill beyond. As you descend and the woods rise on either side, you will find it very easy to forget that you are anywhere near civilization.

At 0.3 miles, turn right at the blue blazes and cross Stemmers Run using the rocks as convenient stepping-stones. (All the water crossings

DIRECTIONS

Take I-695 to Exit 31, Harford Road south; go 1.8 miles and turn left onto Putty Hill Avenue. Go 0.2 miles and turn right onto Fowler Avenue; park where Fowler Avenue ends at Hiss Avenue. The trail starts just behind the brown Double Rock Park sign.

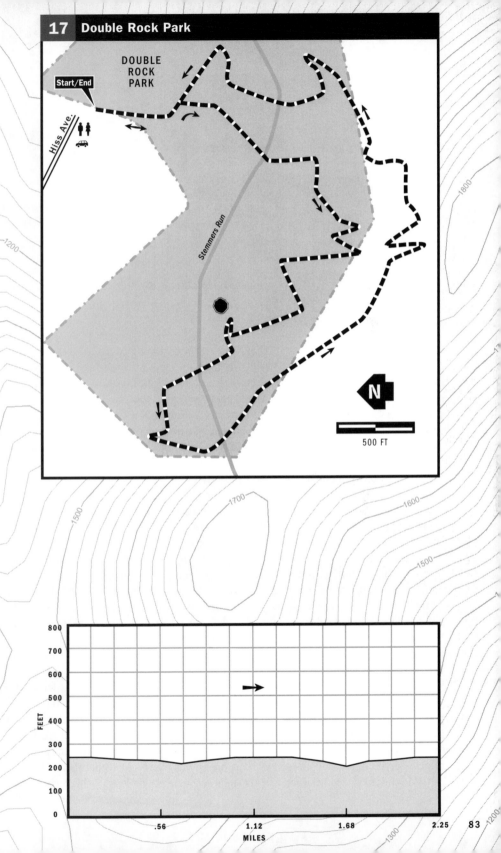

DOUBLE
ROCK
PARK

Start/End

Hiss Ave.

Stemmers Run

N

500 FT

Rock perch at Double Rock Park

on this hike can be easily negotiated using the many rocks that lie in Stemmers Run.)
Bear slightly to the left and follow Stemmers Run as it winds around to the left. You'll
see big fish darting around in the water below where it pools and a beautiful area of
striated rock above, where the water trickles through. You'll see more blue blazes
straight ahead on the trail. At 0.4 miles, head left, crossing Stemmers Run once again,
and pick up the trail on the other side. Continue heading right; pass by the red-
blazed cut into the woods to the left, and follow the blue blazes as they wind up the
hill and rise above Stemmers Run and the valley.

At 0.7 miles, you'll see a huge rock outcropping to the right. This perch makes
a wonderful place to sit and absorb the beautiful scene below: Stemmers Run spilling
over huge chunks of rock. It's a little slice of Appalachia in the crowded Baltimore
suburbs—quite literally since the park's western boundary forms the city line.

Head back up the hill and continue to the right on the blue-blazed trail. At 0.8
miles, the blazes turn to yellow at the dam (to the right) on Stemmers Run. You'll see
an immediate split to the red trail, but stay on the yellow. On this section of the trail,
Stemmers Run is now fronted by posts strung with a steel cable. As the trail gradually heads uphill, it begins to parallel a chain-link fence, which delineates the park
border. The trail winds its way between tall oaks and at 1.2 miles heads downhill and
up rather quickly; be especially careful on a muddy or snowy day since this section
can be quite slippery.

At 1.4 miles, the trail heads downhill and ends at the water. Head left as the
water snakes around and then splits, take a right over the water at 1.5 miles. Once
you're on the other side, go left and then quickly right; you'll see yellow blazes again.
Many fallen trees block the trail here, and you'll have to negotiate a few obstacles; be
on the lookout for the snakes and turtles that find shelter in the crooks of the prone
branches (you don't have to worry about poisonous snakes too much here, though).

As the trail becomes increasingly tight and overgrown, keep a sharp eye out for a faded white blaze on an oak tree to the left. If you miss it, you'll come to a clump of vegetation, at 1.6 miles, where the trail ends abruptly; just turn around and look for the white blaze to the right. It's a mere 200 feet from the trail end. This white-blazed section was clearly once a maintained trail, but it doesn't see heavy use anymore; the blazes are faded and the trail is generally grown over. Most of the white blazes are on beech trees, so look for those. It's easy to lose, but if you keep heading uphill, you'll see occasional white blazes and white arrows to keep you on track. The underbrush is minimal, so you won't have to do much bushwhacking. At the top of the hill, you'll see an arrow pointing to the left; it isn't much of a trail, but if you just head in that direction anyway, you'll very quickly merge onto the well-maintained blue trail again. Take a right onto the blue trail.

At 1.7 miles, you'll see a pavilion to the right and you'll come to a Y intersection just beyond; head right. After a few hundred feet, you'll see an orange post on the left. Go to the left; you're now on a gravel and sand road that leads out to an open field and the back of the garden plot you saw at the trailhead. Go left and follow the gravel trail back to your car.

▶ NEARBY ACTIVITIES

If you've built up an appetite, you won't have any problem finding something to eat. Go either direction on Harford Road for a multitude of dining options. For more hiking, head south on Harford Road to Herring Run Park (see page 55) or continue past Herring Run for a round of golf on the public course in Clifton Park, between Harford Road, Belair Road, and Erdman Avenue.

EASTERN REGIONAL PARK

▶ IN BRIEF

Spot a great blue heron wading in Saltpeter Creek among the rushes and cattails.

▶ DESCRIPTION

Head left on the trail at the wooden fences where tall cattails sway in the breeze. This network of paved paths runs between the park's ball diamonds and athletic fields, and is full of walkers, joggers, in-line skaters, and bicyclists. Note that the mileage markers on the asphalt won't correspond in distance to the hike described here; the markers indicate distances on a 1-mile circuit through the ball fields.

Pass by the soccer fields on the right and head toward the chain-link fence; when you reach it, go right. You'll see a beautiful old weeping willow to the left and train tracks beyond the fence. At the 7/10-mile marker on the asphalt, you'll see arrows pointing to the right, but continue straight. At 0.3 miles, the asphalt stops at a mowed section of grass among the tall, willowy aquatic plants, evidence that water is very close. Sure enough, at 0.4 miles, hop onto the wooden lookout point to the left to get a good view of Saltpeter Creek, coveted by local fishermen for its generous stock of largemouth bass. A nearby Baltimore Gas and Electric power plant heats the surrounding waters, which attracts bull minnows, thus providing a convenient feast for the bass.

▶ DIRECTIONS

Take I-695 to Exit 36, Southeast Boulevard (MD 702) and go 1.3 miles to Eastern Boulevard (MD 150); turn left and continue east toward Chase. In approximately 4 miles, you will see Chase Elementary School Recreation Center; the park entrance is on the right just past the recreation center. The trail starts just off the parking area to the far left, flanked by willow trees close to the gazebo marked "D."

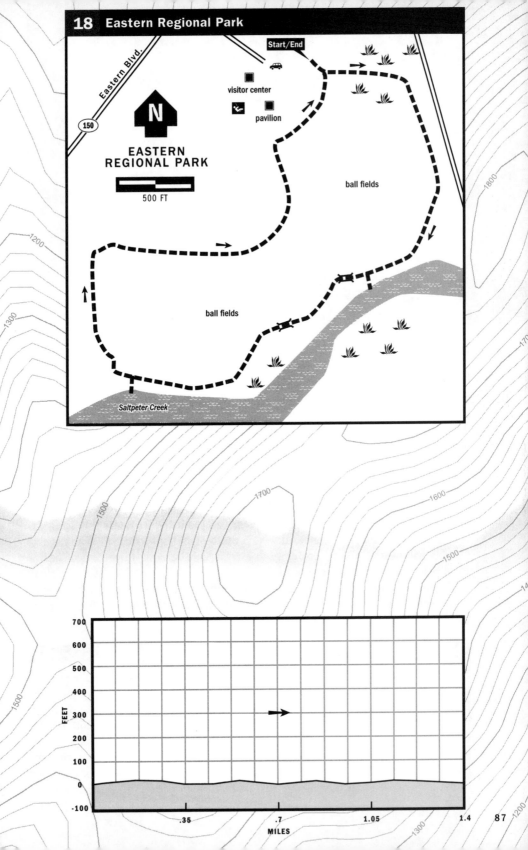

Eastern Blvd.

150

Start/End

visitor center

pavilion

N

EASTERN
REGIONAL PARK

500 FT

ball fields

ball fields

Saltpeter Creek

1200

1300

1800

1700

700
600
500
400
300
200
100
0
-100

FEET

.35   .7   1.05   1.4
MILES

1500

1700

1600

1500

1400

1300

1200

Saltpeter Creek

Coming back from the overlook, head left; when you come to the wooden bridge, turn left, cross the bridge, and pick up the trail on the other side. You'll cross another wooden bridge at 0.6 miles; the willows and rushes here reach as high as 6 or 7 feet. When you see softball fields on the right, at 0.65 miles, cross the wooden boardwalk; in 0.75 miles you will come to a wooden overlook that will give you a slightly different view of Saltpeter Creek. If you didn't see a heron at the first overlook, you may see one here; if you strike out both times, you'll probably at least see red-winged blackbirds overhead and turtles, snakes, frogs, and fish below.

Coming back from the overlook, you'll see a little gravel path heading into the woods just beyond the end of the fields. Take this path into the forest, which has many tall, straight, thin trees, most of them beech and holly. While this is a nice spot, it's close to Eastern Boulevard, which can be busy and loud; you won't see it, but you will hear it. You're also close to Martin State Airport, so you might hear a small plane or two buzzing overhead.

After a quarter-mile, you'll emerge from the woods and pick up the asphalt trail. Head left to go back to the playground; then head right and complete your circuit back to the parking area.

▶ NEARBY ACTIVITIES

Take Eastern Avenue east, turn right onto Marshy Point Road, and follow the signs to nearby Marshy Point Nature Center. Located on a 500-acre site on Dundee and Saltpeter creeks, the center features an exhibit hall and an auditorium for audiovisual presentations. I couldn't include the trails that were being developed in 2004–2005; they should be completed by the end of 2006. In addition to hiking opportunities, you can rent a canoe and explore the coastal forests and marshes along the two creeks. The area hosts a wide variety of birdlife and is very popular with birders. The center is open every day from 9 a.m. to 5 p.m.; for information call (410) 887-2817.

FORT HOWARD PARK

▶ IN BRIEF

Meander along the well-fortified confluence of the Patapsco River and Chesapeake Bay.

▶ DESCRIPTION

Fort Howard traces its beginnings to 1896, when the U.S. government began purchasing land on North Point in preparation of fortifying the area essential to repelling naval attacks on the City of Baltimore. Originally called North Point Military Reservation and renamed Fort Howard, for Colonel John Eager Howard, in 1904, it served as the headquarters of Baltimore's coastal defenses from the time the first troops arrived on June 27, 1899, until the last troops left in August 1940. The Veterans Administration (VA) acquired the property, and now a chain-link fence separates the grounds of the VA Hospital from the park.

From the trailhead, you'll immediately see a red blaze on a beech tree to the right. Go straight, passing the grounds of the VA Hospital on the right and a thick section of woods on the left. After just 600 feet, you'll come to Battery Nichol-son, named for the general who fought in the Bat-tle of Fort McHenry in the War of 1812. Built in 1900, the battlement was armed in 1902 with two 6-foot disappearing rifles.

Just beyond, at 0.2 miles to the right, hike up the hill and head toward the water, the conflu-ence of the Patapsco River and the Chesapeake

▶ DIRECTIONS

Take I-695 to Exit 40, North Point Boulevard (MD 151) south. Go 3.8 miles; just after the I-695 overpass take a left onto North Point Road. Continue 4 miles to the park entrance next to the VA Hospital; follow the road to the parking area. The trail starts next to the large park map (see "Special Comments") beyond the wooden swinging gate at the far end of the parking lot.

ⓘ KEY AT-A-GLANCE INFORMATION

LENGTH: 1 mile

CONFIGURATION: Loop with 2 short spurs

DIFFICULTY: Easy

SCENERY: Historic battlements, Patapsco River, Chesapeake Bay

EXPOSURE: More sun than shade

TRAFFIC: Heavy

TRAIL SURFACE: Asphalt, grass

HIKING TIME: 30–45 minutes

ACCESS: 7 a.m. to dusk

MAPS: USGS Sparrows Point

FACILITIES: Restrooms, water

SPECIAL COMMENTS: Ignore the large park map to the left of the trailhead—it's crude and grossly inaccurate. I made many attempts to locate the long, circular green trail depicted on the map, and I couldn't find anyone who knew anything about it.

Fort Howard

UTM Zone (WGS84)   18S

Easting   375358

Northing   4339759

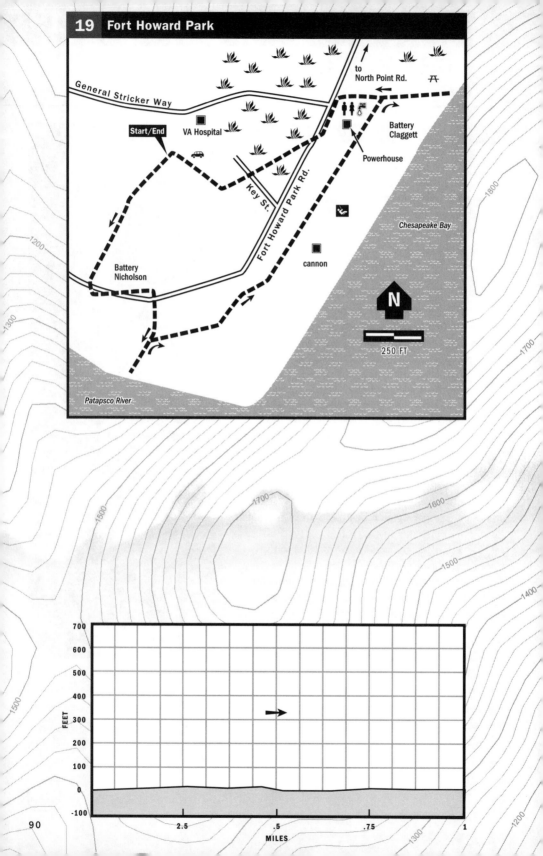

General Stricker Way

to
North Point Rd.

Start/End

VA Hospital

Battery
Claggett

Powerhouse

Key St.

Fort Howard Park Rd.

cannon

Chesapeake Bay

Battery
Nicholson

Patapsco River

N

250 FT

1200

1300

1800

1700

1600

1500

1400

1300

1200

1700

700

600

500

400

300

200

100

0

-100

FEET

2.5

.5

.75

1

MILES

1500

1500

90

Patapsco and Chesapeake confluence

Bay. Besides being a beautiful spot, it's easy to see why government leaders considered it to be such an important area to defend: this spit of land commands a perfect view of the wide waterway that must be navigated to attack Baltimore by sea. You probably won't see British warships sailing by today, but you're likely to see sail and motorboats instead.

Walk along the water for a while; although there is no actual "trail" here, the many sunbathers, picnickers, and others who come here to enjoy the sea breezes have made it a well-trodden area. Also walk out onto the pier. Keeping the water on your right, you'll eventually swing back up the hill and join the asphalt path above. Several playgrounds and pavilions sit between the path and the water, and as you continue along the trail, you'll notice the interesting juxtaposition of the cold steel of the antique cannons and hard stone of the battlements and the gleaming plastic of the playground equipment.

Less than a half-mile down the path, the trail splits into a V; head slightly to the right. You can take one of the many cuts to the right back toward the water before continuing along the asphalt trail. In another half-mile, you'll come to Battery Claggett, which was also built in 1900 and also named for a general who fought at Fort McHenry; it was armed with three rapid-fire guns. Head straight toward the battlement onto a dirt trail that leads to the water. The path soon disappears under vegetation, but you will enjoy nice expansive views of the water, a nice complement to the open-water area you saw earlier. You won't see sunbathers here, only fishermen casting their lines off the seawall.

Retrace your steps back to the paved trail, go to the right, and at three quarters of a mile, you'll pass the fort's powerhouse on the left. It now houses restrooms and water fountains, but it once supplied power for gun emplacements. Head to the right at 0.8 miles farther down the trail, and you will reach the parking area at 1 mile.

On the way out of Fort Howard Park, don't miss historic Todd's Inheritance. It sits half a mile north on North Point Road and is clearly marked with a historical marker. Thomas Todd settled on this spot in 1664. Retreating British soldiers, defeated at the Battle of Fort McHenry, burned the original Todd home; the house standing here now was built on the original homesite in 1816 and was remodeled in 1867.

▶ NEARBY ACTIVITIES

Linking Fort Howard and Todd's Inheritance with nearby North Point State Park (see page 122) provides good hiking as well as excellent history lessons. North Point remains something of a historical shorthand in the Baltimore area for the bravery shown by the Maryland citizen militia and its stand against invading British troops during the War of 1812. At North Point State Park, you can also see the remnants of Bayshore Amusement Park, which operated from 1906 to 1947. When Baltimoreans rode the #26 trolley car to play here for the day, the fare was 30 cents.

GUNPOWDER FALLS STATE PARK (HEREFORD AREA): GUNPOWDER NORTH–SOUTH CIRCUIT

► IN BRIEF

Circle Gunpowder Falls at arguably its prettiest and most scenic section.

► DESCRIPTION

The wrought iron Masemore Road Bridge was built in 1898. A wooden pole sits just to the left of the bridge, pointing out the white-blazed Gunpowder South Trail. Follow the trail upstream over mossy rocks and fallen tree trunks for 500 feet to the blue-blazed Highland Trail to the left. Head uphill through mountain laurel and along a ridged groove; you'll see a valley dropping off to the right and Bush Cabin Run heading into Gunpowder Falls. Although mountain laurel is by far the dominant flora along this hike, if you complete the entire circuit, you'll also pass by river birch, cherry, oak, hemlock, dogwood, and witch hazel.

At 0.3 miles, it looks as if the trail is straight ahead, but you'll see lots of fallen trees in the way—the trail actually heads to the right and narrows as it leads deeper into the woods. When you reach Bush Cabin Run, cross over it to the right. You'll come to a power line cut at 0.5 miles; as you cross it, look to the right—you may see cows grazing at the farm. Once back in the woods, the trail widens significantly and leads through stands of pine and cedar.

You'll reach the narrow Falls Road and a small parking area at 1 mile. Cross the parking area and get back on the trail, which leads downhill;

► DIRECTIONS

Take I-83 to Exit 27, Mount Carmel Road west. Go 0.6 miles and take the first right onto Masemore Road. Follow Masemore Road as it winds past Fosters Masemore Mill (built in 1797); look for the parking area on the right at the bottom of the hill. Walk toward the bridge and pick up the trail there.

ⓘ KEY AT-A-GLANCE INFORMATION

LENGTH: 13.2 miles

CONFIGURATION: Loop

DIFFICULTY: Moderate to strenuous depending on length

SCENERY: Gunpowder River, Prettyboy Dam, wildflowers, rock formations

EXPOSURE: Shade

TRAFFIC: Moderate

TRAIL SURFACE: Packed dirt, rock

HIKING TIME: 6–7 hours

ACCESS: Sunrise to sunset

MAPS: USGS Hereford

FACILITIES: None (restrooms available at the south side of Bunker Hill Road)

SPECIAL COMMENTS: Several bridges and parking areas make it possible to vary the length of this hike. Bunker Hill Road, in the middle of the hike, used to be the most logical starting point, but the bridge there has washed away, so you'll have to begin at one of the other crossings-parking areas. The hike described below begins at the Masemore Road parking area, west of Bunker Hill.

Gunpowder Falls State Park (Hereford Area): Gunpowder North–South Circuit

UTM Zone (WGS84) 18S

Easting 355493

Northing 4385991

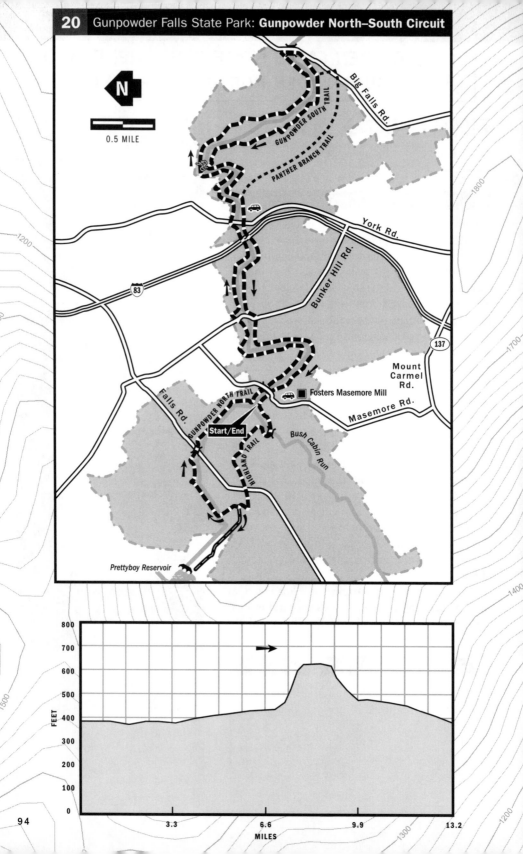

you'll see the horseshoe curve of the Gunpowder Falls straight ahead. At 1.2 miles, the trail splits; head left to reach Prettyboy Dam. The path to the dam is a treat—narrow and winding through and over exposed roots, moss, mountain laurel, erosion-resistant mica schist, trees with bulbous knots, and hemlocks. If you're hiking in the spring, you can be treated to a variety of wildflowers as well—hepatica, bloodroot, spring beauty, rue anemone, and pink lady slippers. You will reach the dam at 1.7 miles; if it's a summer day and you're lucky enough to catch the dam with one of the valves open, enjoy the cooling spray, which you'll begin to feel some 500 feet away.

Turn around and head back; you'll come to the trail split again at 2.2 miles. Head left and you'll soon reach river level. You'll see lots of little ripples; the rocky river has a series of little bends. The trunks of many of the trees along riverbanks bear the telltale beaver gnaw scars. By 2.5 miles, the trail turns into a jumble of rocks, which requires a bit of scrambling. You may think that some major tectonic activity had ceased just before you arrived, and this image of raw nature at work only increases as tree roots spill over the rocks and spongy moss covers the ground beneath the canopy of mountain laurel.

You'll reach Falls Road again at 2.9 miles; cross the steel bridge and pick up the Gunpowder North Trail. Both the river and trail level out a bit here, making a relatively easy stroll along the riverbanks in the grass. Summer blooms in this area include woodland sunflowers, aster, and goldenrod. You'll come to a little bog at 3.3 miles, and you'll pass through a stand of pines before reaching Masemore Road again at 3.5 miles. Your car is just on the other side of the road, but if you want to continue hiking, stay along the river; the trail will take you through stands of oak and tulip poplar. Soon, the river becomes quite shallow and you can see a multitude of pretty light-colored stones in the water. A little farther, the trail runs beneath a limestone rock base, some 30 feet in height.

You'll reach Bunker Hill Road at 4.7 miles; you can't cross here since the old bridge washed out, leaving only two stone abutments. Continue along the river, where the trees crowd the riverbanks a bit more, providing some wonderful canopy. Unfortunately, the only unpleasant stretch of this entire hike awaits—you'll hear it first and then pass under I-83; but you'll quickly leave this area behind. You'll reach York Road at 5.9 miles; you'll see a parking area across the bridge on the right. Cross York Road and pick up the trail at the break in the guardrail; you'll see a series of white rocks leading toward the river, and blue blazes will quickly follow.

It's initially uphill and down, but it quickly settles down to water level at 500 feet. At 6.4 miles, the trail swings around at a big hemlock, which leans out over the water. Very soon after, you will cross a little stream. The trail begins to feel more isolated here, and the river finally completely overtakes the faint echoes of the traffic on I-83.

At 6.8 miles, you'll pass Raven Rock Falls on the left. It's not a high vertical waterfall, but rather a riffle of rock that ends at the trail. Cross a little stream immediately beyond the falls; the trail soon heads up a little higher on the hill among big rocks, moss, ferns, and, of course, more mountain laurel. Some of the schist columns in this area rise about 25 feet. The trail goes a bit deeper into the woods and reaches a trail split at 7.3 miles, right after another stream. Go straight uphill, following the blue blazes; it's a fairly steep climb, and you will cross several deer paths.

Limestone columns along
Gunpowder River

Coming back down the hill, the trail levels out at 7.7 miles and reaches a big river curve at 8 miles. This is a great spot to take in the topography of the area—mid-sized hills rolling gently. You'll soon come to a gravel park road; head right, passing a marshy bog on the other side. The gravel road ends at Big Falls Road Bridge at 8.3 miles. Cross the bridge and pick up the white-blazed Gunpowder South Trail on the other side. This section is one of the many trout catch-and-return areas.

Now walking upstream, the trail on the south side of the river really hugs the edge of the water and is much more narrow than the other side. At 9.2 miles, the trail splits; The Panther Branch Trail, named for a panther that once lived in a cave visible from the trail, goes to the left and loops into the woods, eventually rejoining the Gunpowder South Trail. If you take Panther Branch Trail, be on the lookout for the remains of two old mills, built in the mid-1700s and destroyed in 1874. The entire length of the Panther Branch Trail covers 2.2 miles, and taking it will give you a half-mile less of total hike than if you remained on the Gunpowder South Trail.

Taking either option will bring you to the Sandy Lane Trail (0.3 miles in length), which connects Panther Branch Trail and Gunpowder South Trail. Back on the Gunpowder South Trail, go past a stand of holly and a little stream; you'll soon see Raven Rock Falls across the river. At 9.6 miles, you will come to a nice big rock that the trail goes right over. From this vantage point, you're afforded great views of the river in both directions.

The last trail split comes at 9.8 miles. Follow the right turn toward the river; going the other way takes you into the woods over the hill. The trail along the river gets very narrow, becoming at some points just an eroded knife-edge hanging over the water. You should not have trouble keeping your footing, but be very careful—you can slip and fall into the river here.

Beyond this narrow section, the trail widens and joins the other end of the Panther Branch Trail. Cross the Panther Branch; you'll come to York Road just ahead.

This section of the trail back to Bunker Hill changes only when it runs away from the river and through forest, where wildflowers and ubiquitous rocks reappear. For the next 3 miles you will follow the same route as before toward the turnaround, just on the other side of the river. For some reason, the south side between York Road and Masemore Road hosts many more pines than the north side; even so, in general the two sides of the river in this stretch differ little, and both are beautiful. You will reach Masemore Road and your car at 13.2 miles.

▶ NEARBY ACTIVITIES

To reach Woodhall Winery, one of Maryland's best, head east on Mount Carmel Road and turn right (north) onto York Road. Follow York Road across Gunpowder River and look for signs to the winery.

GUNPOWDER FALLS STATE PARK: JERUSALEM
VILLAGE TRAIL WITH JERICHO COVERED BRIDGE TRAIL

KEY AT-A-GLANCE INFORMATION

LENGTH: 4.8 miles

CONFIGURATION: Out-and-back with loop, plus added loop

DIFFICULTY: Moderate

SCENERY: Little Gunpowder Falls, wetlands, mixed hardwoods, historic sites

EXPOSURE: Shade

TRAFFIC: Moderate

TRAIL SURFACE: Packed dirt

HIKING TIME: 2 hours

ACCESS: 7a.m.-to dusk

MAPS: USGS White Marsh; trail maps at bulletin board at parking area

FACILITIES: Restrooms in park headquarters, open Monday–Friday, 8 a.m.– 4:30 p.m.; museum open Saturday and Sunday 1-4 p.m.; portable bathroom at parking area

SPECIAL COMMENTS: For more information about this hike, visit **www.dnr.state. md.us/outdooradventures/jerusalemhike. html.**

▶ IN BRIEF

Leave from historic Jerusalem Village and follow the floodplain of Little Gunpowder Falls before returning for a trip to the Jericho Covered Bridge.

▶ DESCRIPTION

You can spend hours in historic Jerusalem Village alone, and the fact that some fantastic hiking opportunities lie all around offers a wonderful bonus. The grist mill, now Gunpowder Falls State Park headquarters, was built in 1772 and continued operations until the last miller died in 1961. Employees of the Gun/Cooper Shop, behind the mill, produced walnut gunstocks for the Maryland militia during the Revolutionary War. Spread out from the mill, all within easy walking distance, stand the Tenant House, Lee Mansion, McCourtney's Store, Spring House, "Dwelling," and, of course, the Blacksmith Shop, also built in 1772, where the hike begins. Each historic building tells a fascinating story.

Pick up the trailhead at the edge of the woods behind the blacksmith shop. Initially, this white-blazed trail has cedar chips and packed dirt as it winds through a stand of oak. At the T intersection at 150 feet, take a left toward Little Gunpowder Falls, which you'll eventually follow upstream. You'll see ruins of the millrace at 0.1 mile. The path is very well maintained, but it feels nicely isolated because it's ridged on both sides.

When the trail splits at just under 0.2 miles, with white blazes to the left and blue to the right,

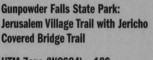

Gunpowder Falls State Park:
Jerusalem Village Trail with Jericho
Covered Bridge Trail

UTM Zone (WGS84)   18S

Easting   380391

Northing   4369102

▶ DIRECTIONS

Take I-695 to I-95 north. Take Exit 74 (MD 152) north toward Fallston. Go 2 miles and turn left onto Jerusalem Road; continue 1 mile to the parking area on the right. The trail starts at the edge of the woods behind the blacksmith shop, to the left of the parking area.

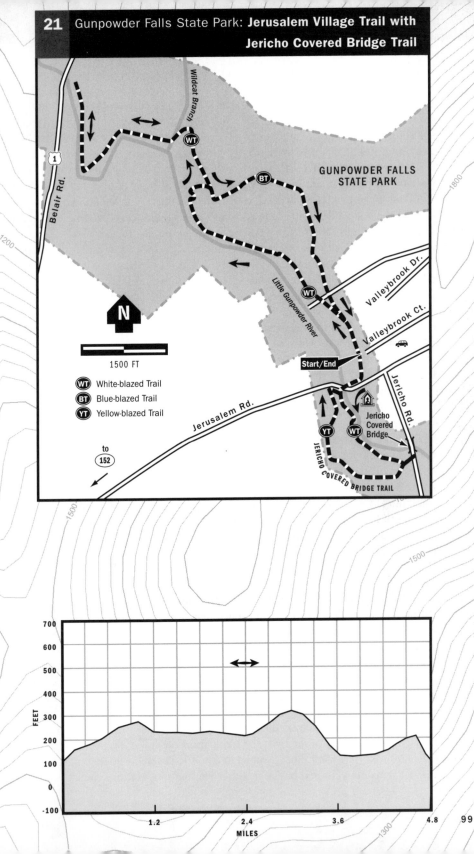

stay on the white-blazed trail but take note of the blue—it will be your return route. The river soon comes into view; it's shallow here, and very rocky, and roughly 150 feet across. You'll see big chunks of granite interspersed with ferns, sycamore, and sumac on the hill on the right. The understory thrives with mountain laurel and spicebush. Even though the river is not far away on the left, the trail often winds away from it, but the many path offshoots make a quick trip to the river possible.

At just under 0.4 miles, ford a little creek by stepping on the rocks. Beech, hickory, tulip poplar, and red and white oak abound here. As the trail winds uphill, you'll have good views of the river, especially in winter. At 0.5 miles, you will pass a bog on the right filled with cattails, ferns, and wildflowers; towering walnuts and some of the largest beeches I've ever seen crowd the bog on every side. The trail is very well maintained; huge trees fall on the trail, but they are quickly cut and pulled to the side. You will see some of them on the edge of the trail, covered in lichen and mosses and sprouting white, flaming red, and orange fungal growth.

At three-quarters of a mile, pass by the cutoff path leading left toward the water and continue on the white trail as it heads uphill. Once you reach the top, you can either head right on the blue trail to return to your car or stay on the white to continue the hike. At just over 1 mile, come down the hill to Wildcat Branch. Cross it by stepping on the big rocks; the water runs clear and swift toward Little Gunpowder River to the left. On the other side of Wildcat Branch, the trail splits; turn left (the trail to the right ends abruptly). When the trail meets Little Gunpowder River, head right to continue paralleling the river. The trail then heads uphill and winds away from the river; you will pass more millrace ruins on the left. You will come to a beautiful stretch of river at 1.4 miles; it's rock free and glass smooth for about 100 feet. Unfortunately, you'll begin to hear auto traffic in this area, though you won't be able to see any cars through the thick woods. The trail comes to a disappointing end at Belair Road at just under 1.7 miles at the "Harford County Welcomes You" sign. It's something of a shock after the incredibly rugged feel of the hike, but the good news is that you have to backtrack—and a good chunk of the return route will be different.

Heading back you'll reach the trail split at just under 2.5 miles; this time take the blue-blazed trail instead of the white—you'll be paralleling the edge of the woods at a power-line cut. The trail heads to a wide open area and picks up on the other side in the woods; if you're hiking in autumn, the foliage provides a very nice view to the right. Back in the woods, the trail heads uphill and becomes very rocky. Cross a little stream and at 3 miles, when the trail splits, head right to rejoin the white-blazed trail. The river comes into view on the right as you go down the hill—the next quarter-mile affords fantastic views of the water. When you rejoin the white-blazed trail, head left toward the parking area. This time, however, instead of heading to your car, go straight toward the mill. Head to the right, cross the bridge on Jerusalem Road, and then cross at the trailhead to reach the Jericho Covered Bridge Trail, denoted by wooden steps, white blazes, and a marker pointing to the covered bridge.

The trail initially follows the river downstream, with thick woods on the hill on the right. At the bend in the river, the trail climbs the hill, giving you a great view. At 0.3 miles from Jerusalem Road, you'll come to the covered bridge; built in 1865, it's the last remaining covered bridge in either Baltimore or Harford county.

On the way back, take the yellow-blazed trail instead of the white—it heads to the left up the hill when the trails split, 250 feet from the road. You'll pass through a stand of tall, thin oaks, and at the top of the hill, red cedar takes over the landscape, and you'll see a farm field to the left through the woods. The trail follows the inside edge of the tree line about 10 feet from the field. White-tailed deer love this border area, and you're likely to see loads of them. You will also see lots of pine, fir, red cedar, and sumac.

At just under 0.8 miles from the beginning of this portion of the hike, you'll come to Jerusalem Road. To avoid walking on the road, which does not have shoulders, head right to pick up the white-blazed trail at the river; then head left. You will rejoin Jerusalem Road at 0.9 miles; turn right to return to your car.

▶ NEARBY ACTIVITIES

To visit the nationally award-winning Ladew Topiary Gardens, get back on Mountain Road (MD 152) north toward Fallston; turn onto MD 1 north. Bypass Bel Air by heading north on MD 24; then turn quickly onto MD 23 west. Follow the signs to the gardens; for information visit **www.ladewgardens.com** or (410) 557-9466.

IRVINE NATURE CENTER

KEY AT-A-GLANCE INFORMATION

LENGTH: 1.1 miles

CONFIGURATION: Loop

DIFFICULTY: Easy with some moderate parts

SCENERY: Towering oaks, wildflowers including several varieties of coneflowers, black-eyed Susans, sunflowers, bluebonnets, and morning glories

EXPOSURE: Mostly shade

TRAFFIC: Light on the trail, moderate near the nature center

TRAIL SURFACE: Packed dirt, exposed roots, rocks, cracked asphalt

HIKING TIME: 1 hour

ACCESS: Only walk on trails when the nature center is open; Tuesday-Saturday, 9 a.m.-4 p.m. and Sunday, noon-4 p.m.

MAPS: USGS Cockeysville, White Oak trail map in nature center

FACILITIES: Restrooms, water

SPECIAL COMMENTS: Register inside the nature center when using the trails; no vehicles and no pets allowed on the trails (although you might see some leashed dogs)

Irvine Nature Center

UTM Zone (WGS84) 18S

Easting 354779

Northing 4363480

IN BRIEF

Stroll through mature forest, orchard, wildflower meadow, and gardens extended with a hike uphill and down through bucolic Greenspring Valley.

DESCRIPTION

Go inside the nature center to register—but don't be so quick to head out. The center itself has some wonderful displays. The live animals exhibited include poisonous dart frogs, snakes, turtles, and hissing cockroaches from Madagascar. Counted among its preserved specimens are native birds, including waxwings, finches, warblers, geese, as well as a red fox, which are indigenous to the immediate area.

The trail starts behind the nature center to the right, next to the barn. Immediately to the right, you'll see a sign pointing to the Irvine Wildlife Garden down the hill to the right. Take time to sit on the shaded benches tucked among the flowers in this lovely spot, filled with black-eyed Susans, sunflowers, bluebonnets, and morning glories.

Walk back up the trail the way you came and then head downhill to the right, paralleling a stream and Greenspring Avenue beyond that. The trail here is grass, and you'll see an organic garden on the left. At 450 feet up the hill in front of you will be an open area with a fence (ok, it's a sewage treatment facility, but you'd never know it if I didn't tell you). The trail becomes packed dirt

DIRECTIONS

Take I-695 to Exit 22 onto Greenspring Avenue. Go north 0.7 miles and turn left at the signs for Irvine and St. Timothy's School. Coming in from Greenspring Avenue, pass by the horses on the hill to the left and the gatehouse; when you see the pond to the left, turn right into the parking area for the nature center.

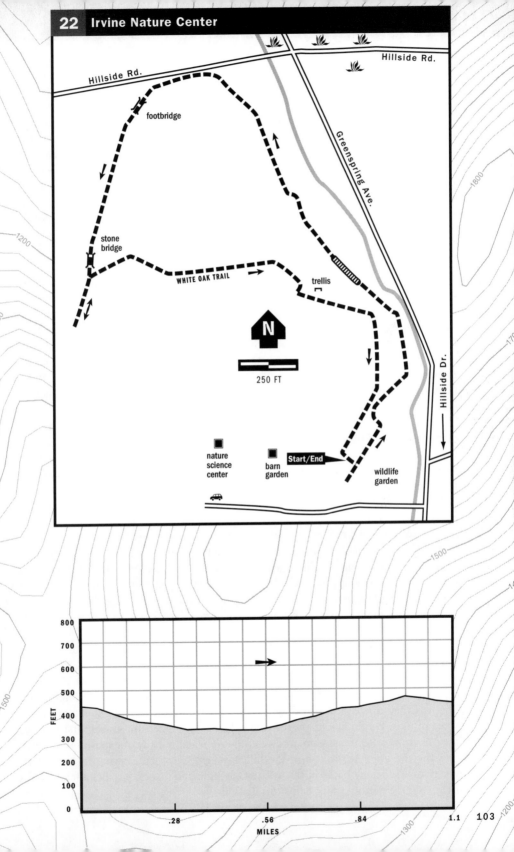

and splits at 0.12 miles; head to the right at the wooden marker labeled no. 2. The trail, which has white blazes, takes you into thick woods; Greenspring Avenue runs beyond a wooden fence.

At 0.17 miles, the trail splits a second time; again, stay to the right, the trail nearest the stream. At 0.24 miles, take the raised wooden boardwalk over wet, marshy land with massive oaks towering above, complemented with an abundance of beech and pine. At 0.3 miles, at wooden marker no. 10, the trail heads left—if you take it, you'll cut your hike in half; to complete the entire walk, go straight. A steep, rocky hill lies straight ahead, and the hiking becomes moderate. You'll gain altitude quickly, and if you're still clutching your white oak trail map, pocket it now—you're now well off the map. The traffic becomes light if not nonexistent, as the multitude of spiderwebs strung across the trail attests. Ferns, moss-covered rocks, and fallen trees flank the trail here.

The sporadic yellow blazes seem random; in fact, you're as likely to see as many white-tailed deer as yellow blazes. As you approach the intersection of Hillside Road and Greenspring Avenue, go through the woods and buy some fresh local produce from Joan if you're hiking in the summer or fall; if you're hiking in the winter, enjoy the views of beautiful Greenspring Valley and marvel at how this large patch of land so close to the city has managed to stave off development. Head left away from the intersection toward a small footbridge; cross the bridge and veer to the left. You're now walking on an old paved road, but it has been almost entirely reclaimed by groundcover and moss.

At 0.45 miles, you'll come to a beautiful old stone bridge to the left. This part of the trail is full of red oaks. If you follow the trail over the bridge and up the hill toward the right, you'll soon come to a sign that reads, "No Public Access Beyond this Point." Even though you'll have to turn around here, take advantage of this good opportunity to sit and absorb the scene. You'll likely not see nor hear any signs of humanity along these hillsides covered with sun-dappled ferns. You will also see a stand of American holly and cork trees next to the sign.

Return to the stone bridge you crossed earlier and take a right up the hill. Red blazes appear suddenly, and at 0.7 miles, you'll come to a gazebo and swing in an open area. Just beyond you'll connect with the White Oak Trail just a few hundred feet uphill from where you would have been earlier if you had turned left at the no. 10 wooden marker instead of heading deeper into the woods.

A paved road and some private houses immediately come into view. When you see these, head left back into the woods, and you'll soon see a white blaze. Head right; on your left you will see a wildflower meadow that's sure to be full of birds and butterflies in the warmer months. A quick right yields an interesting niche created by a fallen tree trunk that has splintered and is covered by a cluster of vines.

Just beyond that, at 0.8 miles, you'll see a makeshift trellis with benches inside. The trail then opens up, providing a good opportunity to see just how magnificent some of these centuries-old yet thriving oaks can be. When the trail splits; head up the hill, away from the stream, and carefully walk along loads of exposed roots criss-crossing the trail. At the top of the hill, bear left; if you are trying to keep track, you're now officially back on the White Oak Trail. You'll soon parallel a fence to the right, and the nature center is just up the hill.

If you're hiking in late spring or summer, you'll see a multitude of barn swallows that visit every year. A series of cages between the nature center and the barn house a broad-winged hawk that was hit by a car and is being rehabilitated, a barn owl that is also being rehabilitated, two screech owls, and an opossum. Down the hill stands a hothouse filled with native plants, with another small garden with benches below, next to the parking area.

▶ NEARBY ACTIVITIES

While a drive through Greenspring Valley any time of the year promises to be a treat, you can't match it for enjoyment in autumn. This is, quite simply, one of the most beautiful areas anywhere near Baltimore. A brand-new regional park, Meadowbrook, has been constructed at the corner of Falls Road and Greenspring Valley Road. The park includes a 0.8-mile loop trail, picnic pavilions, and ball fields. It sits right across Falls Road from upscale shopping and dining at Greenspring Station. Also nearby is the Cloisters Children's Museum at 10440 Falls Road; from Irvine, go south on Greenspring Valley Road to the stop sign, take a right onto Hillside, and continue until it ends at Falls Road; the museum is 300 feet to the right. The museum, set in a castle used for weddings (Will Smith and Jada Pinkett's, among others), encourages hands-on learning with unique exhibits; call (888) 330-9571 for more information.

LOCH RAVEN RESERVOIR: DEADMAN'S COVE TRAIL

LENGTH: 1.7 miles

CONFIGURATION: Out-and-back

DIFFICULTY: Easy

SCENERY: Loch Raven Reservoir, pine forest, hardwoods

EXPOSURE: Shade

TRAFFIC: Light

TRAIL SURFACE: Packed dirt

HIKING TIME: 1 hour

ACCESS: Dawn to dusk

MAPS: USGS Towson

FACILITIES: None

SPECIAL COMMENTS: Several months after completing the hike described here, I noticed a "No Parking" sign at the parking area. The sign was bent, scraped, and had a bullet hole in it. Also, there were several cars there, so parking is a judgment call. Despite the presence of other cars, I'd recommend parking elsewhere, riding a bike, and locking it up at the trailhead.

Loch Raven Reservoir:
Deadman's Cove Trail

UTM Zone (WGS84) 18S

Easting 363036

Northing 4368523

▶ IN BRIEF

Find some solitude at Deadman's Cove, inside the heavily visited Loch Raven Watershed.

▶ DESCRIPTION

The trail initially runs along an old fire road through tall grass. It's very wide, and though in the woods, it's also well exposed. At first you'll hear lots of traffic noise, but that will quickly disappear. By 200 feet, as the trail heads down a little hill, the sounds of the woods take over. Tall oaks dominate, rising above thick underbrush.

At 0.2 miles, you'll parallel a dry creek bed to the left. Though the trail is still very wide, it's now shaded due to the height of the trees. The grass is very tall, so expect a few shin scrapes during summer. By a quarter-mile, you'll see lots of pine along with plentiful white oak, hickory, and sycamore. These woods, like much of the Loch Raven watershed, provide a haven for white-tailed deer, and you're likely to scatter more than a few. Woodpeckers make their homes here too, and the sound of their tree pounding echoes all along the trail. To the left, an interesting wall of trees fronts the creek bed; their uniformity suggests that they

▶ DIRECTIONS

Take I-695 to Exit 27, Dulaney Valley Road north. Cross Timonium Road and look for the signs for the entrance to Stella Maris Hospice. Roughly a quarter-mile past Stella Maris is the parking area for the trailhead; if you come to the light at Old Bosley Road, you've passed it. Once you see the parking area on the left, find the closest place to turn around and then park on the right side of Dulaney Valley Road. The trail starts opposite the parking area across Dulaney Valley Road; it is marked by an orange cable and a sign reading, "Woods Road Closed to Bikes." Note: take great care crossing Dulaney Valley Road.

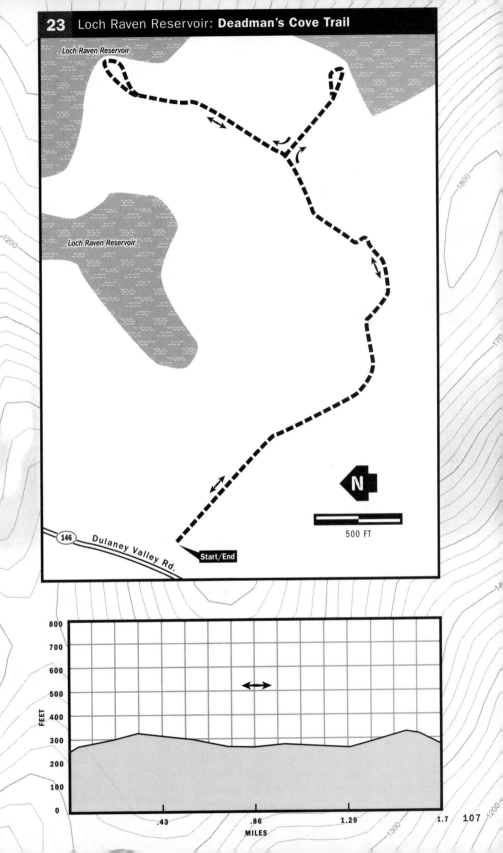

Loch Raven Reservoir

Loch Raven Reservoir

N

500 FT

146 Dulaney Valley Rd.

Start/End

800
700
600
500
400
300
200
100
0

FEET

.43   .86   1.29   1.7   **107**
MILES

Fire road

were planted here long ago. At just over 0.3 miles, head left and follow the tire tracks. Soon after, you'll have your first glimpse of the water through the trees on the right.

As you approach 0.5 miles, a vein of large rocks cuts across the path. When you see a particularly large rock at a trail split, head to the right. The trail gets lost a bit in the tall grass, but the water comes into better and better view, so it's easy to tell where you're going. You'll reach the water at 0.6 miles. Here, you'll have clear, good views across the reservoir—you may see a few people in boats, rowing or fishing. More than likely, you'll have the view all to yourself. The water here is clear, and you'll probably see many fish swimming around at your feet.

When you've had your fill, go back up the trail and after another 0.1 mile, head right at the large rock in the path you hiked earlier. (You can attempt to walk along the water's edge, but it requires a serious bushwhack—heading back up and around is the better, more pleasant option.) Be careful as you walk; tall grass covers rocks and fallen tree trunks in the path. You'll reach the water again at 0.9 miles. The water's edge is entirely surrounded by pine, and it smells wonderful. A rock-studded ravine on the right slopes gently downhill toward the reservoir. Head back up the trail, returning to the point where you originally headed to the water at 1.1 mile; follow the trail all the way back to your car.

▶ NEARBY ACTIVITIES

The Fire Museum of Maryland, the largest such museum on the East Coast, houses 40 pieces of firefighting apparatus dating from 1822. The museum, which also has the largest working telegraph system in the United States, is open weekends May to October and daily June to August, Monday to Saturday, 11 a.m. to 4 p.m. and Sunday, 1 p.m. to 5 p.m.; 1301 York Road; (410) 321-7500. Head south on Dulaney Valley Road and turn right onto Seminary Avenue; turn left onto York Road. The Fire Museum is three quarters of a mile on the left.

LOCH RAVEN RESERVOIR: GLEN ELLEN–SEMINARY TRAIL

Follow the natural contours of the southeastern edge of Loch Raven Reservoir before ascending the hills above to come back through upland forest.

▶ DESCRIPTION

At the trailhead, you'll see a bulletin board explaining which trails are open to mountain bikes and which aren't. Be aware: these are largely ignored. According to the sign, bikes are allowed only on the wide fire road that begins to the right of where you stand. Even though you are heading left at 200 feet on the narrower dirt path, expect a few bicyclists.

You immediately enter thick woods, full of oak and tulip poplar. The first view of the reservoir comes at 0.3 miles as you begin to parallel a stream to the left. It gets very marshy as the water expands into the main body of the reservoir. The trail is flat and level as it winds through the woods, and the water before you gets wider and wider. Before you momentarily wind away from the reservoir at 0.5 miles, expect to scatter frogs, turtles, and an occasional water snake from the thick underbrush that crowds the edges of the trail.

Hundreds of offshoots lead in both directions from the trail; these single-track bike cuts

▶ DIRECTIONS

Take I-695 to Exit 27, Dulaney Valley Road north. Go five blocks and turn left onto Seminary Avenue (after Meadowcroft Lane); park immediately on the right shoulder in front of the Church of Latter-Day Saints. Carefully cross Dulaney Valley Road and pick up the dirt path paralleling Seminary Avenue; follow the path until it comes out to Seminary Avenue and then quickly ducks back into the woods on the left. Two orange posts strung with a steel cable mark the trailhead.

ⓘ KEY AT-A-GLANCE INFORMATION

LENGTH: 9 miles

CONFIGURATION: 2 loops with an extended spur

DIFFICULTY: Moderate

SCENERY: Loch Raven Reservoir, upland forest

EXPOSURE: Shade

TRAFFIC: Light to moderate (mostly bicycle)

TRAIL SURFACE: Packed dirt

HIKING TIME: 3 hours

ACCESS: Dawn to dusk; the Maryland Transit Administration (MTA) bus #8 runs along Dulaney Valley Road and crosses Seminary Avenue; for a complete schedule, visit **www.mtamaryland.com** or call (866) RIDE-MTA.

MAPS: USGS Towson, stationary trail map at trailhead

FACILITIES: None

SPECIAL COMMENTS: Though the majority of the trail traffic is bicycle, cyclists tend to be considerate and usually alert you to their approach.

Loch Raven Reservoir:
Glen Ellen–Seminary Trail

UTM Zone (WGS84)   18S

Easting   362700

Northing   4365199

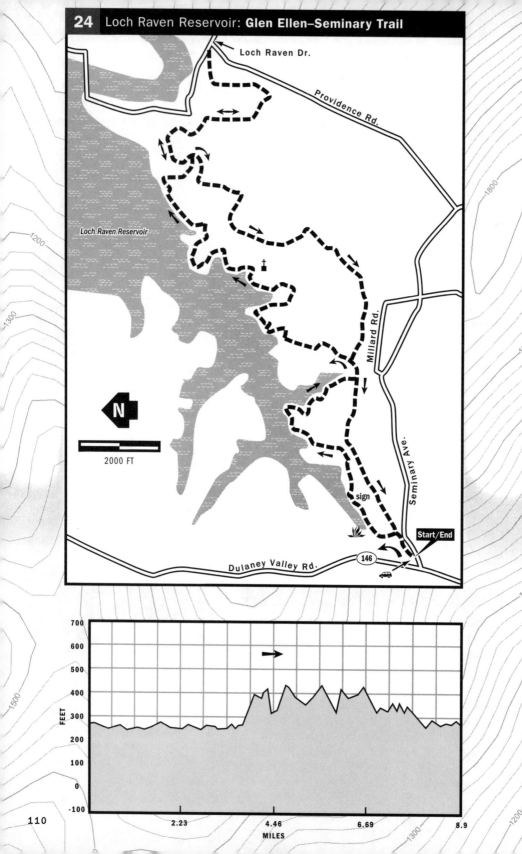

24 Loch Raven Reservoir: **Glen Ellen–Seminary Trail**

lead to some nice scenery, but I discourage taking them because they cause environmental degradation. Besides, staying on the path yields some fantastic views.

Cross over a small stream at 0.7 miles and then head slightly to the right into a grove of pine trees. This is part of the fire road, and it is accordingly wide—only a thin strip made by tire tracks cuts a path in the middle. After another tenth of a mile, you will come to a T intersection; head right, keeping the water on your left. Look for the "Don't be a Fink, Litter Stinks—Friends of the Loch Raven Reservoir" sign; go to the right here as the trail heads slightly uphill.

At 0.9 miles, the trail runs to the water's edge. Shaded by mature pines, this nice spot stays cool even on a hot day. For the next half mile, the trail runs along the edge of the reservoir, following its natural contours. At 1.4 miles, the trail moves away from the reservoir and rejoins the fire road; this is the edge of the watershed property, and you'll see a few private homes to the right as you head left.

Immediately cross over a swiftly moving stream filled with big concrete slabs and head uphill. At the split at 1.5 miles, head left; at 1.7 miles, take the narrow foot trail to the left. You will parallel a very small creek to your left, and the reservoir soon comes back into view through the woods. This trail ends at the water's edge and affords some magnificent views of the reservoir. Head back and take a left at the first opportunity (200 feet from the water's edge). For the next 2 miles, the trail literally is the reservoir edge; often you're separated from the reservoir only by a few washed up tree branches.

Along this section, you'll pass through nice pine groves, over small creeks (where fish and frogs abound), and riparian buffers where lily pads and other aquatic plants grow. At the one and only Y intersection, head left. Expect to see a few white-tailed deer leaping about. At 2.8 miles, you'll pass a collection of rocks decorated with a leash and plastic toys, and you'll come to a similar site at 3 miles, where a small tombstone reads: "Here lies Sam. A great dog. 1975–1989." Another small rock pile with a cross on top sits just beyond. One couldn't wish for a nicer final resting place.

At 3.6 miles, the trail heads abruptly uphill over a clear stream. Rocks and ferns dominate the banks, and trees dangle their roots over the water. As you head up the hill, the ecosystem changes drastically. Alongside the mica-flecked trail, the pines fall away and are replaced by oak, sycamore, maple, and beech. When you reach the top of the hill at 3.8 miles, you will have a few options. It was a beautiful day when I hiked this trail and the thought of heading back seemed a bit of a downer, so I continued the hike by heading left and reaching the turnaround point (Providence Road) at just over 5 miles. But you can turn right at the fire road to go back to Seminary Avenue and your car, yielding a solid hike of roughly 7 miles.

Admittedly, the scenery doesn't vary much along the fire road between the trail intersection, Providence Road, and the trailhead, but it does make a pleasant walk through upland forest. By going to Providence Road before heading back to Seminary Avenue, you'll cross over no fewer than seven rock-strewn, clear streams, and they're often very lovely, cutting banks along the side of the hills.

You have one other option—as you head toward Providence Road, you'll see a red-blazed trail to the left at 4 miles. Surrounded by beech trees, it heads downhill to the water's edge before heading back up to the fire road.

Loch Raven Reservoir

Going back to Seminary Avenue and your car, the trail is very wide and rocky, full of exposed roots, with lots of fallen, decaying tree trunks and ferns on both the right and left. At 7 miles, a few private homes begin to appear on the left. You'll see cleared areas that delineate the edge of the watershed property and the beginning of private property, an occasional stand of bamboo, and some cuts in the woods on the right. More and more backyards appear as you descend the final section of the fire road and return to the trailhead at just under 9 miles.

▶ NEARBY ACTIVITIES

The Fire Museum of Maryland, the largest such museum on the East Coast, houses 40 pieces of firefighting apparatus dating from 1822. The museum, which also has the largest working telegraph system in the United States, is open weekends, May to October and daily June to August, Monday to Saturday, 11 a.m. to 4 p.m. and Sunday, 1 p.m. to 5 p.m.; 1301 York Road; (410) 321-7500. Head south on Dulaney Valley Road and turn right onto Seminary Avenue; turn left onto York Road. The Fire Museum is three quarters of a mile on the left.

Hampton National Historic Site, a stately home that was once the largest mansion in the United States, is also within easy driving distance. Built with a fortune amassed during the Revolutionary War, the site boasts extensive gardens on what was once the northernmost slave-holding plantation in the country. Head south on Dulaney Valley Road from Seminary Avenue; go three blocks and turn left onto Hampton Estate Lane. You will see the mansion and grounds entrance on the right.

LOCH RAVEN RESERVOIR: MERRYMAN TRAIL

▶ IN BRIEF

Arguably the prettiest trail in the Loch Raven Reservoir watershed. Follow it to Merryman Point, where the reservoir spreads out in several directions.

▶ DESCRIPTION

From the parking area, you have several options to begin the hike—the trailhead farthest to the right leads to a narrow path that runs alongside the reservoir, the farthest to the left runs to a fire road, and the second to the left (the one I take) runs along a wide path but not before going along a narrower path, which will eventually afford nice views of the reservoir and give you the option of linking with the fire road. This, I find, is the most diverse and pleasant route.

Swing around a hill and cross a little creek bed at 0.3 miles. Oak, beech, sycamore, and tulip poplar populate the hillside, and spicebush abounds as well. You will have an immediate view of the reservoir, which is fed by the many creeks running alongside the hills. Cross another one of these creeks at 0.4 miles.

Next you'll come to a narrow ridge that acts as the trail. It gets so narrow that it even becomes a bit harrowing in places; it wouldn't take much to slip and fall down the hill to the right. If you did, you'd be sliding among the oak and tulip poplar trunks all the way to the edge of the reservoir, some hundred or so feet down. Be careful to pay attention to where you are walking and do not let the reservoir views and the many birds flitting

▶ KEY AT-A-GLANCE INFORMATION

LENGTH: 9.8 miles

CONFIGURATION: Out-and-back

DIFFICULTY: Moderate

SCENERY: Loch Raven Reservoir, upland forest

EXPOSURE: Shade

TRAFFIC: Moderate

TRAIL SURFACE: Packed dirt, crushed rock

HIKING TIME: 3.5 hours

ACCESS: Dawn to dusk

MAPS: USGS Towson

FACILITIES: None

SPECIAL COMMENTS: Parking at the Dulaney Valley parking area is very limited; to park at Warren Road and do the hike in reverse, take I-83 to Exit 18, Warren Road east, and once you've passed Bosley Road, look for the gravel parking area just before the steel bridge over Loch Raven Reservoir.

▶ DIRECTIONS

Take I-695 to Exit 27, Dulaney Valley Road north and go 3.5 miles. The parking area is on the left just after Bosley Road and just before the bridge over Loch Raven Reservoir. The trail begins just beyond the parking area at the edge of the woods.

Loch Raven Reservoir: Merryman Trail

UTM Zone (WGS84)   18S

Easting   363549

Northing   4369361

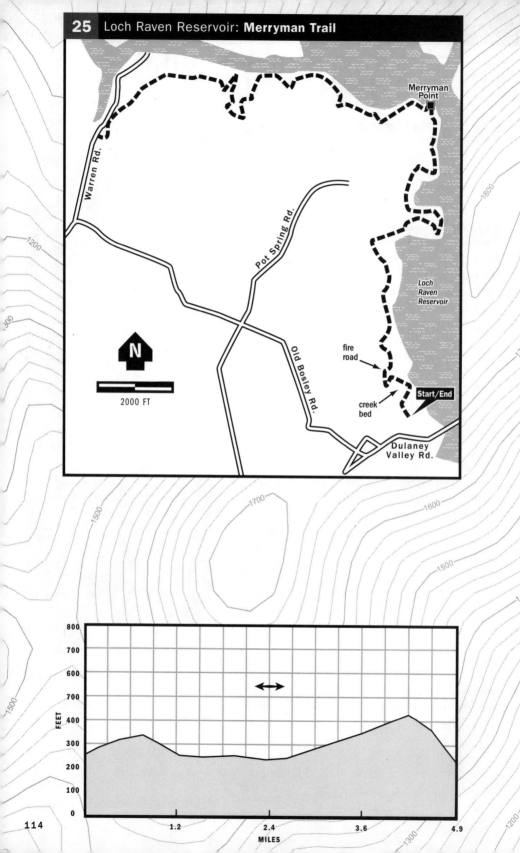

overhead distract you. As you continue along the ridge, your sightline will run along the tops of many of the trees rising up from water level.

You will rejoin the fire road at 0.6 miles. This wide, more level, crushed rock trail heads downhill and crosses a beautiful little stream. On the other side of the stream, you'll come to a T intersection; head right as the path runs through a large patch of greenbrier. After roughly three-quarters of a mile, you'll see the Dulaney Valley Bridge over the reservoir; winter will give you the clearest view of the bridge, which is about a mile away, close to where you parked.

As soon as you spot the bridge, start watching for a little cut path at 0.8 miles. The main fire road trail branches to the left and seems the obvious choice to follow, but if you look closely straight ahead, you'll see the cut path running through a thicket of mid-level growth of thin tulip poplar, grapevine, briers, and spicebush. Taking this path allows you to head to the edge of the reservoir and walk along the water; at one point, the path runs right alongside the water and heads out to a series of large rocks. Since the breeze invariably comes from the east over the reservoir, the water constantly laps against the rocks at your feet. If you close your eyes, you would think you're at the edge of a relatively calm ocean. Aside from hearing the pleasing sound, you'll also have a great view over the reservoir.

Moving on, you'll continue to skirt through the woods along the edge of the reservoir, and in many places, a mere foot or two separates you from the water. You will come to a thick stand of evergreens and just beyond, at 1.5 miles, a power-line cut. A carpet of pine needles lies about, and you can see wide expanses of the reservoir to both the east and west. This is Merryman Point, which gives the trail its name.

At 1.9 miles, cut up the hill and rejoin the fire road, which is essentially a very rocky trail bed, with lots of ferns and oak down the hillside. You will come to a lovely stretch between 2 and 2.5 miles as you go up and down the hills. The very rocky, very thickly wooded trail offers constant sweeping views of the reservoir. You will cross a creek and go under a fallen tree at 2.3 miles and then walk around a big cut gully. At the top of the hill, at 2.7 miles, cross the gully and pick up the trail on the other side on the right. Back on the fire road, the scenery doesn't change much for the hike's duration, but you'll come to one rather dramatic curve at 3.5 miles, where you'll have to make a steep climb up the hill.

A private home now stands where the path once ran, and you'll have to cut around it. This requires a strenuous climb of about 150 feet before heading back down and rejoining the fire road at 4.2 miles. You'll actually remain at this altitude (just shy of 500 feet) for almost the rest of the hike before gradually descending at the trail's end at Warren Road.

Before you reach the fire road, at 4.7 miles, look through the woods on your right to see the steel bridge on Warren Road that runs over a relatively narrow section of the reservoir. You will reach Warren Road at 4.9 miles and a parking area across it diagonally to the left; you can park here if the more popular parking area at Dulaney Valley is full.

You could also set up a shuttle to make the hike one way. If you did set up a shuttle, here's how to return to the Dulaney Valley parking area from Warren Road: go left (west) on Warren Road, turn left onto Bosley Road, and continue until it ends

Loch Raven Reservoir

at Pot Spring Road. Take a right and then a left onto Old Bosley Road and continue until it ends at Dulaney Valley; you will see the parking area on the left.

▶ NEARBY ACTIVITIES

The Fire Museum of Maryland, the largest such museum on the East Coast, houses 40 pieces of firefighting apparatus dating from 1822. The museum, which also has the largest working telegraph system in the United States, is open weekends, May to October and daily June to August, Monday to Saturday, 11 a.m. to 4 p.m. and Sunday, 1 p.m. to 5 p.m.; 1301 York Road; (410) 321-7500. Head south on Dulaney Valley Road and turn right onto Seminary Avenue; turn left onto York Road. The Fire Museum is three quarters of a mile on the left.

Hampton National Historic Site, a stately home that was once the largest mansion in the United States, is also within easy driving distance. Built with a fortune amassed during the Revolutionary War, the site boasts extensive gardens on what was once the northernmost slave-holding plantation in the country. Head south on Dulaney Valley Road from Seminary Avenue; go three blocks and turn left onto Hampton Estate Lane. You will see the mansion and grounds entrance on the right.

NCRR (NORTHERN CENTRAL RAILROAD) TRAIL

▶ IN BRIEF

Choose what length hike you want to take and go—logical, well-spaced turnaround points and parking areas make this the perfect trail for anything from a quick walk to an all-day trek.

▶ DESCRIPTION

The entire NCRR Trail covers some 40 miles. I especially like the section described below because it avoids the crowds that frequent the trail's southern terminus and the suburban feel that too often encroaches on its northern sections in Pennsylvania. The trail itself resulted from one of the better ideas in recreation: turning abandoned rail beds into hiking and biking trails. European settlers came here as early as the 1600s, and by the mid-1800s an established rail line bisected the stream valley, linking Baltimore with the northern industrial states. Union troops were stationed here during the Civil War.

Head right (north) from the White Hall parking area; small trees and the narrow Little Falls to the left dominate the scenery here. You will cross Graystone Road just 0.4 miles after leaving White Hall; be careful—it's easy to lose yourself in the width of the trail and forget that the road you're crossing is a functioning through road, and there is traffic—although it's usually minimal, (you will come to similar road crossings every few miles along this trail). Once you cross

▶ DIRECTIONS

Take I-83 to Exit 31, Middletown Road east and go 0.7 miles to a stop sign on York Road; turn right and go 0.3 miles. Turn left onto Weisburg Road and continue 1.3 miles and bear right at the stop sign; continue on Weisburg Road an additional 0.3 miles to reach the White Hall parking area, on the right just past White Hall Road. The trailhead sits parallel to the parking area.

ⓘ KEY AT-A-GLANCE INFORMATION

LENGTH: 18.5 miles

CONFIGURATION: Out-and-back

DIFFICULTY: Moderate to strenuous, because of length

SCENERY: Little Falls and Bee Tree Run, mixed forest, riparian buffers, rural landscapes, wetlands

EXPOSURE: More sun than shade in winter; reverse in summer

TRAFFIC: Moderate (mostly bicycle) to heavy traffic near the Ashland section of the trail, its southernmost point

TRAIL SURFACE: Crushed rock

HIKING TIME: 6.5 –7.5 hours

ACCESS: Sunrise to sunset

MAPS: USGS New Freedom; you can find excellent virtual maps of the Maryland section of the trail at **www.john carterphoto.com/ncrr/virtualmap.html** and maps with less detail but with more parking, directions, and facilities information at **www.dnr.state.md.us/greenways/ ncrt_trail.html.**

FACILITIES: Most parking areas, including the Parkton area across the trail from a general store, have either flush bathrooms or portable ones. Some also include a public telephone.

SPECIAL COMMENTS: The NCRR Trail runs 40 miles from Ashland, Maryland, to York, Pennsylvania. Frequent parking areas all along the route make choosing shorter or longer lengths easy; for information, call (410) 592-2897.

NCRR (Northern Central Railroad) Trail

UTM Zone (WGS84)   18S

Easting   360160

Northing   4387046

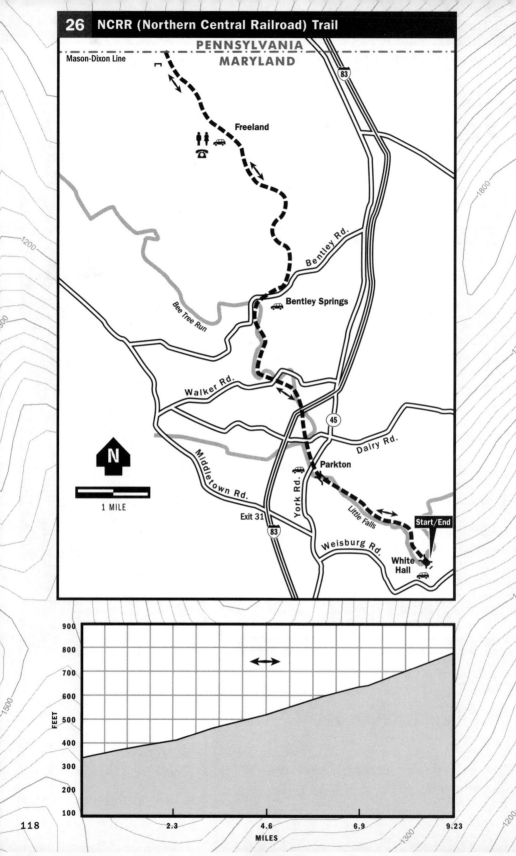

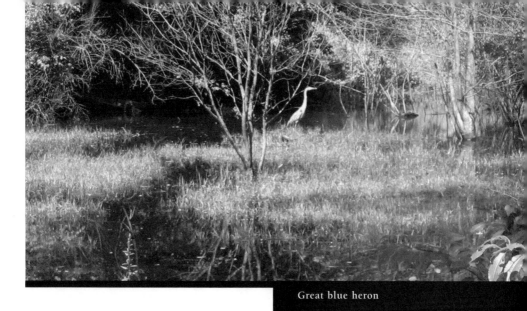
Great blue heron

Graystone Road, rock formations will flank the trail, making it easy to imagine the blast engineering involved in creating the rail bed. Fortunately, enough time has passed that these rock walls are no longer naked and exposed; straggly roots of clinging trees that perch atop the rocks have taken hold, and wildflowers pepper the area, giving splashes of white, yellow, and purple in the summer.

It may take you a while to get used to the occasional whiz of a passing bicyclist. While you'll certainly see walkers and hikers and even people pushing strollers, the majority of the trail traffic consists of bicyclists. This doesn't necessarily make for unpleasant walking, though, because the trail is wide and flat, giving ample opportunity for wide berths—plus people enjoying the trail generally have a happy demeanor, so walkers rarely feel squeezed out.

At 0.6 miles, you will cross a wooden bridge over Little Falls; you'll see the remnants of old railroad tracks on the left. At 0.8 miles, you'll cross the water again and have great views of Little Falls pouring over the rocks below. As you parallel the falls on the left heading upstream, thick woods and ferns along the hillsides will surround you. You will come to a put-and-take trout fishing area and bench at 1.2 miles. Soon after, at 1.4 miles, you'll find a little overlook area that provides a great view of the clean water spilling over the rocks. A sign here warns about poisonous snakes. Only two such snakes live in Maryland: the timber rattlesnake (extremely rare in this area) and the northern copperhead. Your chances of being bitten by either snake are very slim; if you do spot a snake, leave it alone.

After crossing a bridge at 2.1 miles, you'll come to the Parkton parking area, which has a small general store on the left and an old train depot on the right. Mileage markers here tell you that it's 1 mile to Dairy Road and 1.4 to Walker Road; a few private houses appear to the right as you continue on the trail and cross Dairy Road. An exercise course appears on the left, and you will soon see I-83 ahead; it gets

Little Falls

a bit loud for a moment, but you will soon leave the highway behind and regain serenity after you walk under the I-83 ramp.

Cross Walker Road at 3.6 miles; the next parking area is Bentley Springs, a little more than a mile away. You will enjoy the shaded stretch of trail beyond Walker Road; first you will cross water and then the trail opens up, letting you see a farmhouse up the hill on the right. You will cross water again at 4 miles and come to a shaded bench just beyond. Mountain laurel abound here, making this a truly lovely spot when it is in bloom.

You will reach Bentley Road at 4.5 miles; cross Bee Tree Run, and you will see Bentley Springs parking area just ahead, with restrooms and a public telephone. Turning around here gives you a 9.5-mile hike; the next parking area is at Freeland, 2.8 miles away.

At 4.8 miles, the trail gets very boggy, and you'll pass a nice marsh on the left where you're likely to see great blue heron, as I did when I hiked. Other prominent fauna along the NCRR Trail includes monarch butterflies, white-tailed deer, red foxes, raccoons, and Eastern box turtles. At 5.7 miles, you will cross Bee Tree Road and arrive at your next mileage marker: "Freeland: 2 miles, Pennsylvania line: 3.3 miles." Soon after, you'll cross what's left of an old railroad bridge. Watch out for occasional horse manure piles—this section of the trail is used by equestrians from the nearby camp in Bee Tree Reserve. The path cut in the woods on the right just beyond an informational bulletin board, at 5.8 miles; leads through the 263-acre reserve.

The trail soon opens up in an area dominated by wildflowers and the trunks of dead trees that now host birds. The trail then plunges back into the woods; in fact, between 6 and 7 miles, you will see no sign of humanity, aside from the trail and the folks you pass along it, as you walk through the very thick wooded area. Bee Tree Run, when it comes into view, is narrow and pretty tame in this section; a smattering of ferns winds up the hill on the left.

You will reach the Freeland parking area at 7.3 miles; the parking area has a restroom as well as a public phone. The gas station up the road on the left also has public facilities. The Pennsylvania state line is less than 2 miles away.

As you walk away from Freeland, you'll see an open marshy area on the right. Soon you'll cross into Oakland, where you'll see a beautiful old barn to the left. As the trail opens up again, you will get a good sense of the rural nature of the immediate area. At 8.5 miles, the trail begins to resemble the section where you began at White Hall, with blasted rock and clinging tree roots. You will reach the Pennsylvania line from this point at just more than 9 miles. Here you'll find benches and a rest area—a perfect place to relax, eat your lunch, and enjoy that particular thrill one gets from walking from one state to another. You've reached the Mason-Dixon Line, created between 1763–67 to settle a dispute between the Maryland and Pennsylvania colonies. Stones marking the line carry William Penn's seal on the north and Lord Baltimore's on the south. It's a long hike back, but it's downhill; you probably didn't realize you were going uphill when you were heading north, but you'll see it more easily as you head back south and bikes whiz by you.

▶ NEARBY ACTIVITIES

Morris Meadows Recreation Farm with its Historic Preservation Museum, off Freeland Road between Middletown Road and York Road, features early American antiques and artifacts; take I-83 and exit at either Middletown Road (Exit 31) or Freeland Road (Exit 37). If you're into buying antiques instead of just looking at them, head to Monkton, off Exit 27 from I-83, Monkton Road east. To see the nationally award-winning Ladew Topiary Gardens, take I-83 to MD 439 (Exit 36) and go east about 6 miles to a dead end at MD 23; turn right and go approximately 3 miles to the junction of MD 146 (Jarrettsville Pike); turn right onto Jarrettsville Pike and continue to Ladew Gardens, about 3 miles ahead on your left; for information, visit **www. ladewgardens.com** or call (410) 557-9466.

NORTH POINT STATE PARK

▶ IN BRIEF

See how things have (and haven't) changed in an area of undeveloped bay-front property where evidence of human habitation dates back 9,000 years.

▶ DESCRIPTION

The white-blazed gravel-and-grass trail behind the portable bathroom spits you back onto the road at the gatehouse after just 75 feet. From there, take an immediate left onto the trail, which is initially shaded by tall, thick trees but opens up at 0.2 miles into the 232-acre Black Marsh. The marsh and forested buffer surrounding, protected as a Wildland and Natural Heritage Area, provides a haven for birds. According to the Maryland Department of Natural Resources, the birds found in and around the marsh include bald eagles, rare American bitterns, Northern harriers, great horned owls, red-tailed hawks, and elusive black rails. The marsh also serves as home to wading birds such as herons and egrets as well as waterfowl such as canvasbacks, goldeneyes, ruddy ducks, mergansers, and scaup. In summer, the white blooms of rose mallows, one of the eight species of rare or endangered plants in the area, cover the entire marsh.

At 0.3 miles, to the left, you will come to Observation Trail, which has light blue blazes and leads you to an overlook where you can view the Black Marsh Wildlands (it's a short 0.6-mile

▶ DIRECTIONS

Take I-695 to Exit 40, MD 151 south (North Point Boulevard). Go south 3.8 miles and take a left onto North Point Road just after the I-695 overpass. Go 1.8 miles to the park entrance on the left at Bay Shore Road; pass the gatehouse to the parking area on the left. The trail starts at the edge of the parking area behind the portable bathroom.

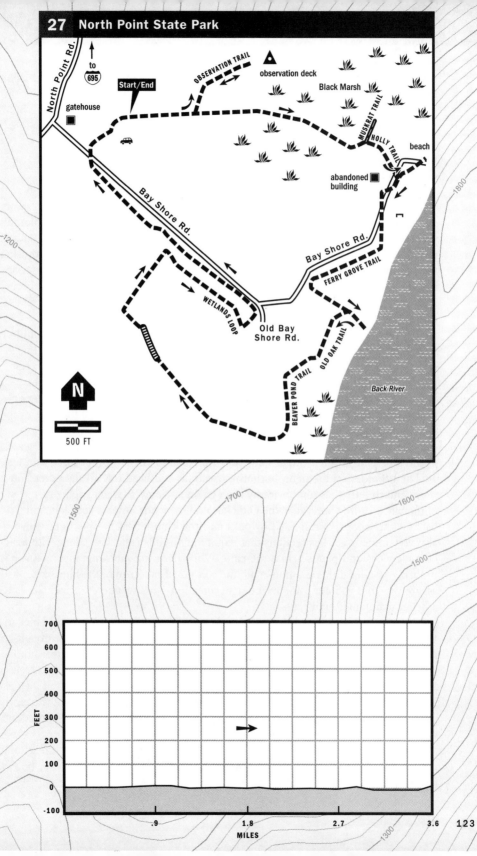

round trip to the observation deck and back). You will likely see herons and wood ducks here.

Back on the main trail, cut left at the yellow-blazed Muskrat Trail, at 1.1 mile. This trail brings you right to the edge of the marsh, where the remains of a small boat, complete with wooden oar and almost completely overtaken by vegetation, sits inexplicably by the water's edge. In addition to muskrats, you will also have a decent chance of spotting beavers, foxes, and otters.

Coming back from the end of the Muskrat Trail, you'll see the purple-blazed Holly Trail about 200 feet to the left. Take the Holly Trail and soon you'll see more and more sky as things begin to open up, and you'll begin to hear a faint rumble. You will see red blazes on this section of the trail, but it looks very underused and is muddy, tight, and overgrown. Go left at the T intersection, and you'll soon learn what the rumble is and why the sky has come into view. While this often indicates roads and development ahead, in this case, the trail leads to a beautiful little rocky beach, and what you heard were waves. You'll see a lonely lighthouse and the wide Chesapeake Bay.

When you're ready to head back, return on the red trail but now continue straight at the T intersection where you went left earlier. You will pass by an old, cavernous abandoned building posted with "No Trespassing. Private Property" signs; please heed the signs. Once you've passed the building, take a left onto the red-blazed Powerhouse Trail as it widens considerably. A bench at 1.5 miles overlooks Chesapeake Bay and commands a really nice view. Continue around the edge of the hill overlooking the water; be on the lookout for bald eagles in this area.

After reentering the woods, you will see white blazes again. At 1.6 miles, go left at the blue-blazed Ferry Grove Trail; you will come to the sky blue-blazed Old Oak Trail at 1.8 miles on the right, but for now, pass it and head toward the water. You'll see a sunken jetty that you obviously can't go on anymore as well as some nice views of the bay. Heading back, take the Old Oak Trail, which is now on your left. You'll be back in the woods, surrounded by oaks and thick underbrush. This trail, which is also very underused, has sections that require minor bushwhacking along with loads of spiderwebs and plants across the path. While there are moments in which you'll probably wonder if this is a trail at all, the continued presence of the blue blazes will assure you that you are going in the right direction. This section eventually leads to a better maintained trail.

When you see a blue blaze on a beech tree after 2 miles, head right and pick up Beaver Pond Trail to the left. This wide, exposed trail follows cut grass through an area that provides good habitat for raccoons, gray squirrels, cardinals, great horned owls, red foxes, red-tailed hawks, spotted salamanders, American kestrels, killdeers, plovers, and robins.

If you want to make a loop with the hiker-biker trail, take a left when you reach the paved road; it leads to the ultra-busy swimming beach area, trolley house, and visitor center. Take a swim if you'd like.

If you wish for more solitude, however, as I did, head right when you reach the paved road. You can always drive to the public area after you complete your hike. I find staying in the woods more pleasant.

So if you choose to head right, you will pass a grove of black cherry covered with white flowers in spring and black fruit in summer. At 2.4 miles, the trail opens up and becomes marshy again. You will cross over a wooden boardwalk at 2.5 miles and pass a big cornfield on the left as you head to the right. When you see a paved road ahead, take a right into the stubby woods—this is the Wetlands Loop. You'll see an open area on the right with lots of bird feeders. Head left at the V. If you wish to make a complete loop of the wetlands, keep going to the right when you reach the paved road at 2.8 miles; otherwise, turn left onto the road and head back to the parking area. Straight ahead on the road, you will see a bulletin board and the trailhead for the white-blazed Wildlands Loop, a big portion of which you covered at the beginning of the hike.

Heading back to the parking area along the road isn't nearly as unpleasant as it sounds. You will parallel a cornfield on the left, but a big buffer separates the cornfield from the road. In summer, the sounds of the grasshoppers and crickets will drown out the noise of the cars going by at low speed. You can follow the paved road around to the parking area where you began.

One of the nice things about North Point State Park is that the vast majority of visitors come here for the beach, which means that the trails are fairly free of traffic. When you're finishing hiking, though, you can head down to the beach area for a pleasant diversion. The new visitor center mimics the original Bayshore Park Restaurant, built by United Railways Electric Company in 1906. The nearby large ornamental fountain, originally built in the early 1900s as part of the Bayshore Amusement Park, operated between 1906 and 1947. The park also included a dance hall, bowling alley, restaurant, gardens, and a pier jutting into Chesapeake Bay. You can still crab and catch catfish, white perch, and striped bass here today. The swimming beach (unguarded) is also nearby, and in between sits Trolley Station Pavilion, a holdover from the days when passengers paid 30 cents to ride the #26 trolley car that ran between Baltimore and Bayshore Amusement Park.

▶ NEARBY ACTIVITIES

The route for British troops to Baltimore during the War of 1812 passed through North Point. Linking nearby Fort Howard and Todd's Inheritance with this hike provides additional good hiking as well as excellent history lessons. Fort Howard is another 2.2 miles south down North Point Road. You'll find Todd's Inheritance a half-mile north of Fort Howard on North Point Road. Thomas Todd settled on this spot in 1664. Retreating British soldiers, defeated at the Battle of Fort McHenry, burned the original Todd home; the house standing here now was built on the original homesite in 1816 and was remodeled in 1867.

OREGON RIDGE PARK

KEY AT-A-GLANCE INFORMATION

LENGTH: 4.2 miles

CONFIGURATION: Loop

DIFFICULTY: Moderate

SCENERY: Upland forest, Baisman Run, historic structures

EXPOSURE: Shade

TRAFFIC: Moderate

TRAIL SURFACE: Packed dirt with many sections of exposed roots

HIKING TIME: 2 hours

ACCESS: Dawn to dusk

MAPS: USGS Cockeysville; trail maps at nature center

FACILITIES: Restrooms in the nature center and lodge at main park entrance; take a right at the split in the road to go to the nature center; the park includes a swimming beach, playgrounds, restaurant, and theater.

SPECIAL COMMENTS: The nature center is open every day except Monday from 9 a.m. to 5 p.m. No bikes are allowed on the trails; dogs must be leashed.

Oregon Ridge Park

UTM Zone (WGS84)   18S

Easting   354694

Northing   4372885

IN BRIEF

Hike up and down hills in one of the Baltimore area's most popular parks.

DESCRIPTION

Oregon Ridge has become well known around Baltimore for many things: its annual Fourth of July celebration with a performance by the excellent Baltimore Symphony Orchestra, its cross-country skiing trails, the swimming beach, the restaurant, and the theater. Hiking doesn't usually make the top of the list, and that's a shame because the trails in the park offer a great trek.

Since you're starting from the nature center, it makes sense to stop in for a moment or two. Inside, you'll find live animals—turtles, red spotted newts, bullfrogs, a bee colony, hissing cockroaches, American toads, crayfish, bullhead catfish, snakes (including the copperhead, the only poisonous snake inhabiting Baltimore County)—as well as stuffed owls, fox, elk, European starling, and woodpeckers. You can also walk through a hothouse and see sliders and diamondback terrapins.

If you're facing the entrance of the nature center, head toward the long wooden bridge to the left to start your hike; stop to pick up a brochure and follow the self-guided nature trail before you cross the bridge. While you're still on the bridge, look out over the valley below to see what's left of the iron ore pit from the mid-1800s;

DIRECTIONS

Take I-83 to Exit 20, Shawan Road west. Take a right on Beaver Dam Road and follow the signs to the park entrance. Once inside the park, head right at the split in the road to go to the nature center; park in the nature center parking area beyond the bathhouse. The trail starts at the end of the long wooden bridge to the left of the nature center.

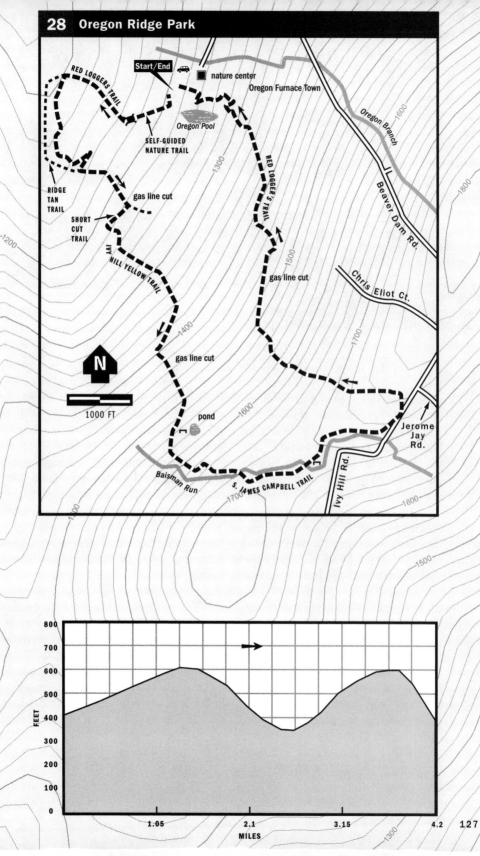

Start/End

nature center

Oregon Furnace Town

Oregon Pool

RED LOGGERS TRAIL

SELF-GUIDED
NATURE TRAIL

RED LOGGER'S TRAIL

Oregon Branch

Beaver Dam Rd.

RIDGE
TAN
TRAIL

gas line cut

SHORT
CUT
TRAIL

IVY HILL YELLOW TRAIL

Chris Eliot Ct.

gas line cut

N

1000 FT

gas line cut

pond

Jerome
Jay
Rd.

Baisman Run

S. JAMES CAMPBELL TRAIL

Ivy Hill Rd.

800

700

600

500

400

FEET

300

200

100

0

1.05   2.1   3.15   4.2

MILES

127

Resting spot shaded by hemlocks

it's heartening to see what 150 years of nature's reclamation has done to restore this area's natural beauty. This mined pit yielded primarily goethite, one of the main ingredients in the manufacture of pig iron. Now you can see relatively uncommon American chestnut trees growing here; a plague wiped out more than 95% of these trees east of the Mississippi River, making them rare today. You will also see sassafras, black tupelo, two types of wild blueberries, red oak, white oak, ash, red maple, dogwood, tulip, beech, and sarvis trees in the valley. On ground level, you may catch a reflected glimmer of Loch Raven schist, which contains mica, garnet, feldspar, and quartz crystals.

Head right after the wooden bridge onto Red Loggers Trail (marked correspondingly with red blazes). The name "Loggers Trail" might give you pause, but don't worry—despite the name, you're not going to happen upon hideous sections of clear-cut forests, but don't expect to see old growth either. The trees are mostly tall, thin oak mingled with lots of ferns along the hillsides.

After 900 feet, the trail splits at Ridge Tan Trail, which takes a higher elevation than Loggers Trail; the two link after 0.3 miles. If you stayed on Loggers Trail, it heads downhill at 0.25 miles. Be careful here—lots of big rocks lie in the trail. At 0.3 miles, you'll begin to parallel a little stream on the right that cuts through the center of the valley; hills rise on either side of you. At 0.6 miles, the trail begins heading uphill and soon becomes rather precipitous. It's very rocky and very rooty, which would make it tough to hike in ice and snow. You'll come to a T intersection at 0.8 miles; take a right and head toward the red blazes (to the left is where you would have come from if you took the tan Ridge Trail earlier). Over the last half-mile, you've gained more than 250 feet of elevation.

Although the scenery is beautiful, it doesn't change all that much from the beginning of the trail. So when you come to the gas line cut line at 0.9 miles, it actually looks pretty nice. You'll come to a total of four gas line cuts (four altogether) along this trial, and they pleasantly mix things up a bit since they provide sections of high grass that shelter a host of insects, which in turn attract birds. When you enter the woods on the other side, at 1 mile, take a right on the Short Cut Trail—don't worry, despite the name, you're not shirking any challenges. Loggers Trail begins to loop back to the nature center here; by taking the Short Cut Trail, you'll link with Ivy Hill Yellow Trail, which extends the hike.

The Short Cut Trail takes a gradual descent through a grove of ferns before it links with Ivy Hill Yellow Trail, at 1.2 miles. Take a right and for the first time, you'll be on level ground. Walking through here on a windy day is heaven—the sound of the branches and leaves swaying hundreds of feet above your head is magical (of course, if it's winter and there are no leaves and that same wind gives a chill below zero, "heaven" might not be the best description). You will come to another gas line cut at 1.4 miles, and after 100 feet, you'll be back in the woods.

At 1.6 miles, the scenery begins to change a bit as low-lying bushes and pines make an appearance. Listen closely—you'll probably hear hawks calling. The trail descends, heads left, and becomes very rocky again. Many of the rocks at your feet shine with quartz and feldspar. Heavy rains may wash out this section of the trail a bit.

Suddenly you will hear the sound of running water, and Baisman Run appears on the right. You'll see a rickety wooden bridge going over the run, but stay on the trail—you'll cross it at places that offer much more secure footing.

You will cross Baisman Run at 1.75 miles and come to a T intersection on the other side; head to the left up the railroad ties to the pond. With a nice wooden bench to sit on and beautiful hemlocks lining the other side of the pond, this is a lovely spot to rest a while. Continuing on, you'll soon see a sign for the S. James Campbell Trail, which also has yellow blazes. Despite the two names, this and the Ivy Hill Trail are actually the same, so if you stay on yellow-blazed paths, you'll be fine. At 1.9 miles, you will cross the quick-moving but shallow Baisman Run on a series of rocks; be extra careful if the rocks are submerged—they can be very slippery. You'll most probably get the soles of your boots wet, and even if you step on the stream bottom, the only "harm" will be that you'll scatter tadpoles, minnows, and skimmers.

When you see a jeep trail straight ahead up the hill, take a left; a sign points you again to the S. James Campbell Trail. Cross Baisman Run again; there are no rocks here, so you'll get a bit wet. The trail gets tight and woodsier, but it soon opens up again with thin small trees, some of which have fallen and are lying across the trail; you'll have to hurdle them as you walk beside Baisman Run heading downstream. The sound of the stream belies its size; the many rocks and swiftness of the water make it sound much larger than it is. Cross the stream again at 2.1 miles; this time, there are several large rocks, so you won't have any problem even if the water is high. Cross yet again about 70 feet later; you might want to stop here and sit on the bench while you listen to the wonderful sounds of nature.

At 2.3 miles, the trail heads uphill to the left as Baisman Run turns to the right; you'll suddenly be thrust into civilization again when Ivy Hill Road appears through the woods to the right. You're skirting the park boundary here, but you won't see or hear much traffic, and you'll soon be heading away from the road again as you go uphill. Like earlier in the hike, it's very steep here, and you'll gain more than 200 feet of elevation very quickly. Go through another gas line cut, and, at 3 miles, you'll come to an intersection and Loggers Trail once again. Head right and go down the hill into a section that is thickly wooded, much more so than the top of the hill on Ivy Hill Trail.

Cross another gas line cut again and head toward the lake. You'll see a sign for the nature center and lake access. Go down the hill over railroad ties; if it's swimming season (April to October), you'll hear people playing in the water. At the sign that points to the frog pond, go straight; you'll see a playground on the left, along with volleyball courts. This isn't so much a trail anymore, even though some of the trees here and there bear red blazes; essentially you're walking through the area between the lake and bathhouse—if it's in season, you'll have to exit through the gate and head back to the car, just a few hundred feet ahead to the left; if it's not season, the red blazes run right beside the lake and lead out a door in the wooden fence around the lake area. You'll find concessions, water, and bathrooms here, and the parking area and nature center are just on the other side of the bathhouse.

Before you leave, check out the re-created Oregon Furnace Town, just down the hill to the right of the nature center entrance. This area includes the Tenant House Museum, with historical exhibits on woodsman's tools and the clothing worn by the men who mined the pits here in the 1800s. The 1850 census data shows that approximately 225 people lived here, mostly Irish and German immigrants and emancipated black slaves.

▶ NEARBY ACTIVITIES

The Oregon Grille, at 1201 Shawan Road, offers an expensive but wonderful dining experience; housed in a restored 19th-century stone house, it boasts a five-star rating. You can reach the Maryland State Fairgrounds by taking Shawan Road right and turning right onto York Road. Generally speaking, there's something going on at the fairgrounds all year long, but if you are there in late August or early September, you can enjoy the state fair, which draws people from all over Maryland and adjoining states.

PATAPSCO VALLEY STATE PARK: GLEN ARTNEY AREA

> ▶ **IN BRIEF**

Take in the best of the Glen Artney Area: two branches of the Patapsco River, mature forest, and Lost Lake.

> ▶ **DESCRIPTION**

The trailhead leads onto Soapstone Branch Trail. A long, flat ridge drops off both sides of the trail, with Soapstone Branch to the right and very big beech trees all around. Just before 0.2 miles, the trail heads into a very deep gully; follow it down to level ground. Soapstone Branch is just a trickle here—small and narrow, but running clear.

At 0.25 miles, you'll see the trail's first purple blaze. Mid-level growth includes mountain laurel and sumac, with oak and beech towering above. This is a good place to consider the drastic contrast between the nearby city and this natural area: here you are, less than half a mile from a major highway, a Park and Ride lot, residential neighborhoods, schools, and churches, but you can see nothing but thick woods, much of it old growth. It serves as an important reminder of the value of Patapsco Valley.

Near a trail sign, you'll see how the water has cut under a big oak and the root system hangs over. As you move on, huge rocks dominate the trail. You will make several very easy crossings over Soapstone Branch in this section. At 0.7 miles, up the hill to the right, you will come to

> ▶ **DIRECTIONS**

Take I-195 west toward Catonsville–Park and Ride; continue toward the Park and Ride to where I-195 ends at Rolling Road. Turn left and continue on Rolling Road; after it turns into Selford Road, immediately look for the gravel parking area on the shoulder of Selford Road across from the Park and Ride lot. The trail starts just off the parking area.

> ℹ **KEY AT-A-GLANCE INFORMATION**

LENGTH: 4.9 miles

CONFIGURATION: Out-and-back with 2 loops

DIFFICULTY: Moderate

SCENERY: Soapstone and Santee Branches, Patapsco River, mature forest

EXPOSURE: More shade than sun

TRAFFIC: Moderate

TRAIL SURFACE: Packed dirt

HIKING TIME: 1.5–2 hours

ACCESS: 9 a.m. to sunset

MAPS: USGS Relay; you can also purchase an excellent map of the entire Patapsco Valley State Park trail system at the park or from the Maryland Department of Natural Resources online at **www.trailmapsetc.com** or **www.dnr.maryland.gov.**

FACILITIES: Restrooms, water, pavilions, and playground at the paved area at 0.8 miles of this hike

SPECIAL COMMENTS: The official park entrance for the Avalon, Orange Grove, and Glen Artney areas can be reached by taking I-95 to Exit 47 (BWI Airport) and traveling east on I-195. Take Exit 3 to Elkridge. Turn right on US 1, heading south, and take the next right onto South Street. The park entrance is immediately on the left. Note: For this hike, with its extension, follow the directions below.

Patapsco Valley State Park: Glen Artney Area

UTM Zone (WGS84) 18S

Easting 351634

Northing 4345360

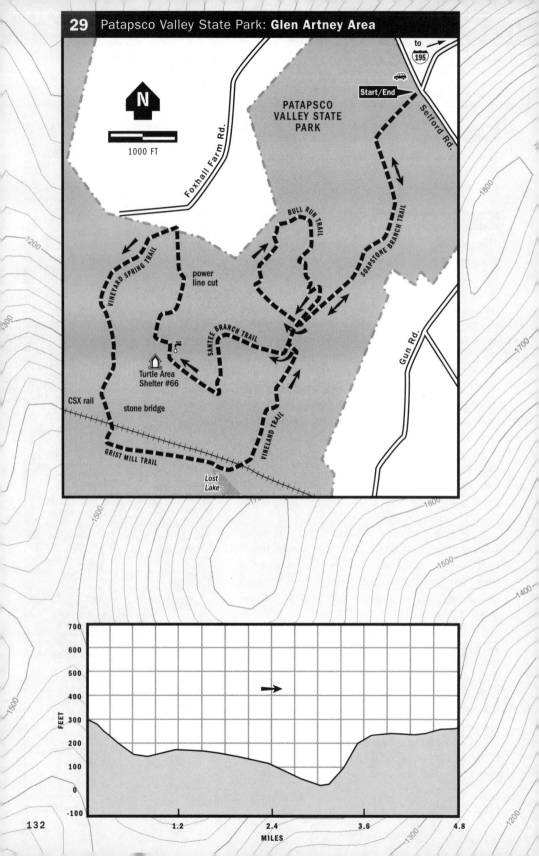

N

1000 FT

PATAPSCO
VALLEY STATE
PARK

Start/End

Selford Rd.

Foxhall Farm Rd.

BULL RUN TRAIL

SOAPSTONE BRANCH TRAIL

power
line cut

VINEYARD SPRING TRAIL

SANTEE BRANCH TRAIL

Turtle Area
Shelter #66

Gun Rd.

CSX rail

stone bridge

GRIST MILL TRAIL

VINELAND TRAIL

Lost
Lake

700

600

500

400

300

200

100

0

-100

FEET

1.2   2.4   3.6   4.8
MILES

the orange-blazed Bull Run Trail; take note that this trail will be part of your return route. For now, stay on Soapstone Trail. Immediately after the Bull Run Trail cut, you will come to the longest crossing over Soapstone Branch; the large rocks here make this easy, too. On the other side you'll come to a little parking area that has a pavilion and bathrooms, as well as a playground.

From the parking area, head diagonally up the hill to the right to stay on Soapstone Trail. On the right at 0.9 miles, you'll see Santee Branch Trail at the top of the hill. Abandon Soapstone Trail (it heads back down the hill to the left and ends in a section where you will be later), and take Santee Branch Trail to a road and parking area. Walk along the road to continue the hike. Since this is a park road, it's narrow, doesn't have a lot of traffic, and is bordered by thick woods on either side, making it actually quite pleasant. At the split in the road, head right and go past the Do Not Enter (for car traffic) sign.

Old-growth forest of Glen Artney Area

At the wooden posts to the right at 1.25 miles, pick up the trail (barely discernible, but among spread-out trees and easy to navigate) and then go left up the hill. You'll come to the Turtle Area Shelter, #66. Turn right back onto the asphalt. You'll find a water fountain here next to the parking area on the right; expect these parking areas to be empty during the week. Across from the parking area you will see a little dirt trail heading into the woods, at just under 1.5 miles; take the trail and you'll soon see white blazes on the trees.

The topography changes drastically—before it was soaring old growth; here it's short, with nubbly trees and lots of underbrush. Obviously people used this area as an open field sometime in the last 20 or 30 years, but the native vegetation is now filling it in nicely. You will cross through a power line cut with its nice views of the forest on the right, and then pass a circular brick structure to the left; this section feels eerily isolated and exposed. You will come to a trail intersection at about 1.6 miles; go straight and link with the red-blazed Vineyard Spring Trail. Be sure to stay on the red-blazed trail; if you head to the right here, you would come to the park boundary and eventually join Santee Branch Trail, which heads northward to the Hilton Area of the state park (see page 135). You'll be rewarded with another beautiful area, dominated by tall, thin tulip poplar. This spot attracts many kinds of birds, and during fall and spring migrations, you may see bluebirds, scarlet tanagers, and Baltimore orioles. The trail here has lots of rocks and exposed roots, and it also has very distinct levels—lots of underbrush, mid-level shorter trees and hanging vines, and soaring older ones.

At 1.8 miles, you'll see a cut to the right, which will also take you to Santee Branch Trail. Pass that cut and head steadily down into a valley, where a trickle of water flows on the left. At just over 2 miles to the left you'll come to the loop cut for Vineyard Trail; continue straight on the red trail (taking Vineyard Trail would lead you back to the white-blazed trail where you were before). At 2.1 miles, you'll pass, on the right, the concrete slabs and foundation of some long-gone building, now covered in moss.

At 2.25 miles, go under a stone bridge on a boardwalk (above you is the CSX rail line); you'll emerge at the paved, wheelchair-accessible Grist Mill Trail. Go left on this trail, which is popular with walkers, bikers, and in-line skaters. It's something of a shock to land here after the isolation of the trails from which you've just come, but that's not to say that Grist Mill Trail isn't nice. It's quite scenic, with nice shade trees to the right fronting the Patapsco River as well as the rising hill to the left where the trains run infrequently.

At a little over 2.5 miles, you'll come to a parking area with bathrooms fronting Lost Lake, an interesting fishing lake reserved only for people who are 61 years of age or older, are under 16, or have disabilities. As soon as you pass the lake, head left under the stone bridge and railroad tracks at the sign that points toward Glen Artney and Lower Glen Artney. On the other side of the bridge, look for the crossing over Soapstone Branch. Since there are no large rocks in the water here, you will not be able to cross in high water; if you can't cross, head straight to get back to the road and ultimately reach the same place as you would crossing Soapstone Branch. Clearly the more pleasant option is to take the narrow trail on the other side of Soapstone Branch if water levels allow. Once you cross the branch, head left on the purple-blazed Vineland Trail.

At 3 miles, the trail runs left into Soapstone Branch. You'll have to cross here, but big rocks make it easy. Head up the hill and go right; you'll soon emerge at the parking area you came across at 0.8 miles. Backtrack from where you came before, crossing Soapstone Branch again, but this time head left up the hill on the orange-blazed Bull Run Trail. (If you're short on time, you can go straight; your car is just 0.8 miles ahead.)

Bull Run Trail splits immediately. In fact, it will split several times—it's a loop, so you can go either way; I took the leftward choice each time to make the longest loop possible, which totals not much more than a mile. The trail goes quickly and steeply uphill among mostly tulip poplar. At the top of the hill, you'll come to a power line cut; follow the tree line for a while and cut back into the woods when the trail ends at the power tower. Now the path becomes pebble and rock. You'll come to another split here; again I took the left, onto the dirt trail. This upland forest consists of mostly beech and oak, with poplar still popping up here and there. Some of the enormous trees here are at least second growth, if not old growth.

At 3.9 miles, the trail turns rock and pebble again. When it does so, take a right and soon after (about 1,000 feet) take a left onto the packed dirt trail down the hill. You will come to a little switchback; when the trail splits again, head left. Now the trail runs through a deep-rutted gully as it continues down the hill; you'll soon come to the other side of Soapstone Branch from where you began the hike. When the trail ends at 4.2 miles, cross Soapstone Branch for the last time and head left; you'll be back on the way to your car.

PATAPSCO VALLEY STATE PARK: HILTON AREA

Even though this is one of the more popular sections of Patapsco Valley State Park because of its camping infrastructure, you can still get a few of the trails to yourself.

▶ **DESCRIPTION**

On the Forest Glen Trail, you'll initially walk downhill on a wide, packed dirt trail through lots of sassafras, oak, and tulip poplar. At 0.2 miles, go straight instead of cutting off to the right. You'll walk along a ridgeline and soon end at an overlook that provides a nice view of the Patapsco Valley below, especially if you're hiking in late fall or winter. Turn around and return to the righthand cut you just passed.

Walking on a ridge of rock heading downhill, you'll hear Santee Branch and soon come to an absolutely gorgeous spot: moss-covered rock thick with ferns and underbrush and clear water dripping down the hillsides, eventually making its way to the stream valley. Redbud, sassafras, and dogwood thrive in this area. Parallel Santee Branch on your right as it joins with Sawmill Branch. At half a mile, you will come to a big stone bridge. Cross Sawmill Branch just before the bridge, and once on the other side, you'll see Sawmill Branch Trail to the right; don't take it now—you'll be on it later. Instead head straight up the hill on the yellow-blazed Buzzards Rock Trail (you'll see the CSX rail line to the left). Be

▶ **DIRECTIONS**

Take I-695 to Exit 13, Frederick Road west. After 2 miles, turn left onto South Rolling Road. At the first intersection, bear right on Hilton Avenue. Continue 1.5 miles until you reach the park; turn right and follow the park road around to a parking area, about 0.2 miles. A sign on the right marks the trailhead: "Forest Glen Trail."

ⓘ KEY AT-A-GLANCE INFORMATION

LENGTH: 3.4 miles

CONFIGURATION: Jagged loop with internal loop and out-and-back

DIFFICULTY: Moderate to strenuous

SCENERY: Buzzards Rock, Santee and Sawmill Branch, upland forest

EXPOSURE: Mostly shade

TRAFFIC: Light to moderate near campground

TRAIL SURFACE: Packed dirt; small section of crushed rock and gravel

HIKING TIME: 1.5–1.75 hours

ACCESS: 9 a.m. to sunset

MAPS: USGS Relay, Savage, Ellicott City, Baltimore West; you can also purchase an excellent map of the entire Patapsco Valley State Park trail system at the park or from the Maryland Department of Natural Resources online at **www.trailmapsetc.com** or **www.dnr.maryland.gov.**

FACILITIES: Telephone to the left just before park entrance; restrooms up the hill from the parking area; campsites, pavilions, playgrounds

SPECIAL COMMENTS: There is a $2 per day use fee, usually operating on an honor system; place the money in an envelope at the toll gate and put it in the box.

Patapsco Valley State Park: Hilton Area

UTM Zone (WGS84) 18S

Easting 349083

Northing 4345288

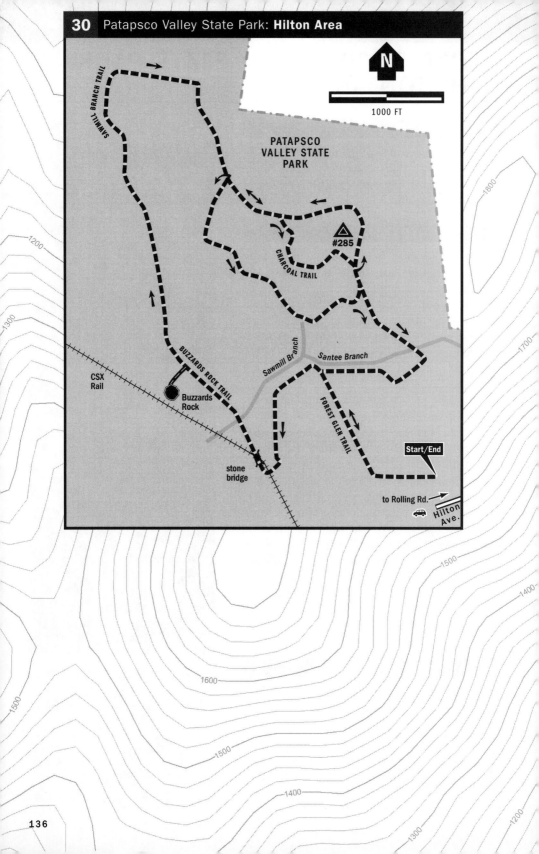

N

1000 FT

PATAPSCO
VALLEY STATE
PARK

SAWMILL BRANCH TRAIL

⚠ #285

CHARCOAL TRAIL

CSX
Rail

BUZZARDS ROCK TRAIL

Sawmill Branch

Santee Branch

Buzzards
Rock

FOREST GLEN TRAIL

Start/End

stone
bridge

to Rolling Rd.

Hilton
Ave.

warned: Buzzards Rock Trail involves a very steep climb over rocks and tree branches; you'll gain about 200 feet in elevation in less than two-tenths of a mile.

As you climb, you'll rise higher and higher above the train tracks; the Patapsco River lies just on the other side of the tracks. At 0.6 miles, the trail levels out a bit, providing a reprieve from climbing; you will see lots of oak and beech here. On the left at 0.7 miles is Buzzards Rock, named for the birds that used to congregate there. It's easy to see why they did—the spot commands a sweeping view, making it easy to spot prey.

The yellow trail continues to the right of the rock. You'll come to a power-line cut at 0.9 miles. Go through the open area and pick up the trail on the other side at the edge of the woods. The trail becomes crushed rock and gravel here and looks like an old fire road. At 1.1 miles, go right (south) on Sawmill Branch Trail at the trail sign; unimproved sections of Sawmill Branch Trail go north over South Hilltop Road. At South Hilltop Road, you can also head west to continue on Buzzards Rock Trail as it winds downhill toward the Ilchester Rocks and the paved Grist Mill Trail that runs along the Patapsco River. The southward section of Sawmill Branch to the right, however, winds through mature upland forest and is virtually untraveled compared to the popular Grist Mill Trail. (A portion of the Grist Mill Trail is part of the Patapsco Valley State Park–Glen Artney hike described on page 131.)

Sawmill Branch soon comes back into view on the left as you swing around to the right and head back into the valley. You will begin zigzagging down the hill. At 1.3 miles, you will come to a little clearing on the right where the valley opens up in front of you, and you will soon cross Sawmill Branch, where you will see a slew of minnows and tadpoles.

At 1.5 miles, you will come to the family campground area through the woods on the right, and you'll cross the road to the camping area at 1.6 miles. Once on the other side, take the orange-blazed Charcoal Trail on the right. Pass through the power- line cut again and pick up the trail on the other side at the edge of the woods. You'll very quickly loop around and spit back out to the power-line cut at 1.9 miles, but this time, you parallel the tree line along the cut downhill into the valley to where it bottoms out at Santee Branch. Cross the Branch here—it's not very deep, but the rocks are spread out, which requires a bit of a well-coordinated leap.

When you reach the other side, go right, and at the trail split, head right again. You'll soon come to a section of the trail where you were before, but you'll just as quickly hit new sections. At 2.1 miles, look for a barely discernible path through the woods to the right that will lead you to the paved loop road of the camping area. Take a right onto the loop road at campsite #285, head right into the woods, and pick up the trail on the other side. Of course, if this campsite is occupied, you're not going to want to walk through it; instead, you can follow the loop road around and when you come to the road crossing where you last hit at 1.6, take it into the woods. You'll soon come to the Charcoal Trail again, but this time, pass it instead of taking it. If the campsite is unoccupied and you head straight, you'll soon see the obvious trail; in another 100 feet, you will pass Charcoal Trail as it heads to the left. In either case, you're now passing Charcoal Trail and following the path that swings away from it to the left.

This very rocky section becomes very wet after rain or when snow melts and the hills drain. At particularly wet sections, cut logs laid across the path will make it easier to continue on the trail. You'll see the purple-blazed Pigs Run Trail at 2.25 miles;

turn right onto it. You'll cross through a power-line cut and then take the wooden footbridge into the woods. The trail goes downhill; it's very rocky and tough on the knees here. A thick, full upland forest surrounds you; the trees are primarily oak, but you'll also see tulip poplar, beech, dogwood, maple, sassafras, redbud, and sycamore. Many wildflowers also abound here, including lady's slipper, jack-in-the-pulpit, mayapple, bloodroot, mountain laurel, goldenrod, black-eyed Susan, and Indian pipe. At the trail split at 2.7 miles, head left up the hill to return to your car.

▶ NEARBY ACTIVITIES

You might enjoy hiking through the nearby Orange Grove and Glen Artney sections of Patapsco Valley State Park; for hike descriptions and directions, see pages 131 and 139. Also nearby is historic Ellicott City; the former mill town, founded in 1772, has been immaculately preserved, and you will find shops and restaurants on the main street. To reach Ellicott City from the Hilton Area, reverse the directions given above to Frederick Road and head west (instead of east back to I-695); Frederick Road turns into Main Street in Ellicott City.

PATAPSCO VALLEY STATE PARK: McKELDIN AREA

▶ IN BRIEF

Walk to Liberty Dam on unmaintained trails, which take you to the developed, popular McKeldin Area of Patapsco Valley State Park.

▶ DESCRIPTION

Starting at the trailhead, you will walk on a rocky, packed dirt trail that parallels the North Branch of the Patapsco River. After about 300 feet, much of the rock spreads across the trail and into the water. You will see massive ferns and mountain laurel on both sides of the trail.

At 0.3 miles, you'll see the first sign of the great contrasts this area offers—while you will walk much of this hike through upland forest, here you are in riverine wetland. A low-lying marsh and boggy area sits to the left, while the trail rises and crosses over a few feeder streams and brooks. Head up the hill to the right at 0.4 miles, and soon after cross a stream in a pine forest. A cut path to the right goes to the top of Liberty Dam; head straight and you'll come to the bottom of the dam, where the trail ends. Liberty Reservoir sits on the other side. When you've reached the dam, turn around and go right toward the river; at a little over 0.7 miles you'll come to a spit of rock and sand that allows you to cross in one jump.

On the other side you have some options. You can take a right turn that leads to the dam. You can also take a rocky path up the hill; if you

❶ KEY AT-A-GLANCE INFORMATION

LENGTH: 6.3 miles

CONFIGURATION: Combination

DIFFICULTY: Moderate to strenuous

SCENERY: Patapsco River, Liberty Dam, McKeldin Rapids

EXPOSURE: Shade

TRAFFIC: Light to moderate

TRAIL SURFACE: Packed dirt with a short section of asphalt

HIKING TIME: 2.5 hours

ACCESS: Open Memorial Day to Labor Day from 8 a.m. to sunset and from 9 a.m. to sunset the remainder of the year

MAPS: USGS Sykesville, Finksburg; you can also purchase an excellent map of the entire Patapsco Valley State Park trail system at the park or from the Maryland Department of Natural Resources online at www.trailmapsetc.com or www.dnr.maryland.gov.

FACILITIES: Restrooms and water at maintained area; also camping, picnic facilities, and disc golf

SPECIAL COMMENTS: To bypass the first part of this hike and go directly to the maintained area and the official McKeldin entrance, follow the directions below but stay on Marriottsville Road another 0.4 miles from the gravel road; the entrance will be on the left. There is a $2 per day use fee for vehicles.

▶ DIRECTIONS

Take I-695 to Exit 18, Liberty Road west, toward Randallstown. Go 4.5 miles and turn left onto Marriottsville Road. Go 3.9 miles and turn right onto a little gravel road just before the Patapsco River; go straight to the little parking area. The trail starts just beyond the parking area at the edge of the woods.

Patapsco Valley State Park: McKeldin Area

UTM Zone (WGS84)   18S

Easting   337574

Northing   4359214

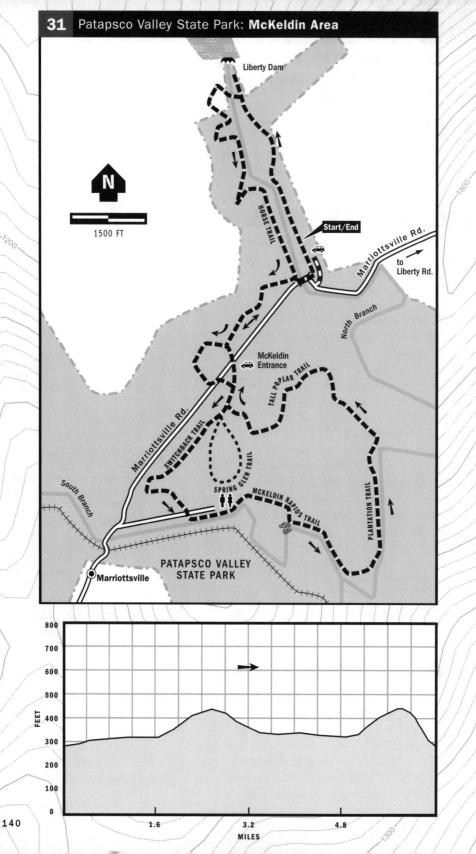

N

1500 FT

Liberty Dam

HORSE TRAIL

Start/End

Marriottsville Rd.

to Liberty Rd.

North Branch

McKeldin Entrance

TALL POPLAR TRAIL

Marriottsville Rd.

SWITCHBACK TRAIL

SPRING GLEN TRAIL

MCKELDIN RAPIDS TRAIL

PLANTATION TRAIL

South Branch

Marriottsville

PATAPSCO VALLEY STATE PARK

800
700
600
500
400
300
200
100
0

FEET

1.6   3.2   4.8

MILES

stay on this path, when it heads left it will lead you along horse paths toward the official McKeldin Area entrance. Or you can take the more interesting option that lets you walk astride the river along unmaintained trails. Be aware that these unmaintained trails become easy to lose and require more strenuous hiking than the horse trails, but they offer nicer scenery and will link to the horse trail in half a mile. To take the river trail, head left down the hill on a barely discernible groove in the grass and dirt; if you lose the trail, follow the deer paths, which are easily detectable.

You'll be above the river walking away from the dam. You'll have to skirt your way around a big gully until you find a good place to cross and then follow a narrow stream to the left, which you'll cross at 1.2 miles. Next, head up the hill to the right where the path stops at the river. Go around another little stream full of moss-covered rocks and cross at 1.4 miles. Once you are across the stream, the trail becomes very discernible—this is the horse trail that you skipped earlier. Take a left, passing a series of hillside mini-waterfalls. For the next 0.8 miles, this trail can be muddy and ground up because of equestrian use.

When you see the bridge over Marriottsville Road at 1.8 miles, the trail splits. Head right to stay off the road and in the woods. This area is marked by low-level growth: spicebush, greenbrier, and bloodroot. At 2.2 miles, things open up at a power-line cut, and a fire road heads to the left up the hill and swings around to Marriottsville Road at the McKeldin Area entrance. Don't take the fire road now—you'll be on it coming back; for now, head left through the woods and cross Marriottsville Road a few hundred feet west of the entrance. This will take you into the pine plantation, a beautiful area with towering pines planted in neat rows. Looking straight on, it seems almost impenetrable, but turn 90 degrees and you'll see order. Take the path here right toward the entrance road for the McKeldin Area and then turn left up the hill; this is the maintained area, and if you've driven here, go to the toll gate and pay the entrance fee of $2.

On foot, you'll have two options when you reach the McKeldin Area entrance: the purple-blazed Tall Poplar Trail and the white-blazed Switchback Trail. Take the Switchback Trail. Despite the presence of people in this area, the wildlife seems undeterred; rabbits, gray squirrels, woodchucks, and white-tailed deer run about. You may even spot a shy red fox.

Though you bypassed the Tall Poplar Trail, the Switchback Trail also winds among tall poplars; taking the Switchback Trail simply yields a much larger hiking loop. At 2.9 miles, the trail runs very close to Marriottsville Road, but fortunately it soon turns away toward the river. When you come to a bulletin board and trail split, take a left; you'll pass the other side of the Tall Poplar Trail at 3.1 miles. At 3.2 miles, at a big bamboo grove where mallards congregate, the trail splits again; stay on the white-blazed trail (to the right) up the hill, giving you a great view of the river. You will come to a paved park road at 3.4 miles, and you'll see a restroom on the right.

Cross the park road and pick up the white-blazed trail again; just 0.1 mile later, down the hill, you'll see a sign for the orange-blazed McKeldin Rapids Trail. According to the Maryland Department of Natural Resources, "The trail's name hints at its destination . . . a cascading rapid on the Patapsco River that flows into a large, deep pool of water." True enough—it's a beautiful spot. Though swimming is prohibited due to strong undercurrents, fishing is very popular, and the park service stocks the river each spring and fall with adult rainbow and brown trout. Smallmouth and largemouth bass, bluegill, redbreast sunfish, and rock bass reproduce in the river.

Turning to the left away from the rapids, you'll cross great rock formations. At one point, the trail itself is a huge rock slab. Be aware that these exposed rocks are favored spots for snakes, including the copperhead, one of only two venomous snakes in Maryland. If you see a snake and it has an hour glass-shaped head, give it a wide berth.

At 3.8 miles, you will reconnect with Switchback Trail, and you'll be standing at a point of interest: while the hike began in Baltimore County, it moved into Carroll County at the first river crossing at Liberty Dam and is now right across the river from Howard County. This is the only place in Patapsco Valley State Park where the three counties converge, the confluence of the north and south branches of the Patapsco River.

Go left at the split and follow the river. When you reach the red-blazed Plantation Trail, take it as it heads gradually up the hill into upland forest. (You could have continued to hug the river on the white-blazed trail—both options will eventually take you to the same place, but taking the red varies the scenery.) The forest here is primarily oak, but you'll also see tulip poplar, beech, dogwood, maple, sassafras, redbud, and sycamore. Many wildflowers also abound here including lady's slipper, jack-in-the-pulpit, mayapple, bloodroot, mountain laurel, goldenrod, black-eyed Susan, and Indian pipe.

When you reach the top of the hill and a cleared area, you'll see the southern edge of the pine plantation; hawks like to congregate on this tree line. Head left toward the paved park roads, past a basketball court on the left and restrooms on the right. Cross the park road and pick up the purple-blazed Tall Poplar Trail at 4.8 miles. When you see a chalet-style shelter straight ahead and the trail goes in two directions, head right. At another split at 4.9 miles, continue right.

You will see holly trees on the left and the toll gate and contact station on the right, and you'll reach the paved park entrance road at about 5 miles. (You've now completed the outermost loop of the McKeldin Area, but if you still want more, there's a 0.7-mile blue-blazed Spring Glen Trail loop to the left.) This time, follow the entrance road straight across Marriottsville Road and pick up the fire road; follow it down the hill along the power-line cut to where you were earlier. (If you hear gunshots, you might feel unnerved, but don't fear being hunted or shot; the shots are coming from a nearby firing range.) At 6.1 miles, take a right toward Marriottsville Road and you'll see a river crossing in the shadow of the bridge. Cross the river and head left; your car will be just ahead.

▶ NEARBY ACTIVITIES

You can enjoy more great hiking (as well as fishing) at nearby Liberty Reservoir, just to the north; please see pages 173 and 177.

PRETTYBOY RESERVOIR: CCC (CIVILIAN CONSERVATION CORPS) TRAIL

▶ **IN BRIEF**

Enjoy a solitary stroll through a pine forest on an old fire road. The out loop will tease you with water views, and the return loop will lead you to the water's edge.

▶ **DESCRIPTION**

Beginning at the trailhead, you'll enter the forest on a very wide path, cut by the Civilian Conservation Corps (CCC), the Depression-era jobs program. The dirt and gravel trail here has two clearly discernible tire tracks with higher grass in the middle. Deep woods flank the trail, but the width of the path gives you open walking space.

You'll pass through areas with very tall pines and dense underbrush on either side of the trail. Even though you've just left the road, you probably won't hear any traffic at all; this section of Baltimore County is still very rural. At 0.2 miles, the woods open up a bit, exposing the trail even more. You'll begin to see cuts and side trails on the left and right, but stay straight for now; you'll take one of the cuts on the return trip. At 0.3 miles, an interesting phenomenon occurs that's easy to miss. On the right, the forest is almost entirely pine, but on the left, oaks, hickories, and maples dominate with very few pines at all—the trail creates the dividing line.

Though it almost defeats the purpose of a hike to keep your eyes on the ground, if you're

▶ **DIRECTIONS**

Take I-83 to Exit 27, Mt. Carmel Road west. Go 3.6 miles and take a right on Prettyboy Dam Road. Go 1 mile and take a left onto the unmarked Tracey's Store Road. Go 1.1 miles where the road turns sharply to the left; you'll see a small parking area on the right where the road bends. Wooden posts strung with an orange cable mark the trailhead.

ⓘ **KEY AT-A-GLANCE INFORMATION**

LENGTH: 3.7 miles

CONFIGURATION: Out-and-back with a loop and spur

DIFFICULTY: Easy

SCENERY: Pine forest, Prettyboy Reservoir

EXPOSURE: Mostly shade

TRAFFIC: Light

TRAIL SURFACE: Packed dirt, gravel

HIKING TIME: 1.5 hours

ACCESS: Dawn to dusk

MAPS: USGS Hereford, New Freedom

FACILITIES: None

SPECIAL COMMENTS: You'll probably have the entire trail to yourself; the trailhead is easy to miss, so pay particular attention to the directions below; the difficulty in finding the trail and the rural nature of the area almost guarantee solitude.

Prettyboy Reservoir: CCC (Civilian Conservation Corps) Trail

UTM Zone (WGS84)   18S

Easting   351076

Northing   4387054

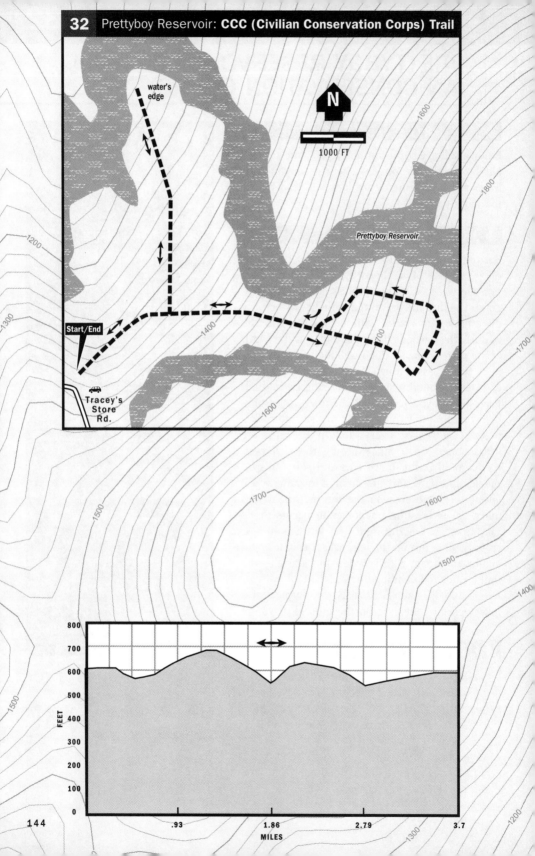

hiking the CCC Trail in summer, you may want to keep a look out for a legion of tiny frogs congregating in the grooves of the path. When I hiked this in July, I scattered thousands of tiny frogs, and I had to go slowly to avoid crushing dozens at a time. They are especially prominent in areas when the trail is exposed, such as the section between 0.45 and 0.55 miles.

Beyond this point, oaks and hickories overtake the previously dominant pines, and while this results in something of a barren view in the winter, the payoff comes in autumn when the trees explode in vibrant colors. You'll begin to see the reservoir through the woods on the left, even though the water is pretty far away and it's difficult to get a good view.

By 0.6 miles, the tire tracks fade away, but the trail remains wide. The loop begins here; you can go in either direction since you'll come back to this same spot regardless. When I walked this part of the trail, a young white-tailed deer was eyeing me warily off to the left, so I decided to head right. In that direction, the trail rises gradually, and a hill drops off to the right. At just under 1 mile, the trail splits; you want to head left to complete the loop. The reservoir is down below you to the right, but it's something of a tease here as you'll never get a great view through the woods; you can head toward the water on the return trip.

The grass grows much higher here on the path, signaling a lack of use. Continue heading around the loop; you'll complete it by rejoining the trail at 1.4 miles. Walk another half-mile, and then take the wide main trail to the right. The scenery is essentially the same as the trail you've been on, but this time you'll reach the water's edge after 0.6 miles. This area won't afford any sweeping views of the reservoir, but it's a nice little spot where you can dip your toes into the water. You might see someone fishing here. When you've had your fill, head back and turn right on the main trail to walk back to your car.

▶ NEARBY ACTIVITIES

You can sample Maryland wines and tour the facilities where they're made at two area wineries. You can reach Basignani Winery at 15722 Falls Road in Sparks by taking Exit 20B off I-83; call (410) 472-0703 for more information. Take Exit 27 off I-83 to reach Woodhall Winery at 17912 York Road in Parkton; call (410) 357-8644 for more information. If you want to do more hiking, opportunities abound at Prettyboy Reservoir (see pages 146 and 150).

PRETTYBOY RESERVOIR: GUNPOWDER RIVER

Prettyboy Reservoir: Gunpowder River

UTM Zone (WGS84) 18S

Easting 347529

Northing 4394504

IN BRIEF

Feel the temperature drop as you descend from wooded hills to the swift Big Gunpowder River, scrambling through an untamed and isolated section along the way.

DESCRIPTION

As you enter the woods on a fire road, you'll be surrounded by a thick vegetation of oak, pine, flowering dogwood, maple, and poplar above, with several varieties of ferns, raspberry bushes, and honeysuckle below. Many cardinals, jays, thrushes, woodpeckers, warblers, and vireos avail themselves of this great habitat, and they even have their pick of relatively rare black walnut and very rare American chestnut trees.

With the profusion of trailside poison ivy here, you'll be glad that the trail is very wide. You'll see a cut to the right at 0.4 miles, but pass it as well as several more cuts to the right that follow soon after; these lead to Big Gunpowder River, but you're headed there on a more scenic route. The fire road narrows a bit to a foot trail for about two-tenths of a mile and then widens again along the edge of the watershed boundary; you will see a farm field on the left beyond a buffer of

DIRECTIONS

Take I-83 to Exit 31, Middletown Road west. Go 4.6 miles to Beckleysville Road and take a left. At 0.2 miles, the road bears left; continue going straight. The road name changes to Cotter Road and then to Clipper Mill Road at 1.9 miles at a stop sign. Go straight and cross Prettyboy Reservoir on a white bridge. Go 0.4 miles and take a right onto Gunpowder Road. After 0.5 miles, pass Hoffman Cemetery and park at the bottom of the hill on the right. Walk across the road; you will find the trailhead leading into the woods behind an orange cable.

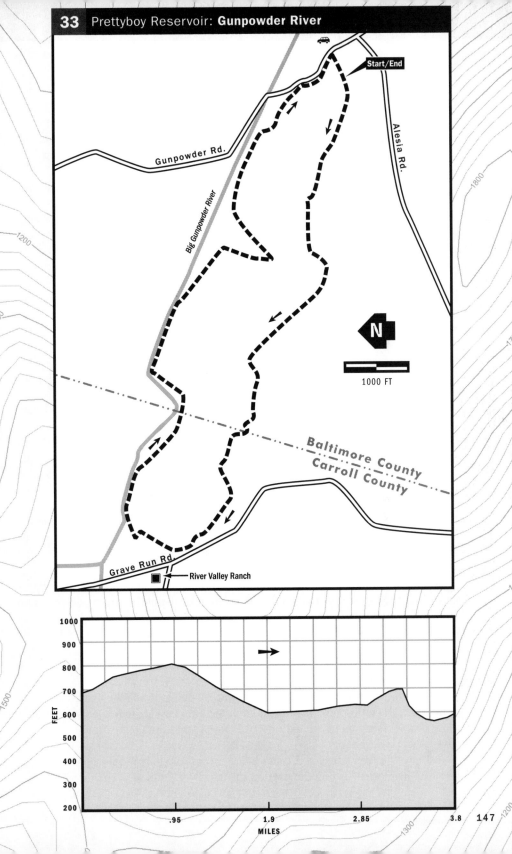

trees. You will also see mountain laurel and blackberry; if you are hiking in the summer and you didn't fill up on the raspberries along the trail earlier, the blackberries here will be a special treat.

There's a Y intersection at 1.25 miles; continue left, passing a deer blind in a tree on the right. The trail narrows and becomes increasingly rocky as you leave Baltimore County and enter Carroll County (don't worry; you won't see any intrusive signs telling you that fact).

You will approach Grave Run Road at 1.6 miles. On the right you will see the entrance to River Valley Ranch, a resort and Christian youth camp founded in 1952 by two Irish immigrants. When you reach the road, turn around and you'll see a different path heading into the woods about 10 feet from the one you just left; Big Gunpowder River will be flowing below you on the left. Here the narrow, twisty river is carving banks out of the meadow. The trail you're now on is twisty and narrow as well; unlike the fire road coming in, however, this one is spotted with horse manure from equestrian traffic from the nearby ranch. On the right, moss-covered rock outcroppings dot the hillside. If you look through the trees on the left toward the ranch, you might catch a glimpse of the resident bison.

Below you about 200 feet to the left, the river widens considerably and provides a nice loud accompaniment. You will continue to descend and soon reach the river, joining a wide fire road; the aroma of hay-scented fern fills the air here, and a jumble of moss-covered rocks and fallen trees give the area an Appalachian feel.

At 2.1 miles, the trail splits. The fire road heads right up the hill, while a little foot trail heads left toward the river. Take the foot trail, but first pull up your socks or cinch the cuffs of your pants to prepare for the vegetation, including poison ivy and thorny rose, that covers the trail. You will soon be rewarded for your efforts, however—utter isolation comes almost immediately, embodied by a massive rock in the river, a great place to stop and contemplate.

A little bit farther, it looks as if the trail disappears, and you'll have to cross a little island on the right; use the tree trunk there to help you cross safely. Be on the lookout for nesting Canada geese; it's easy to inadvertently sneak up on them and be startled when they suddenly take flight—or worse, become a victim of their maternal aggressiveness. Many mallard ducks also nest here.

Make your way along the hillside through the brush, big rocks, and wildflowers, mostly wild geranium and jewelweed, or "touch-me-not," the name derived from the popping noise that comes when you touch the plant's mature seed pods. As long as you stay near the river, the trail will reappear—it never strays too far from the water. The river alternates between roiling over rocks and then settling into deep flat pools. It's very cool in the river valley; you'll notice the obvious temperature drop in the air after coming off the hill.

Don't be discouraged by all the work you are doing during the first quarter-mile of this hike; the trail soon opens up and becomes much easier to follow. By 2.4 miles, the trail widens to rejoin the old fire road. You'll still have great scenery—now you have easier passage too.

Leave the river valley at 2.6 miles and ascend the hill. You'll begin to see big, beautiful hemlocks shading the river on the left. By 2.7 miles, at the top of the hill, the trail splits; continue straight, cross a stream, and then come to another intersection. Take a left, heading back down toward the river. You'll pass the stream, crowded with hemlock, on the left; by 3.3 miles, Big Gunpowder River comes back into view through those hemlocks. Descend once again to river level, where things open up. You'll reach Gunpowder Road at 3.6 miles; cross the road and walk along the wide grassy shoulder heading right. Before you go too far, look to the left, and you'll see another parking area across the bridge. If you want to add a quick but memorable hike, head there for the Hemlock Trail—see "Nearby Activities" below and page 150. If you are finished hiking for the day, continue on Gunpowder Road; you will reach your car at 3.8 miles.

▶ NEARBY ACTIVITIES

Hike through a hemlock gorge to a spectacular swimming spot on the Hemlock Trail; see page 150. You can sample Maryland wines and tour the facilities where they're made at two area wineries. You can reach Basignani Winery at 15722 Falls Road in Sparks by taking Exit 20B off I-83; call (410) 472-0703 for more information. Take Exit 27 off I-83 to reach Woodhall Winery at 17912 York Road in Parkton; call (410) 357-8644 for more information. If you want to do more hiking, plenty of opportunities abound at Prettyboy Reservoir (see pages 143 and 150).

PRETTYBOY RESERVOIR: HEMLOCK TRAIL

KEY AT-A-GLANCE INFORMATION

LENGTH: 1.25 miles

CONFIGURATION: Approximate out-and-back (see map and "Special Comments" below)

DIFFICULTY: Moderate to strenuous

SCENERY: Hemlocks, Gunpowder River, swimming hole, rock outcroppings

EXPOSURE: Mostly shade

TRAFFIC: Light

TRAIL SURFACE: Packed dirt

HIKING TIME: 1 hour; longer with a swim

ACCESS: Dawn to dusk

MAPS: USGS Lineboro

FACILITIES: None

SPECIAL COMMENTS: It's very difficult to follow precisely the same path out and back; at some points, there seems to be no trail at all, but passage is guaranteed by the open forest floor.

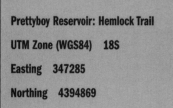

Prettyboy Reservoir: Hemlock Trail

UTM Zone (WGS84)   18S

Easting   347285

Northing   4394869

IN BRIEF

Get a taste of Appalachia within a grove of centuries-old hemlocks. After a hike that can be strenuous at times, cool off with a refreshing dip in the icy Big Gunpowder River.

DESCRIPTION

The trail goes downhill toward the water, and almost immediately you'll see the graffiti-covered underside of the bridge you just crossed in your car. Head left on the little dirt path following the river downstream. The trail is packed dirt and can be very close and narrow, especially in summer; pull up your socks if you don't want to catch poison ivy. Occasionally you'll catch glimpses of the swift, loud river on the right through the thick underbrush. Over the river as well as up the hill on your left, you'll see tall trees, but this part of the path is pretty much exposed to the sun.

At 0.1 mile, the trail opens up a bit, and soon you'll begin seeing beautiful rock formations

DIRECTIONS

Take I-83 to Exit 31, Middletown Road west. Go 4.6 miles to Beckleysville Road and take a left. At 0.2 miles, the road bears left; continue straight. The road name changes to Cotter Road and then to Clipper Mill Road at 1.9 miles at a stop sign. Go straight and cross Prettyboy Reservoir on a white bridge. Go 0.4 miles and take a right onto Gunpowder Road. After 0.7 miles, you'll come to a bridge; park on the shoulder on the left as soon as you cross the bridge. Once you've parked, look for the guardrail on the other side of the road 100 feet or so from the bridge and a sign telling you not to swim, wade, camp, etc.; the trail begins just behind that sign. Be aware: there's another wider path to the left strung with an orange cable. Although that provides a nice little walk, it does not lead to the one described here.

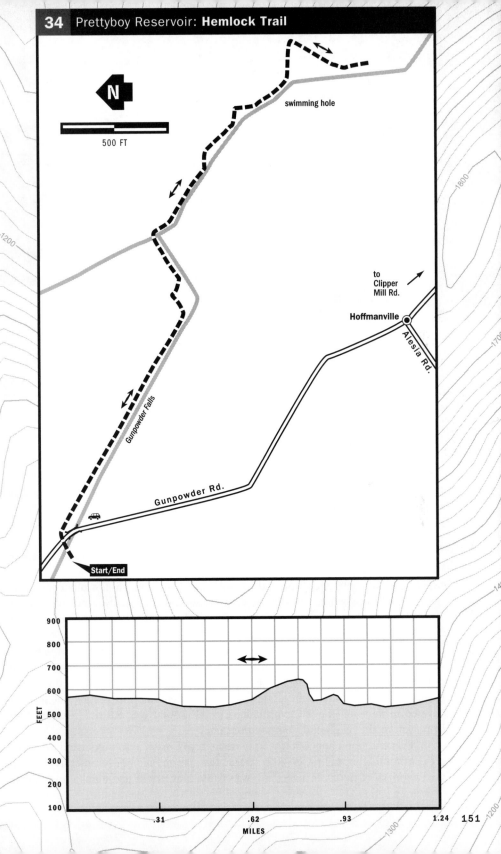

Swimmers in the icy Gunpowder

on the hill on the left. The trail becomes rocky here, and moss abounds. The still well-defined trail heads right to the river at 0.2 miles but heads away from it soon after and goes up the hill. At a quarter-mile, you will cross a stream; use the large fallen tree spanning the water to help you cross. You'll emerge into a hemlock forest, and these beautiful old trees begin to completely dominate the landscape. It's simply breathtaking.

Things begin to get a bit tricky here, and the trail becomes very hard to follow. The thick hemlocks crowd out sunlight, and very little if any underbrush grows. This creates wide alleys between the trees that can look very much like a trail. This, added to the trail's inexplicable underuse, will make it hard for you to see where to go, but as long as you keep the river within view on your right, you'll be fine. In fact, this confusion is half the fun.

For instance, just when it seems that you should head to the water, an eroded bank or a stand of vegetation swallows the path, so you decide to head uphill, clambering over the rocks and through the hemlocks. Depending on how often you decide upon this route, the hike can become very strenuous very quickly. I only had one free hand (the other taken up by my GPS unit), and the going was very difficult at times, but I still had a blast hiking the trail.

Every now and then, you'll find a nice level middle ground between the hill and the river. Here, pine needles carpet the soft soil, and you'll hear that distinctive soft hollow sound of the ground beneath you when you're not on rock. In this middle ground, you'll have the swift, clean river on your right and lots of rock outcroppings covered in moss on the left, with hemlocks all around you. All this zigzagging will bring you to the hike's end point all the same.

That end point appears at 0.5 miles when you reach a deep pool and swimming area surrounded by big rocks—the perfect destination on a hot summer day. Beware: the swiftness of the river makes the water here downright icy, suitable only for the brave or numb. The trail essentially ends in a tangle of vegetation and underbrush after another couple hundred feet. Follow your approximate route back to your car; inevitably, you'll not retrace it exactly, but so long as the river is nearby (this time on your left), you'll make it back ok.

▶ NEARBY ACTIVITIES

You can sample Maryland wines and tour the facilities where they're made at two area wineries. You can reach Basignani Winery at 15722 Falls Road in Sparks by taking Exit 20B off I-83; call (410) 472-0703 for more information. Take Exit 27 off I-83 to reach Woodhall Winery at 17912 York Road in Parkton; call (410) 357-8644 for more information.

If more hiking is your goal, try the easy trek just beyond the orange cable you passed when you started the hike above. The path heads up through the woods to the Hoffman family cemetery. The Hoffmans owned a paper mill that was used to make the first paper currency in the United States, and many of the headstones date back to the 1700s. Additional opportunities abound at other areas of Prettyboy Reservoir (see pages 143 and 146).

ROBERT E. LEE PARK–LAKE ROLAND

KEY AT-A-GLANCE INFORMATION

LENGTH: 6.7 miles

CONFIGURATION: Out-and-back with a loop and spur

DIFFICULTY: Moderate

SCENERY: Jones Falls, Lake Roland, upland forest

EXPOSURE: Mostly shade

TRAFFIC: Light to moderate on the trail; moderate to heavy at the lake

TRAIL SURFACE: Packed dirt, short stretch of asphalt

HIKING TIME: 2–2.5 hours

ACCESS: Dawn to dusk; you can reach the park from the Falls Road Light Rail stop and walking east on Copper Hill Road; this will take you to Lake Roland. The Light Rail runs Monday–Friday, 6 a.m.–11 p.m.; Saturday, 7 a.m.–11 p.m.; and Sunday and holidays, 11 a.m.–7 p.m.

MAPS: USGS Cockeysville

FACILITIES: Water fountain at the lake

SPECIAL COMMENTS: If you are afraid of dogs, be aware that the section of Robert E. Lee Park near Lake Roland just over the Light Rail tracks is a favorite for dog owners who blatantly disregard the leash laws; I've never been attacked here, but I have often had to wipe off the remnants of muddy paws.

Robert E. Lee Park–Lake Roland

UTM Zone (WGS84) 18S

Easting 356778

Northing 4362073

IN BRIEF

Follow an old rail bed along Jones Falls to Lake Roland before returning through upland forest. Along the way, catch sight of rare serpentine landscape.

DESCRIPTION

Climb over the guardrail and head right. Unless there are drought conditions, it's more than likely this beginning section will be full of mud. If it's really bad, a parallel trail heads uphill to the left and eventually rejoins the trail in approximately a quarter-mile when it rises above the low-lying area.

Once above the floodplain, the trail runs along the rail bed of the now-defunct Baltimore and Susquehanna Railroad. You will parallel Jones Falls downriver on the right, and on the left, you'll see rock outcroppings with clinging tree roots. At 0.3 miles, you'll notice the first of many old railroad ties still in the trail. Oak and maple trees dominate this section, offering wonderful, colorful foliage in autumn. At 0.4 miles, you'll come to a big dip in the trail. The bog on the left provides home to a multitude of bullfrogs. Pass by the cut paths heading up the hill on the left; they lead to private land.

At just under 0.7 miles, the trail rises above a precipitous drop on the right; lots of hanging grapevines weigh down some of the smaller trees below. Just beyond you'll see an old steel bridge over Jones Falls. This is a favorite spot for dog owners; expect to see a few frolicking canines in the water. Don't take the path on the left—it runs

DIRECTIONS

Take I-83 to Exit 11, Ruxton Road west. Take an immediate left onto Falls Road. Go 0.3 miles and park on the left shoulder where the road sweeps to the right. The trail starts just beyond the guardrail.

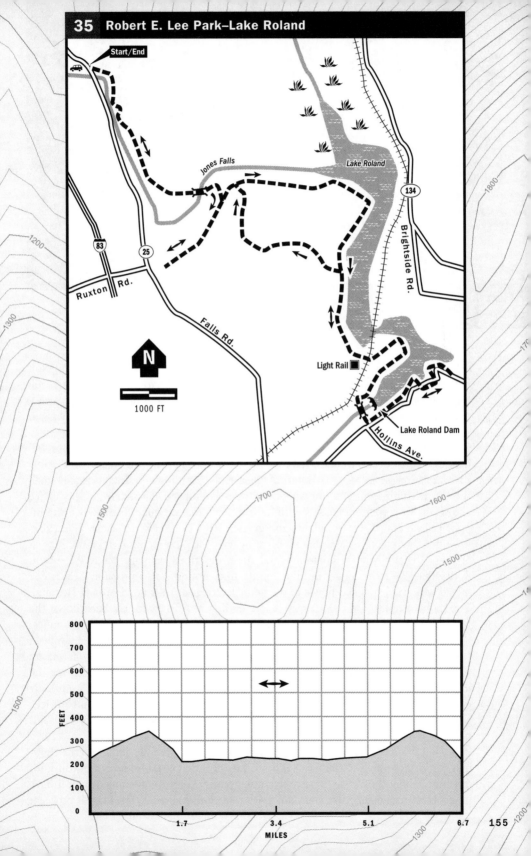

Start/End

Jones Falls

Lake Roland

134

Brightside Rd.

83

25

Ruxton Rd.

Falls Rd.

N

1000 FT

Light Rail

Lake Roland Dam

Hollins Ave.

800
700
600
500
400
300
200
100
0

FEET

1.7   3.4   5.1   6.7

MILES

Steel bridge over the Jones Falls

a little more than a mile along the edge of Lake Roland and follows Roland Run before it dead-ends in a residential neighborhood. Instead, cross the bridge and look for two path offshoots—one to the right leading downhill and one to the right leading uphill; pass both of these and take the next path you see to the right; it's easy to spot, at just under 0.75 miles.

This trail is very rocky and rooty; you'll see a blue blaze or two, but these will die out. At just over 0.8 miles, the trail suddenly opens up and you are in an entirely new landscape in an area that's part of "Bare Hills." You'll see prairie grass and smell the short, stubby pines as you walk over the rocky topsoil. The sharp rocks you see about you are serpentine, or serpentinite, a mineral that produces extremely nutrient-poor soil that supports few plants and grasses. This extremely rare ecosystem exists in only a few places in Maryland. (For a heavy dose of serpentine, take the hike at Soldiers Delight Natural Environmental Area, described on page 159). When you notice that you're no longer heading uphill, turn around. You'll probably hear traffic mixed with the barks and howls of the kenneled dogs at Falls Road Animal Hospital. The trail continues for a short way before ending at Falls Road. Go back down the hill, rejoin the original trail, and head right. This out-and-back spur totals 0.6 miles.

Back on the original trail, you'll pass some man-made berms built by bikers. Just beyond, you'll see yet another cut path on the right; take note of it—it will be your return route. For now, keep going straight. At the railroad ties, you can see the indentations from the rail bed heading straight, but as a hiking path, it eventually gets lost in a tangle of vegetation; so head left instead, keeping the falls on your left. The trail runs through tall, mature oaks. You will see periodic white blazes here, but nothing consistent.

At 1.5 miles, you'll see well-worn paths going down the big gullies on the right; bikers use these. In addition, you will see lots of little cut paths spread out in both directions; bikers also use these single-track paths. Keep going straight; you'll have no problem recognizing the main trail—it's wide and well-trod. The biggest problem you'll encounter along the trail is mud puddles, made worse by erosion-causing mountain bikes (I'm guilty of contributing to this myself, so I shouldn't complain).

At 1.6 miles, Jones Falls comes into better view through tall thin trees. Check out the path down to the water; the river runs nice and clean here. Go back up and rejoin the trail, which heads up and down a bit before opening to a clearing at the edge of the lake at just over 1.8 miles. You will see a bird feeder sticking out of the marshy area; keep an eye out for great white herons—I see one almost every time I hike here. I've also spotted an ibis, but just once.

The trail suddenly drops downhill and rejoins the rail bed on the left. You will have many opportunities to go down to water level to look for that heron. At just under 2 miles you will come to my favorite spot to do just that; you'll see some rail-road ties heading left down to the water—you can go sit at the lake's edge and watch the birds, turtles, and snakes (and though less romantic, I've seen nutria here too). Sit for more than five minutes, and you'll see a Light Rail train gliding by on the tracks on the other side of the lake.

At 2 miles, you'll see the defunct railroad tracks, now covered with plants; you will follow them for a while. You can either stay on this wide path or take the smaller one that parallels it about 10 feet to the left, closer to the water. Either way, the two trails connect at 2.25 miles.

At this point, you'll come to the Light Rail tracks. Of course, use caution when crossing even though this section sits in the middle of a long straightaway, making it impossible for a train to surprise you.

Once you cross the tracks, head uphill. This portion of the trail is badly eroded, and you'll have to clamber over some roots and rocks, but you'll see daylight ahead to the right. Once you reach the top of the hill, you'll see a pavilion and picnic tables. Now you're on a cracked asphalt path; take a left and follow it around the water. Although this is a nice spot to sit waterside and contemplate the lake, I recommend that you keep moving—your chances for solitude here are next to none. It's nearly impossible to escape this section of the park without hearing the screeching tussle of a couple of canines that have been allowed to roam free (see "Special Comments"). So head around on the asphalt path—you'll have the opportunity for good views and solitude on the other side of the lake. Pass the caretaker's house on the left and head down the very steep hill toward the bridge; you will see Lake Roland dam on the left.

Cross the bridge and take the road to the left; you'll see a lovely spot to sit next to the marble building that reads, "Lake Roland 1861," a reminder of the lake's prior use as a city reservoir. Fishermen frequent the pier on the left of the little cul-de-sac. Take the dirt path at the end of the cul-de-sac and head uphill over the rocky path. At the top of the hill, where there's asphalt again, take a left onto the wide dirt path and head uphill again. As the path turns right, you'll have a glorious view of the lake. Usually, the underbrush is cut down; the view is spectacular and offers wonder in all seasons—spring blooms, summer green, fall foliage, and winter barrenness. Turn around at the fire hydrant where Woodbrook Lane begins.

On the return trip, take the detour into an upland forest at 5.2 miles through oak and tulip poplar. The trail, which is narrower and more difficult in places than the trail coming in, is full of rocks and roots, but accordingly it feels wilder and sees less traffic. It loops and rejoins the main trail at 5.9 miles.

You might be interested in visiting two nearby sites that have great historical significance. You can walk from the trailhead to Rockland Historic District, listed on the National Register of Historic Places, at the corner of Falls Road (north of the trailhead), Ruxton Road (to the east), and Old Court Road (to the west). The buildings in Rockland, Baltimore County's first permanent settlement dating back to 1706, remain and have been lovingly maintained, while the mill now houses businesses and shops. From Rockland, you will have a short drive to the Colored Methodist Protestant St. Johns' Chapel of Baltimore County. Built for free blacks in 1833, it has held services continually since 1886. To get there, head north on Falls Road and take the first right onto Ruxton Road; when it ends at a stop sign, go right onto Bellona Avenue, and you will see the church 0.3 miles ahead on the right.

SOLDIERS DELIGHT NATURAL ENVIRONMENTAL AREA

▶ IN BRIEF

Take a quick trip to a look-alike Midwest prairie, where the serpentine landscape provides a rare environment. Then head to the "other side" of Soldiers Delight, which is more typical of the mid-Atlantic.

▶ DESCRIPTION

Many people mistakenly assume that the Soldiers Delight Serpentine Trail is named for its shape. In fact, the name refers to the type of soil in the area. Serpentine, or serpentinite, is a mineral that produces extremely nutrient-poor soil that supports few plants and grasses. Exceptions include the rare examples of serpentine grasslands that grow in Soldiers Delight. Many of these grasses are not only rare in Maryland, but across our entire planet.

Long before Europeans settled in Baltimore County, serpentine grassland covered much of this land, thanks in great part to the Native Americans who fire hunted here. The Native Americans set extensive fires to drive deer toward open areas, and the fires had the secondary effect of establishing the grasslands that still feed the deer. According to the Maryland Department of Natural Resources, even though what serpentine grassland remains in Maryland amounts to less than 5 percent of the original, it harbors no less than 34

▶ DIRECTIONS

Take I-695 to Exit 18, Route 26 west. Go 4.5 miles and take a right onto Deer Park Road. You will see the park entrance at 1.9 miles on the left; park in front of the visitor center. The trailhead parallels the parking lot next to the bulletin board. Alternate directions: Take I-695 to I-795 west to Owings Mills Boulevard. Continue to Owings Mills Center, go past the mall, turn right onto Lyons Mill Road, and then right onto Deer Park Road.

ⓘ KEY AT-A-GLANCE INFORMATION

LENGTH: 6.3 miles

CONFIGURATION: 2 intersecting, jagged loops

DIFFICULTY: Moderate

SCENERY: Rare prairie and serpentine landscape, Chimney Branch, abandoned mines

EXPOSURE: Half and half

TRAFFIC: Light to moderate; you will see more deer than people

TRAIL SURFACE: Packed dirt, rock

HIKING TIME: 3 hours

ACCESS: Sunrise to sunset; visitor center open Wednesday–Friday, 9 a.m.-4 p.m.; Saturday and Sunday, 10 a.m.-4 p.m.

MAPS: USGS Reisterstown; trail maps at bulletin board outside visitor center; and excellent detailed maps of Soldiers Delight can be purchased online at www.easycart. net/MarylandDepartmentofNatural Resources/Central_Maryland_Trail_ Guides.html

FACILITIES: Restrooms, water, vending machines in visitor center

SPECIAL COMMENTS: Wear sturdy hiking boots or trail shoes—serpentine rock is very sharp. The hike consists of two loops of roughly equal length that intersect not far from the parking area, which makes it easy to take only one. To hike only the east side trails, pass the park entrance on Deer Park and go an additional 0.3 miles to the parking area at the overlook; the trail starts across Deer Park Road from the overlook.

Soldiers Delight Natural Environmental Area

UTM Zone (WGS84)   18S

Easting   341930

Northing   4363785

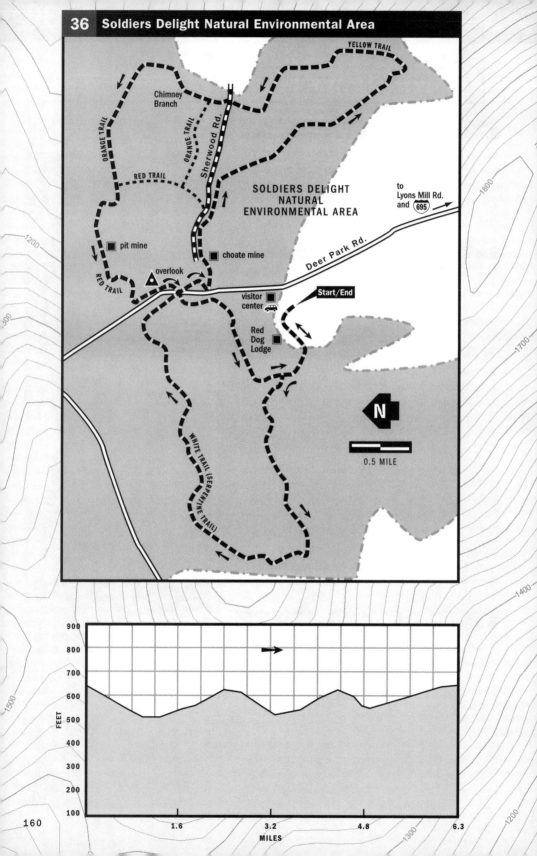

YELLOW TRAIL

Chimney
Branch

ORANGE TRAIL

ORANGE TRAIL

Sherwood Rd.

RED TRAIL

SOLDIERS DELIGHT
NATURAL
ENVIRONMENTAL AREA

to
Lyons Mill Rd.
and 695

pit mine

choate mine

Deer Park Rd.

RED TRAIL

overlook

visitor
center

Start/End

Red
Dog
Lodge

N

0.5 MILE

WHITE TRAIL (SERPENTINE TRAIL)

900
800
700
600
500
400
300
200
100

FEET

1.6   3.2   4.8   6.3

MILES

rare and endangered plant species. Those found in Soldiers Delight include papillose nut rush, serpentine aster, whorled milkweed, grooved flax, and fringed gentian, among others. Not surprisingly, the rare grasses also host rare insects, including Edward's hairstreak, an unnamed leafhopper, and a black pear-shaped beetle, usually found only in deserts. Soldiers Delight remains the largest remaining serpentine area in the eastern United States and is among the most species-rich in the world.

Begin the hike by heading left on the white-blazed trail by the visitor center. Very soon, you'll come to the Red Dog Lodge, an old now-defunct hunting lodge. Pass it and emerge into an open area created by a power-line cut. Inevitably, along the way you're bound to hear a sudden shuffle and then see the bounding hops of the white-tailed deer that thrive in Soldiers Delight.

You will walk through a pine forest, a welcome spot of shade on a hot day. As you turn north, you'll come to a creek where an odd sight greets you—to the left sits an old rusted automobile, with the make no longer distinguishable. It belongs to nature now, with grasses growing through the trunk and hood. It doesn't seem to have much of an effect on nearby stream life, if the thousands of darting minnows, skimmers, and dragonflies are any indication.

Continue your walk up a fairly steep hill. The trail here is entirely loose rocks; this is the serpentinite. If you were barefoot, you'd get an unwelcome understanding of how sharp the edges of this mineral can be. As the trail takes you back into a pine forest at the top of the hill, turn around and enjoy the astounding view—prairieland sweeps in all directions. Red-tipped grasses swaying in the breeze surround you, and depending on the season, you might see yellow from the gray goldenrod and grooved flax, white from the serpentine aster and whorled milkweed, and purple from grass-leaved blazing star and fringed gentian.

Stubs of culled pines dot the prairie: An act of arson didn't damage these trees; rather it is a result of an ongoing attempt to restore the grasslands, free of the invasive and nonnative pines. When you head back into the woods, you'll come to another section of the power-line cut you crossed earlier. Beyond the power-line cut, the landscape still looks pretty stubbly, but oaks and poplars offer shade. Since these trees are native, they are left to grow as best they can in the serpentine soil.

As you approach Deer Park Road, you'll hear quite a bit of noise. You'll come to an overlook on Deer Park Road at 2.1 miles. A historical marker here tells you that chrome was first discovered in Baltimore County in 1808. Chromite mines existed at Soldiers Delight from 1828 to 1850, and they produced almost all the world's chromium.

Cross Deer Park Road and head right to continue hiking on the east side. You will see a series of three trails blazed in red, orange, and yellow that run across landscape far more typical of the Baltimore metro region. Begin on the rocky red-blazed trail. Initially, the landscape looks much as it does in the serpentine section, but there is far less serpentine grassland on this side of Soldiers Delight and mature Virginia pines line both sides of the trail, with wildflowers on the right. Very soon, at 2.3 miles, you'll notice a wooden post pointing to the yellow-blazed trail and the choate mine to the right. The abandoned mine sits within a wooden fenced area, but if you circle around the fence, you can walk inside and approach the mine opening; you'll

Choate Mine

have to stop there since the mine is now filled with water. The mine played a part in the big operation that thrived in this area in the early to mid-1800s, when miners dug for chromite, talc, asbestos, magnesite, and soapstone, among other minerals.

Continuing on, the trail becomes very rocky, and often the entire trail itself is one large slab of rock. The nicely shaded area supports flourishing greenbrier underbrush, which gives the first indication of the difference between these trails and the Serpentine Trail. As I walked, I heard the hoot of an owl, but I couldn't spot it within the thick canopy of pine, poplar, and oak.

At just under 2.7 miles, the trail opens up. You can head left to make a quick loop of the red-blazed trail (1 mile total), diagonally left to head to the orange-blazed trail (2 miles), or keep going straight onto the yellow-blazed trail to make the complete 3-mile circuit. At the beginning of the yellow-blazed trail, you will still see a lot of serpentine rock. Green underbrush lines the right side of the trail, while prairie grass grows on the left, and the dominant pine and eastern red cedar shades both sides. You will also hear and perhaps see the many deer that scurry about in the forest.

At 3 miles, you will cross a small stream and head uphill to the right. At 3.3 miles, you'll come to and cross Chimney Branch, which flows into Liberty Reservoir. Just beyond you'll find an area where lots of pines are being eliminated. Head to the right on the other side of the stream; the trail becomes extremely rocky again here.

You will walk through another open serpentine area before plunging back into the woods at 3.5 miles. The soil is good here and supports lots of underbrush. The trees are still mostly conifers, but they grow much taller here than at other places along the trail. The soil also supports oak, beech, sycamore, and maple. Amazingly (and a testament to the varied nature of Soldiers Delight), there's even enough moisture in this section for ferns and mosses to grow.

At 3.7 miles, you will cross Sherwood Road, a narrow lane that leads to a private home, and the trail will pick up in a field on the other side, among very tall prairie grasses. When you enter the woods again, head left. The path straight ahead leads to private homes; you may find it confusing here because no signs point you in the correct direction. Also, the path ahead is wider than the one to the left, but you should head left anyway. Once you do, you will once again see yellow blazes on the trees. Unfortunately, the trail skirts the edge of the park boundary and lots of back-yards appear on the right among the mixed hardwood.

To connect to the orange-blazed trail, go straight at 3.9 miles; the trail begins to head left away from the houses and over a nice sweeping hill to the right. The next 0.3 miles is pretty hilly, and you will almost immediately notice, aided in part by the appearance of a small stream to the right, the stark contrast between this trail and the Serpentine Trail. But then, at 4.3 miles, you will emerge into a serpentine clearing, with its attendant cut pines. The stream still runs on the right, and the water rippling over its rocky bed fills the air with a pleasing sound.

A little farther down the trail, you'll come to a post indicating the red-blazed trail to the left and the yellow-blazed trail to the right. Take a right and walk past a thick stand of grass-leaved blazing star with its purple blossoms. After crossing a tiny stream, you'll enter an open area as you gradually head uphill. At 5.1 miles, you will come to a fenced area surrounding a pit mine on the right. Even though it's closed off, the pit mine still poses a danger. Peer in the hole, but don't climb the fence. (Inci-dentally, when you see "pit mine" on the trail map, you might expect a massive open pit, but it's actually quite small.) You will reach Deer Park Road at 5.6 miles. Cross the road and head to the left to make your way back to the visitor center on the only section of trail in Soldiers Delight that you haven't yet hiked.

▶ NEARBY ACTIVITIES

Just down the road from Soldiers Delight, you'll find the family-friendly Northwest Regional Park, home to many ball fields, paved paths, and wheelchair-accessible gar-dening plots. From the Deer Park Overlook, head back toward MD 26. The park entrance is approximately 3 miles to the left, just before Lyons Mill Road. For additional information on Northwest Regional Park, contact the park office at (410) 887-1558.

CARROLL COUNTY

GILLIS FALLS

KEY AT-A-GLANCE INFORMATION

LENGTH: 2.7 miles

CONFIGURATION: Combination

DIFFICULTY: Easy

SCENERY: Gillis Falls, mixed hardwoods, rural landscapes

EXPOSURE: Mostly shade

TRAFFIC: Light

TRAIL SURFACE: Packed dirt, grass

HIKING TIME: 1 hour

ACCESS: Trails are open seven days a week, from sunrise to sunset, from February 16 through August 31; they are closed Monday, Wednesday, Friday, and Saturday from September 1 through February 15 for the Cooperative Hunting Program; and they are completely closed for two weeks beginning the Saturday after Thanksgiving for Firearm Deer Season.

MAPS: USGS Winfield; *Guide to the Trails in Carroll County, Maryland* includes excellent maps—contact or visit the Carroll County Department of Recreation and Parks at 225 North Center Street, Room 100, Westminster, MD 21157; (410) 386-2103 or (888) 302-8978.

FACILITIES: None

SPECIAL COMMENTS: Be careful to avoid private farmlands by staying on the trails and keeping to the tree line whenever you emerge into open fields.

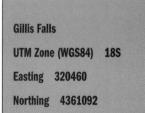

Gillis Falls

UTM Zone (WGS84) 18S

Easting 320460

Northing 4361092

IN BRIEF

Take a short but secluded walk through a varied landscape—river valley, rolling fields, and piedmont forest.

DESCRIPTION

Follow the sign to Gillis Falls Trailhead and go left from the parking area; you'll see a little path to the right heading toward Grimville Road, but stay on the path on the edge of the more pleasant wooded area for a little while longer (you'll come out to the same place either way). You will come to the big open field of the equestrian center on your right before you will enter the woods on a path at 0.3 miles. The nice wide dirt trail heads downhill; at 0.5 miles, at the bottom of the hill, you'll come to a wide fire road. Go right (this is where you would have wound up if you had taken the path to Grimville Road that you passed at the top of the trail). Gillis Falls is on your left; don't expect a waterfall—it's a stream, generally 10 to 20 feet across and a few feet deep at best.

Across the water, you'll see the remains of a fireplace and chimney. It's very boggy between you and the stream, with lots of mountain laurel on the hill on the right. Continue through the woods, a combination of pine, oak, poplar, and dogwood; you'll see many songbirds flitting about in the high grass and ground vegetation.

When the trail splits at 0.75 miles, head left

DIRECTIONS

Take I-695 to I-70 west; continue to Exit 73, Woodbine Road north toward Woodbine. Go 1.8 miles and turn left onto John Pickett Road. Go 1.7 miles and turn left onto Grimville Road. Continue 0.3 miles to a gravel parking area on the right; you will see a sign for Carroll County Equestrian Center—the sign also points left to the Gillis Falls Trailhead.

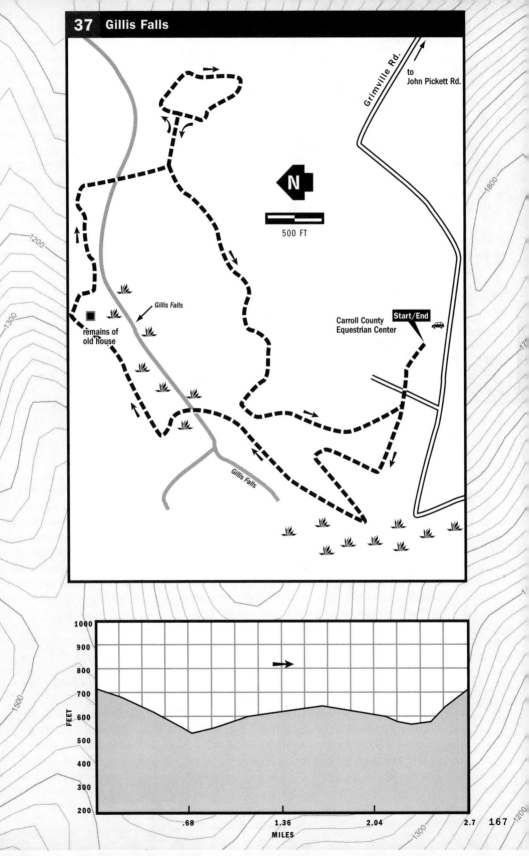

to
John Pickett Rd.

Grimville Rd.

N

500 FT

Gillis Falls

remains of
old house

Gillis Falls

Carroll County
Equestrian Center

Start/End

FEET

1000
900
800
700
600
500
400
300
200

.68   1.36   2.04   2.7   **167**

MILES

Gillis Falls

and cross Gillis Falls; it's pretty shallow and full of rocks here, making it easy get across. At just under a mile, you'll see the remains of jockeys' quarters, now overgrown with vegetation, in the woods to the right. The trail splits again at 1 mile at the remains of an old house; go uphill to the right. (You'll see a narrow footpath straight ahead that leads to the stream, but unless you're on a horse, you won't be able to get across without wading in knee-high or perhaps waist-high water.) At 1.2 miles, at the top of the steep hill, head left at another trail split, and take another left at the T intersection ahead. Pine trees dominate on the right side of the trail, with oaks to the left.

This trail opens into an open field; it's a nice view, with gently sloping hills rolling off into the distance. But if you're standing there, it means you just missed the rest of the trail. Turn around and look for the barely discernible path down the hill to the left. It was once a horse trail but was abandoned after several large trees fell across it; not many hikers use it, so it remains a bit overgrown. If you look closely, you can see the grooves in the trail as it heads back downhill toward the water.

Cross Gillis Falls again at 1.5 miles; again, the water is very shallow and narrow, making an easy crossing. On the other side you'll come to a very obvious, easily discernible trail—take it left, and you'll pass a sizable bog. The trail soon narrows and heads uphill, following a switchback full of rocks. You will emerge into an open field at 1.7 miles; follow the tree line around to the right. Just before 1.9 miles, start looking for a narrow, overgrown footpath that cuts back into the woods. Continue on the path until you link back up with the wide trail you used earlier; turn left—you'll parallel Gillis Falls as it flows downstream. Cross the stream at 2.2 miles and continue walking in the stream valley; you will see beautiful rock outcroppings up the hill on the right and mountain laurel on the left.

You will cross Gillis Falls again at 2.3 miles and then pass the stone foundations of a few old houses on the left. You'll soon reach the trail split you passed earlier; this time take the footpath diagonally left up the hill just before you reach the wide fire road. You'll emerge from the woods once again on the grounds of the equestrian center; while you walk straight across the field, you will have a great view of Carroll County's still-rural landscape. You will come to a little ridge, lined by small pine trees; walk along the ridge until it swings to the left at 2.7 miles. Head down to the tree line and back to the parking area.

HASHAWHA ENVIRONMENTAL APPRECIATION AREA

▶ IN BRIEF

Start at Bear Branch Nature Center and stroll through 10 different examples of environmentally friendly land usages.

▶ DESCRIPTION

Enter the trailhead and follow the sign to the pavilion. The wooden fence flanking the crushed rock trail zigzags to the bottom of the hill. When you see the pavilion on the left, head right through the open field and then left at the sign pointing to the blue-blazed Vista Trail. Almost immediately you will come to a 3-way intersection; take a left up the hill.

You will be on a wide dirt path surrounded mostly by short oaks. The trail quickly heads up and then down as it circles the pavilion you passed at the top of the trail. Head up the hill at 0.4 miles in a grove of pines; you will see the surrounding farmland beyond the pines. Walk through a nice buffer of thick vegetation and emerge at a raptor pen at about 0.6 miles. You will see a number of birds being rehabilitated here, including an American kestrel, eastern screech owl, barred owl, bald eagle (looking very

▶ DIRECTIONS

Take I-695 to Exit 19, I-795 west; continue until I-795 ends at MD 140 (Baltimore Boulevard) north to Westminster. Continue on MD 140 for 12 miles and turn right onto MD 97 north to Union Mills and Gettysburg. Continue on MD 97 (it becomes Littlestown Pike) 2.8 miles and then turn right onto John Owings Road. After 1 mile, you'll see a "Welcome to Hashawha and Bear Branch Nature Center" sign on the left; turn here and then take a right at the sign for the Nature Center. The trail begins on the blue-blazed Vista Trail just to the left of the Nature Center.

ⓘ KEY AT-A-GLANCE INFORMATION

LENGTH: 2.5 miles

CONFIGURATION: Loop with a short spur

DIFFICULTY: Moderate

SCENERY: Wildflower meadows, Big Pipe Creek, raptors

EXPOSURE: Slightly more sun than shade

TRAFFIC: Moderate

TRAIL SURFACE: Packed dirt, crushed rock, asphalt

HIKING TIME: 1.5 hours

ACCESS: Dawn to dusk on trails; Bear Branch Nature Center open Wednesday–Saturday, 10 a.m.–5 p.m. and Sunday, noon–5 p.m.

MAPS: USGS Manchester; trail maps also available in Bear Branch Nature Center; *Guide to the Trails in Carroll County, Maryland* includes excellent maps—contact or visit the Carroll County Department of Recreation and Parks at 225 North Center Street, Room 100, Westminster, MD 21157; (410) 386-2103 or (888) 302-8978.

FACILITIES: Water and restrooms in Bear Branch Nature Center

SPECIAL COMMENTS: The Hashawha Residential Camp, which sits in the middle of the Hashawha Environmental Appreciation Area, is closed to the public; please respect the no-entry areas, which designate the private rental area.

Hashawha Environmental Appreciation Area

UTM Zone (WGS84)   18S

Easting   329583

Northing   4390472

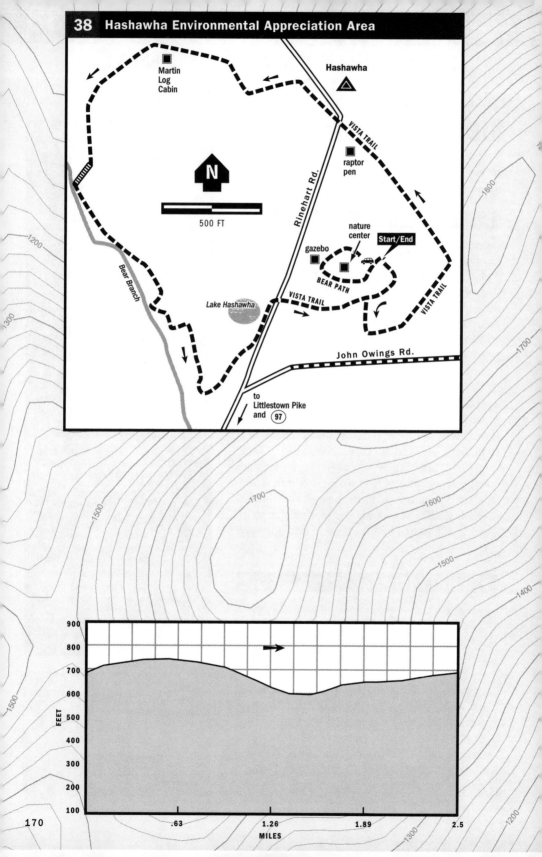

Hashawha

Martin Log Cabin

VISTA TRAIL

raptor pen

N

500 FT

Rinehart Rd.

nature center

gazebo

Start/End

BEAR PATH

Bear Branch

Lake Hashawha

VISTA TRAIL

VISTA TRAIL

John Owings Rd.

to Littlestown Pike and 97

900
800
700
600
500
400
300
200
100

FEET

.63   1.26   1.89   2.5
MILES

majestic even in its confined space), turkey vulture, red-tailed hawk, and broad-winged hawk.

Continue the hike by heading to the right, away from the cages; you will come to a gravel road and then an asphalt road. In about 100 feet, you'll see yellow (Wilderness Trail) and green (Stream Trail) arrows pointing to the right, and straight ahead lies the restricted area of the Residential Hashawha Camp, a camp for Carroll County sixth-graders. Back in the woods after heading right, turn right at the exercise course at just under 0.8 miles, and you will pass the restored Martin Log Cabin at 1 mile. You will parallel a wildflower meadow on the right, filled with goldenrod and cacophonous crickets and grasshoppers in summer. You will reach a boardwalk at about 1.25 miles; take a right over the boardwalk and then a left on the other side through another wildflower meadow.

At 1.5 miles, you'll be paralleling Big Pipe Creek, and you'll come to a beautiful open area where a tremendous old maple shades a picnic bench sitting in a crook of the semicircular sweep of the creek. Take the wooden boardwalk straight ahead over the creek; you'll pass a clump of beech trees as you head up the hill. At the top of the hill, take a right; the trail quickly heads downhill. You will see the creek again on your right as you swing around to the left and head back uphill.

At just under 2 miles, you'll see a gravel road heading left to the camp area and a paved asphalt road heading to the right; take the asphalt road for 500 feet, passing Lake Hashawha on your left. Pick up the Vista Trail again to the right across the road. Pass a marsh on the right, and you'll soon be back at the pavilion you passed at the beginning of the hike. Head left up the hill toward your car; this time, however, take a brief detour by heading left when you come to the parking area. You'll come to an informational sign on "forest edging" and a paved concrete path beyond. Take a left; this is the Bear Path, which winds around the nature center and ends at a gazebo from which you can view examples of land usage that maintain the 10 healthy environments in the Hashawha Environmental Appreciation Area: wildlife habitat, field strip cropping, grass waterway, contour strip cropping, grass diversion, lined outlet (rip-rap), pond, woodland, field border, and nontidal wetland. You can take a mowed-grass path from the gazebo to the nature center, which has exhibits on hundreds of butterflies, as well as live box turtles, stuffed mink, deer, raccoon, and beaver; you can also learn about the interesting changes in the habitat in this area all the way back to the Paleozoic period.

▶ NEARBY ACTIVITIES

Hashawha Environmental Appreciation Area sits within the Union Mills environmental area, which contains approximately 8 miles of hiking trails; please see page 188 for hiking suggestions in Union Mills. For sustenance after a hike at Hashawha, head south on MD 97 into downtown Westminster. Full of restaurants, antiques shops, and museums, Westminster offers many diverse activities. The Maryland Wine Festival takes place each September at the nearby Carroll County Farm Museum grounds in Westminster; for more information, call (800) 654-4645, (410) 876-2667, or (410) 848-7775.

LIBERTY RESERVOIR: LIBERTY WEST–MORGAN RUNS

▶ IN BRIEF

A taste of Loch Raven Reservoir, but without the people.

▶ DESCRIPTION

You may not think highly of starting a hike with busy MD 32 just above you on your right, but you'll quickly move away from civilization. About 900 feet down the fire road, you'll see another fire road heading downhill on your left (a pair of orange cables strung with an orange wire on the right marks the entrance off MD 32). Take the road down the hill, and at 0.25 you'll reach the reservoir; you'll see a thick forest of white pine on the right.

Although you might still be able to hear the traffic on MD 32, when I was here the quacking and wing-beating of ducks, the pounding of a woodpecker, and the whispering glide of a gray heron effectively drowned it out. Moving on, the trail more or less follows the contours of the reservoir. As you walk along, notice the edge of the reservoir as you parallel it; submerged tree trunks give the area a "bayou-ish" look. Ravens and red-winged blackbirds frequent this area.

Unlike the trails at Loch Raven Reservoir, which often run right alongside the water, the trails here, at Liberty Reservoir, run up the hill, away from the water a bit. This is because these trails have remained primarily fire roads, as opposed to cut "single-track" for bikes. Since the fire roads run about a hundred or so feet above

▶ DIRECTIONS

Take I-695 to I-70 West, and continue to MD 32 north; go 10 miles to Liberty Reservoir Bridge. Cross the bridge and immediately look for the gravel parking area to the right; park your car, walk across MD 32, and go over the guardrail. The trail starts on the fire road at the bottom of the hill.

ⓘ KEY AT-A-GLANCE INFORMATION

LENGTH: 6.7 miles

CONFIGURATION: Loop

DIFFICULTY: Easy to moderate

SCENERY: Liberty Reservoir, Morgan Run, Little Morgan Run, white pine plantations

EXPOSURE: Shade

TRAFFIC: Light

TRAIL SURFACE: Packed dirt

HIKING TIME: 2.5 hours

ACCESS: Sunrise to sunset

MAPS: USGS Finksburg

FACILITIES: None

SPECIAL COMMENTS: This hike includes a difficult river crossing at Little Morgan Run; expect wet feet in all but the lowest water levels.

Liberty Reservoir: Liberty West–Morgan Runs

UTM Zone (WGS84)   18S

Easting   333270

Northing   4367091

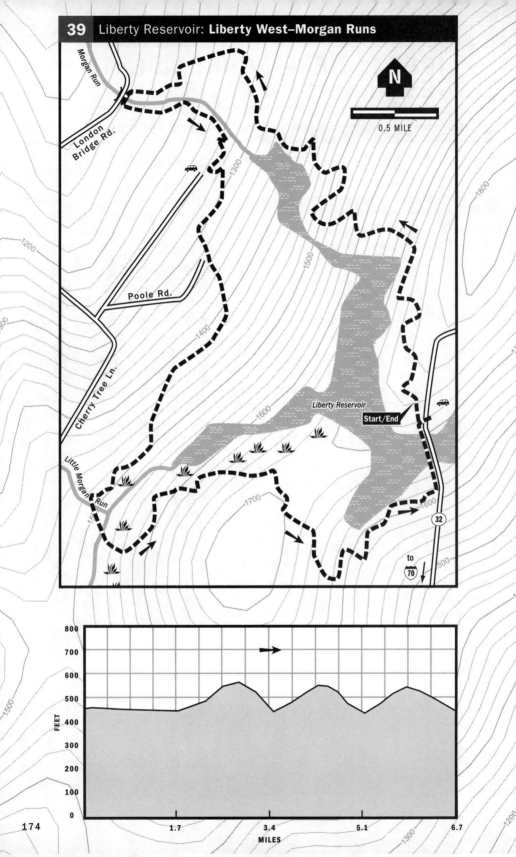

N

0.5 MILE

Morgan Run

London Bridge Rd.

Poole Rd.

Cherry Tree Ln.

Little Morgan Run

Liberty Reservoir

Start/End

32

to 70

800
700
600
500
400
300
200
100
0

FEET

1.7   3.4   5.1   6.7
MILES

the water, you will have many good views of the reservoir spreading out in several directions.

By 0.7 miles, once again the trail runs through the pine forest and will continue so for a while. You will cross a stream at 1.1 miles; look for a bog milkweed swaying in the breeze at 1.5 miles. Here you will head up a steep hill, away from the reservoir; you'll come to a power-line cut at the top of the hill, and you will hear the crackle of electricity in the air—the buzz is a bit unnerving, but it's nothing to worry about. The trail here takes the form of two tire grooves directly under power lines.

At 1.9 miles, the path veers away from the power lines and heads back into the woods; you will cross a little stream and soon after come to Morgan Run, a wide river with small rapids coursing over rocks. You'll hear the wonderful sound of swiftly moving water, which you don't get at the reservoir. The trail, now a footpath, follows Morgan Run upstream to London Bridge Road, a small rural road. Cross the bridge and immediately head back down the other side; you'll now be walking downstream. On your right, moss and fern-covered rock outcroppings line the hills, which are studded with mountain laurel. The narrow trail winds through an area forested mostly with oak trees. This section bears little resemblance to the previous 2 miles, highlighting the varied nature of this hike.

You'll probably see some horseshoe impressions in the dirt path here. At a grouping of fir trees at 2.6 miles, you'll pass a marsh on the left; if you're walking in late spring or summer, the chorus of frogs will be almost deafening. The trail soon splits, and you can either go to the left along the reservoir or straight ahead to rejoin the fire road; take the fire road. You'll soon come to Poole Road, marked by another set of orange cables with a small parking area beyond. Make a U-turn and look for another orange cable; head in that direction. The trail takes you into an incredibly beautiful white pine plantation; you will find it easy to get lost in contemplation here as you walk along a little stream on the left with the pines to the right.

At 3 miles, unfortunately civilization comes into view, and you'll see a few houses on the right beyond the pine forest. Over the next half-mile or so, you'll pass a bunch of trails leading off to the left—these all dead-end at the reservoir. At 3.3 miles, you'll see a wide fire road to the left, the end of a residential road to the right, and a set of orange posts straight ahead. Follow the orange posts, continuing straight alongside the narrow paved road to the right. Though it's a bit disappointing to be passing backyards, if you only look left, it's all pines as far as you can see—and you'll probably hear the hammering of a woodpecker or two.

The trail will take you to a stream valley and across a little stream. Immediately after you will come to Little Morgan Run. As mentioned in "Special Comments" above, you might have difficulty crossing here without getting wet. I hiked it on a cold early spring day, and I spent half an hour throwing rocks in the water to make a crude crossing; it didn't work—I still got wet feet. If the water level is low, however, you should be able to cross more easily and stay dry too.

On the other side of Little Morgan Run, the trail parallels a twisty little stream that empties into a marsh and then bleeds into the edge of the reservoir. You will come to a trail split at 4.9 miles; take the leftward cut to stay in the woods. Over the next half-mile or so, you will go up and down a series of hills, skirting the edge of the

Liberty Reservoir

forested reservoir boundary; houses will reappear through the woods on the right. The trail swings around toward the reservoir, giving you a great view of the water, which here splits off into four directions like a headless body.

At 5.9 miles, you'll come to a T intersection; go left and you'll quickly come to the edge of the reservoir. It offers a nice view, but unfortunately you'll probably also see trash; debris seems to float this way and accumulate here. Head uphill to the right, keeping the reservoir on your left; mountain laurel line the path here. When you reach the fire road at the top of the hill, go left. You'll start to hear the traffic on MD 32 again; take the narrow footpath through the woods. You will come to MD 32 at 6.4 miles; carefully walk along the shoulder of the highway, taking extra care when you cross the Liberty Reservoir Bridge as the shoulder narrows considerably. You will find your car on the right on the other side of the bridge.

▶ NEARBY ACTIVITIES

In addition to the other trails in the Liberty Reservoir watershed, this area offers an abundance of hiking opportunities. To the south, check out the Hugg-Thomas Wildlife Management Area of Patapsco Valley State Park; it is open to hikers on Sundays from February 16 to August 31 (open to hunters only the rest of the year); take MD 32 south to the first right over the Patapsco River and turn left onto Main Street and then right onto Forsythe Road. Also visit Morgan Run Natural Environmental Area to the west (see page 180); take MD 32 south to MD 26 west and continue to MD 97 north. You also have the option of hiking in Piney Run Park (see page 184); take MD 26 west and turn left onto Martz Road into the park.

LIBERTY RESERVOIR: MIDDLE RUN TRAIL

▶ IN BRIEF

An anomaly: despite this hike's location at Liberty Reservoir, it rarely offers views of the reservoir itself. Nevertheless, it's arguably the prettiest and most diverse hike in the Liberty Reservoir watershed.

▶ DESCRIPTION

The trail splits almost immediately; a fishermen's path to the right heads downhill toward the water, and the main trail, a wide fire road, continues straight. If you want to spend a little while by the water, take the cut down to the edge of the reservoir; to continue this hike, go straight.

Pine dominates the landscape here, evidenced by the smell and innumerable needles underfoot. You will also see some hardy holly trees that are managing to eke some living space despite the crowding pines, which block the sunlight from reaching the forest floor. At 0.25 miles, you'll come to a 4-way crossroads; turn right and move away from the pines into a forest of oak, poplar, mountain laurel, and redbud, filled with birdsong.

On the left at 0.4 miles, you'll pass a great rock outcropping rippling down the hill like a dinosaur's spine. When the trees are bare, the tip of the ridge offers a great view of the river valley. Mountain laurel line both sides of the trail. Down the hill on the left you will see the edge of the reservoir, complete with a marshy buffer area

▶ KEY AT-A-GLANCE INFORMATION

LENGTH: 3.7 miles

CONFIGURATION: Out-and-back with a loop

DIFFICULTY: Moderate

SCENERY: Middle Run, pine plantations, mixed hardwoods

EXPOSURE: Mostly shade with some sun in winter and early spring when the trees are bare

TRAFFIC: Light

TRAIL SURFACE: Packed dirt

HIKING TIME: 1.5–2 hours

ACCESS: Sunrise to sunset daily

MAPS: USGS Finksburg

FACILITIES: None

SPECIAL COMMENTS: This hike requires crossing Middle Run four times; although the water is never too wide nor too deep, expect wet feet and legs, perhaps up to your knees.

▶ DIRECTIONS

Take I-695 to Exit 19, I-795 west. Take Exit 7, Franklin Boulevard, but head west to Nicodemus Road just before you get to Franklin Boulevard. Nicodemus Road turns into Deer Park Road after Ivy Mill Road. Cross Liberty Reservoir bridge and continue 1 mile to the big turn to the right; look for the gravel parking area on the left. Walk into the woods behind the parking area and look for the footpath.

Liberty Reservoir: Middle Run Trail

UTM Zone (WGS84)   18S

Easting   336810

Northing   4368285

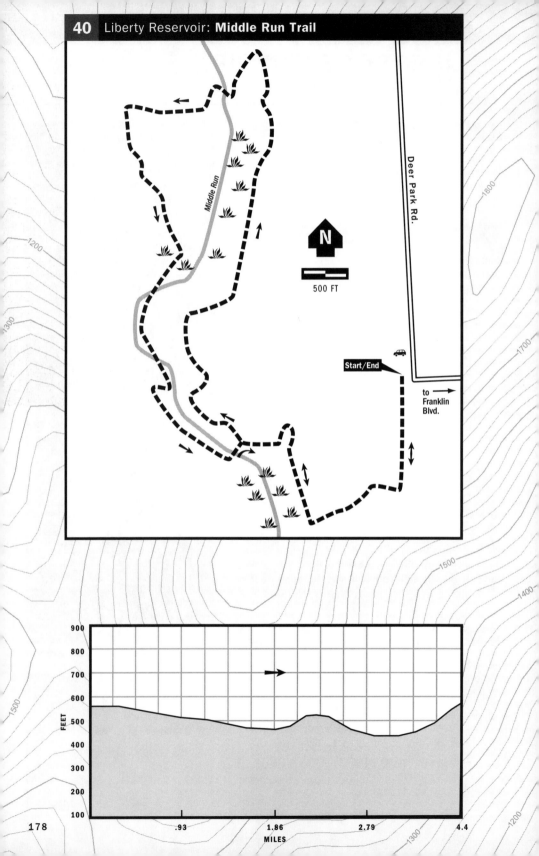

Middle Run

Deer Park Rd.

N

500 FT

Start/End

to →
Franklin
Blvd.

FEET

900
800
700
600
500
400
300
200
100

.93   1.86   2.79   4.4
MILES

between the reservoir's end and the trail; continue along the edge of the reservoir until the trail splits at a jumble of rocks on the right at 0.7 miles. You'll see Middle Run on the left; you will end up here in a few miles.

Middle Run

Go to the right at the split; you'll head gradually uphill, passing through a pine and spruce forest that supports a plentiful white-tailed deer population. You'll cross a modest stream at 1.2 miles—a little warm-up for what's ahead. At 1.3 miles, you'll come to another little stream with a towering cathedral of pine on the other side. You'd be hard pressed to see dirt here—a carpet of pine needles covers the trail. At 1.5 miles, you'll see a power-line cut straight ahead; turn left (turning right leads to another parking area at Deer Park Road, north of where you parked).

Middle Run appears soon after. This decent-sized crossing requires removing your shoes; take time to look in both directions, upstream and down, while you're crossing. The beautiful, meandering stream runs clean and clear. On the other side, the trail splits; keep going straight ahead, moving gradually uphill through more pines. The pine plantation ends abruptly and gives way to oak and poplar, with a few flowering dogwoods here and there.

The trail splits again at 1.8 miles; this time head left. Mountain laurel dominates this section of the trail, and if you're lucky to catch it during spring bloom, you're in for a treat of white clustered flowers. You will cross Middle Run a second time at 2.3 miles; use the fallen tree approximately 50 feet to the right of the trail to help you across. It's not easy, but it's certainly doable if you want to avoid taking off your shoes again; if you do remove your shoes, don't put them back on when you reach the other side—you'll be crossing the water again in a tenth of a mile.

After you cross Middle Run the third time, you will see blue blazes on some of the trees, but they promptly disappear. Pass the trail cut going straight up the hill on the right, and stay on the trail parallel to the stream. At 2.8 miles, you'll notice some nice smooth flat stones leading down to the water; checkered with green moss, they make a perfect place to stand and take in the beauty of the stream valley.

The main trail continues straight ahead at 3 miles, and a cut to the left leads back to the water; follow the cut and cross Middle Run for the fourth and final time. If you've somehow managed to make it this far without removing your shoes, you'll have to do it before crossing here, where the stream is wide. Take extra caution walking over the rocks, which can be quite slick. Once across, backtrack to the parking area, remembering to take a left at the 4-way crossing at 3.6 miles.

MORGAN RUN NATURAL ENVIRONMENTAL AREA

ⓘ KEY AT-A-GLANCE INFORMATION

LENGTH: 5.7 miles

CONFIGURATION: 2 jagged loops

DIFFICULTY: Easy to moderate

SCENERY: Mixed hardwoods, regenerating fields, stream valleys

EXPOSURE: Half shade and half sun

TRAFFIC: Light

TRAIL SURFACE: Packed dirt, grass

HIKING TIME: 2 hours

ACCESS: 7 a.m. to sunset daily

MAPS: USGS Finksburg, Winfield; *Guide to the Trails in Carroll County, Maryland* includes excellent maps—contact or visit the Carroll County Department of Recreation and Parks at 225 North Center Street, Room 100, Westminster, MD 21157; (410) 386-2103 or (888) 302-8978. (Technically, the Maryland Department of Natural Resources, rather than the Carroll County Recreation and Parks department, manages the Morgan Run area, but it is included in this publication.)

FACILITIES: None

SPECIAL COMMENTS: Numerous trails at Morgan Run, many of which are connector trails, provide many different possibilities and configurations for hiking—to make the longest hike, keep heading left whenever you come to intersecting trails. *Guide to the Trails in Carroll County, Maryland* (see "Maps" above) can help you make better sense of the trails that head out in many directions.

Morgan Run Natural
Environmental Area

UTM Zone (WGS84)   18S

Easting   327861

Northing   4370386

▶ IN BRIEF

Morgan Run Natural Environmental Area includes approximately 1,400 acres of wonderful hiking and equestrian trails. The entire area has been blissfully left alone, with well-maintained trails but no unnecessary "improvements," making it a perfect place to "get away from it all."

▶ DESCRIPTION

The first thing you notice at Morgan Run is birds—songbirds flitting about, shuttling from the tall trees to the regenerating fields and their many birdhouses, while within the woods woodpeckers and owls make their incessant noises, hawks and turkey vultures wheel above, and startlingly massive wild turkeys waddle over the trails. Because this hike frequently leads from woods to the edge of fields, you will constantly hear branches cracking and leaves crunching as the creatures move about, but you'll have a hard time spotting them. Abundant life and energy surround you here.

At your first trail split option, head left into the woods; be on the alert for horse manure, evidence of the trail's equestrian traffic. Also be alert for ticks, which lurk in the tall grasses in the treeline buffer, and take extra time looking for and

▶ DIRECTIONS

Take I-695 to I-70 west to Exit 76, MD 97 north to Westminster. After you cross MD 26, turn right onto Bartholow Road and then make an immediate left onto Jim Bowers Road and an even more immediate left onto Ben Rose Lane. Continue straight to the end of the large gravel parking area at the end of the road. At the far left end of the parking area, you will see two picnic benches; the trail begins straight beyond the picnic tables. In about 200 feet you will be able to discern the trail's worn groove in the grass.

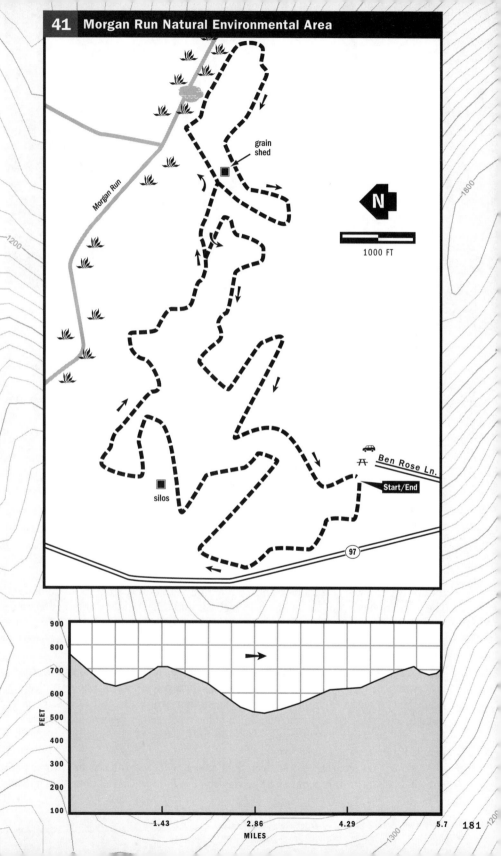

Trailside pond

removing ticks from your clothing and body at the end of the hike. I hiked Morgan Run in the summer and picked off no less than two dozen ticks.

After a quarter-mile, you'll be able to hear the traffic on MD 97 on the left, but a thick buffer of poplar, oak, maple, sassafras, ash, and dogwood prevents you from seeing it. Unfortunately the trail continues toward MD 97, coming as close as 10 feet before heading away at a branch of Morgan Run, which at this point is not much more than a trickle. You will see an overgrown foot trail heading toward the water, but go right instead on the obvious and wide trail that leads up the hill. As you head away from MD 97, the sounds of civilization fade away and isolation returns.

Be on the lookout for some old stone foundations on the right at 0.6 miles. At 0.8 miles, you emerge onto an opening where you have several options; again, head left. Deer favor this habitat, and you'll probably see a few of them. Clumps of isolated vegetation pock the land, and the field on the right, once cleared, is growing back. Unfortunately, autumn olive, an invasive species, has taken over; if you're hiking in the spring, you will smell a pleasant scent reminiscent of lilac from its white flowers. The autumn olives provide habitat for songbirds and other wildlife, and the trees also serve as a windbreak for the area's big pockets of deforested land; on the negative side, the dominating autumn olives do a superb job of crowding out native species, something you will notice as you continue your hike.

You'll see some old abandoned silos on the left at 1.3 miles; continue around and swing back into the woods at 1.4 miles. When you emerge at the next clearing, head right to stay away from MD 97 (going straight will lead you to the same place but add a tenth of a mile to the hike). Just before you reenter the woods, turn around for a great view of a wooded valley—a farm on the right is the only indication that people live in this area.

When you reemerge to the open field, take a left. (You will see an obvious path straight ahead; if you're looking at the *Guide to the Trails in Carroll County, Maryland*, you might be confused because this trail is on that map. It connects to the place you're going to on the lefthand trail.) Swing around where the hill levels a bit, and take a left back into the woods; you'll see oak, maple, and dogwood trees on your left and pines on your right. Take another leftward cut after another 900 feet. You'll quickly come to a rightward cut; pass it and take the next rightward cut instead (continuing straight will eventually loop around and will add another half mile to the hike). The path becomes a well-worn groove in the grass and merges with the more obvious trail and links to the other end of the loop you just skipped. You'll come to another wide path immediately after; take a left, but notice the cut to the right at 2.5 miles—you'll be taking it on the way back.

At 2.6 miles, you'll see an old decrepit garage stable and a newer one closer to the trail. Swing around to the left to continue the hike, and you'll see a corn bin just ahead. Cross a branch of Morgan Run on some logs; once across you can head right to go back or go straight to extend the hike. Be sure to look left to see a beautiful pond in a grove of towering beech trees; you would have a difficult time finding a more peaceful place.

Ultimately, you'll be taking a right, and you have three chances to do so: a path at 3 miles, one just beyond that, and then a third path that will take you to the farthest edge of the trail. I recommend taking the third path because it leads you through thick forest with no sign of humanity even though the park boundary means nearby suburban backyards. You will reenter the woods at 3.3 miles; take a left at 3.4 miles and head deeper into the woods. You will parallel a branch of Morgan Run as you walk upstream. Cross the branch at 3.6 miles. It soon joins the wider Morgan Run, which operates as a catch-and-release trout stream; cross the water again. After making this, you might have some trouble spotting the trail; look for it about 10 feet to the right of where you've crossed.

Go uphill and turn right onto the wider path that runs along a hillside covered with ferns and honeysuckle. You will gradually rise above the stream valley on the right and emerge from the woods at 3.8 miles at the shed you passed earlier. Take a left; you will backtrack a little bit before heading left again, at 2.5 miles, at the cut you noted earlier. At a little over 4 miles, you will come to a T intersection; go left. You'll begin passing cuts to the right at about 4.5 miles; all of these cuts head back to the parking area, but pass them to make the hike longer.

For some variation, turn right at the connector trail at 5.1 miles (otherwise you'll continue to the parking area along the tree line, adding a half-mile to the hike); and then turn left at the central field trail. It will lead you straight to the parking area, affording some nice views of the entire area on the way. Again, remember to check for ticks when you finish hiking this section.

▶ NEARBY ACTIVITIES

In the mood for some fishing? Nearby 300-acre Piney Lake is believed by many to be the best fishery in the state. Head back to MD 26 and take a left. Then take a right onto White Rock Road and follow the signs. For a description of Piney Run's hiking trails and nature center, see page 184.

PINEY RUN PARK

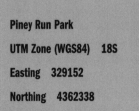

Piney Run Park

UTM Zone (WGS84) 18S

Easting 329152

Northing 4362338

▶ **IN BRIEF**

Leave the boating and fishing crowds behind as you explore the forests around popular Piney Lake.

▶ **DESCRIPTION**

Before you start your hike, stop in the nature center, which features live reptiles and knowledgeable naturalists. The nature center hosts an astounding 300 programs a year, ranging from presentations for toddlers to senior citizens. Make sure you check out the hummingbird garden and aviary; you can see the birds even when the nature center is closed. The birds you might see include black vultures, turkey vultures, barred owls, great horned owls (the largest resident owl in Maryland), red-shouldered hawks, and red-tailed hawks.

Beginning on the Lake Trail behind the nature center, you'll be in thick woods that obscure 300-acre Piney Lake, which many believe to be the best fishery in the state. According to the Maryland Department of Natural Resources, fish species found in the lake include pumpkinseed sunfish, redbreast sunfish, brown bullhead, smallmouth bass, white sucker, spotfin shiner, bluntnose minnow, banded killifish, golden shiner, creek chub, and tessellated darter. These are in addition to the more common largemouth bass, bluegill, yellow perch, channel catfish, black crappie, striped bass, and redear sunfish. In addition, the state Department of Natural

▶ **DIRECTIONS**

Take I-70 to MD 97 north; turn right on Streaker Road and continue until it ends at White Rock Road. Turn right and go 0.4 miles; turn left onto Martz Road and follow the signs to Piney Run Park. Take the first right to the parking area for the nature center; the trail starts 100 feet behind the nature center.

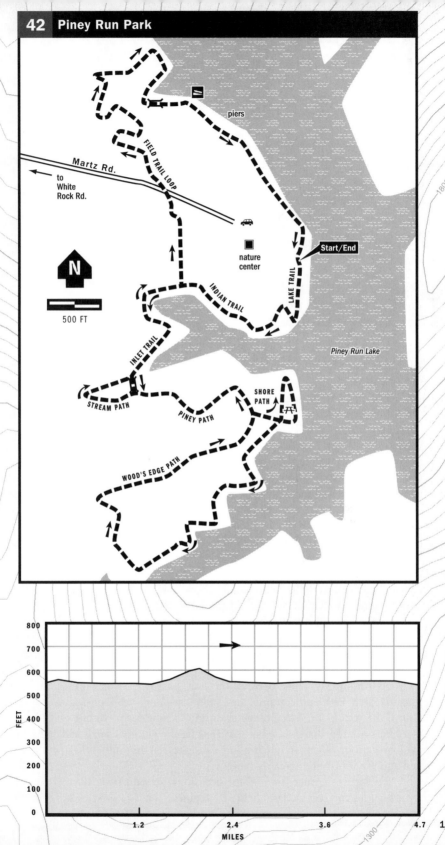

Piney Run Lake

Resources introduced tiger muskie to the lake in 1996 and stocks it annually with rainbow trout.

If you haven't brought your fishing pole, stick to the blue-blazed Lake Trail as it heads right and circles the aviary. After 250 feet, pick up the red-blazed Indian Trail continuing in the same direction. When the trail splits, at 0.2 miles, take Inlet Trail, with yellow blazes, to the left and follow the contours of the lake. You'll soon come to an open field on the right buffered by pine trees and forsythia; an overwhelming smell of pine fills the air here, a sample of what's to come. At 0.5 miles, you will see a "You are here" trail map facing a footbridge; cross the bridge. The trail splits on the other side of the small stream; take the trail to the left now—you'll take the one to the right on your way back.

The trail gradually rises above the lake through an oak and poplar forest with lots of moss, and the trail blazes turn orange as you approach a pine plantation. The trail splits again at 0.7 miles; again, head left and follow the trail to the Shore Path, which dead-ends to the left in just a few hundred feet. Take it for a nice view and an area of contemplation at the edge of the lake, where ducks, geese, and fish congregate. Several gnawed tree trunks in the area indicate that beavers live here too. Heading back, go to the left to the spit of land that juts into the lake. Studded with pines, it's an extraordinarily beautiful spot that boaters often use as a picnic area; but as you know, you can also reach it by foot.

Continuing your hike back on the trail, pass the cut heading to the right that leads to Piney Path and continue along the lake. You'll walk on a short exposed section of the trail before you plunge again into a pine forest with a very high canopy that offers blissful shade on a hot day. Despite the glorious smell and sight, however, the high canopy blocks so much of the sunlight that ground-level growth is very limited and the forest floor is fairly barren.

You will see spruce, fir, and the occasional redbud trees along the edge of the woods before you reach a farm field at 1.6 miles. The trail then swings around to the right and reenters the canopy of pines; take Wood's Edge Path straight ahead (heading left would connect you with the Piney Trail you passed earlier).

Now, on Wood's Edge Path, you are paralleling Inlet Trail. All you see on the left is pine, while the right is mostly oak. At 2 miles, take a left; pass by Inlet Trail to the right, and take Stream Path straight ahead toward the footbridge. Go past this bridge; continue on the trail and cross a different footbridge over a pretty little rock-strewn stream farther ahead and emerge onto an open field full of clover. Take the path back to Inlet Trail, but this time, at 2.8 miles, go straight (instead of heading right where you came in before), cross the footbridge, and swing to the right at the field onto the gravel. Turn left onto the paved park road.

Cross the paved road and head straight toward Pavilion 4; after you pass the boat launch parking, look for a sign for the Field Trail. The sign is some distance from the actual trailhead; if you are confused, just head right toward the new pavilion, parallel the paved road in the grass, and continue past the second pavilion on the right. Here you'll see a sign for Field Trail Loop, which is blazed white.

Be careful at the beginning of this trail—roots cover the eroded path. Red cedar dominates here, and cardinals, jays, ravens, and blackbirds flit about in the branches, while hawks circle overhead. Continue on the carpet of cedar needles, and at 3.1 miles, you will see a sign pointing in both directions for Field Trail. Take a few minutes to sit on the bench straight ahead and enjoy the great views over the lake. Moving on, go to the right, following the signs to Field Trail Loop. At 3.6 miles, cross a footbridge and go left toward the boathouse at the popular fishing and picnic area. Pick up the asphalt path as it heads past the boat launch, where you can rent a canoe or kayak. Traffic is heavy with people and boaters, but a prohibition on gasoline motors helps ensure that at least it's quiet.

You will pass a series of wooden piers on your left; continue straight ahead on the paved road until you see a sign for Lake Trail, marked by a series of 2x4s heading up the hill. This section of Lake Trail takes the form of a very pleasant footpath that winds along the lake. Eventually it heads up the hill and rejoins the wider, more established Lake Trail, but it's easy to miss since fishermen have extended the footpath all along the lake's edge. If you find yourself still on the footpath along the lake, but you can see the nature center through the woods, just find a path and take it up the hill.

▶ NEARBY ACTIVITIES

You can find much more hiking at nearby Morgan Run Natural Environmental Area to the north (see page 180), Liberty Reservoir to the east (see page 177), Gillis Falls to the west (see page 166), and Patapsco Valley State Park's northern sections to the south. If you're looking for a perfect antique for your home, visit the shops in New Market, "Maryland's Antique Capital," just 10 miles down I-70 west in Frederick County.

UNION MILLS

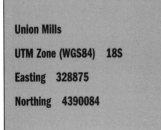

Union Mills

UTM Zone (WGS84) 18S

Easting 328875

Northing 4390084

IN BRIEF

Take a rugged hike through rural northern Carroll County, slogging over creeks, through steep switchbacks, and pleasant rolling fields.

DESCRIPTION

Once past the trailhead, you'll soon see a sign that reads: "Boulevard Trail." The trail, which is dirt and crushed rock, plunges into a grove of pines. Then it runs along a ridge with a slight rise on the left and a steep plunge on the right. At the top of the hill, it opens up, which gives you a nice vista of woods and fields loaded with goldenrod.

As the trail winds up and down the hills, you will see a "Boulevard Trail" sign every 0.3 miles or so. At 1.4 miles, Big Pipe Creek comes into view, and you'll soon see a sign on the right for "Crossover Trail." Take this trail across the creek; there's no natural crossing over the creek, but it often only has 2 inches of water in its shallowest section. Expect your feet to get wet and also muddy; this section is pretty wild, and equestrian use ensures that the creek banks remain soft and muddy. Since you have just begun the hike, it might be best to take off your shoes and put them back on once across the creek.

The trail, sporadically marked with white blazes, parallels the stream to the left on the other

DIRECTIONS

Take I-695 to Exit 19, I-795 west; continue until it ends at MD 140 (Baltimore Boulevard) north toward Westminster. Go 12 miles and turn right onto MD 97 north to Union Mills and Gettysburg. MD 97 turns into Littlestown Pike; go 2.8 miles and turn right onto John Owings Road. Go another 0.7 miles and turn left at the stables and sign for "Equestrian Trail Parking." The trail starts up the hill behind the stables between the two ponds.

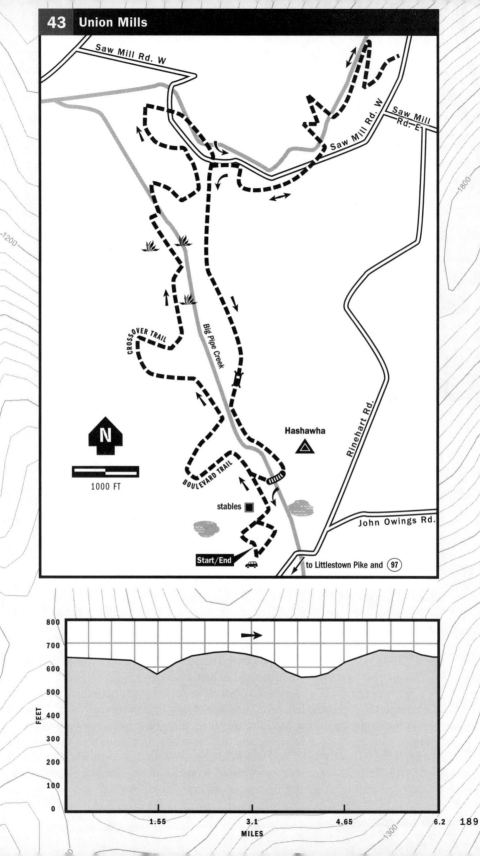

Saw Mill Rd. W

Saw Mill Rd. W

Saw Mill Rd. E

CROSSOVER TRAIL

Big Pipe Creek

Rinehart Rd.

N

1000 FT

Hashawha

BOULEVARD TRAIL

stables

Start/End

John Owings Rd.

to Littlestown Pike and (97)

FEET

800
700
600
500
400
300
200
100
0

1.55   3.1   4.65   6.2   **189**

MILES

Boulevard Trail

side. It's more up and down here, with moderate to strenuous switchbacks. At the top of the hill at 1.8 miles, head left and follow the trail toward a sign that reads: "Loop." It runs through an open field and comes to Saw Mill Road at 2.1 miles. The trail then runs parallel to Saw Mill Road, sometimes running on the shoulder itself, before plunging back into the woods. You will find that this is not nearly as unpleasant as it sounds; the shoulder is wide and the woods are thick all around. Take proper caution here though—the area is rural and not very heavily traveled, but the road has lots of blind curves and folks sometimes take these too quickly.

Just beyond 2.4 miles, you'll see a cut to the right; you can take that trail to begin making the loop back to the trailhead, but to extend your hike, continue along the Saw Mill Road trail. The trail cuts away from the road for good at just under 2.9 miles and crosses the creek—again, expect to get your toes wet. Take the trail up the hill, where a profusion of ferns decorates the hillside. You will emerge into an open meadow full of goldenrod; you'll be on a wide fire road here. Take a left and, at 3.2 miles, cross a stream (you won't get wet toes this time—the stream has lots of rocks you can use as stepping-stones). You will see some beautiful rock formations on your right.

The trail becomes crushed rock before it splits at 3.4 miles. Take a right and follow the trail until you come to a wide grass path; turn right. You will see a steel girder—turn around here (the trail beyond it heads uphill and ends at Saw Mill Road in a little less than half a mile). Retrace your route until you reach the cut to the left, at 4.9 miles, where you continued straight earlier (at 2.4 miles).

Take a right at 5.3 miles, and cross a wooden footbridge; the area opens up into a field of mostly goldenrod. Take a left; you're now in the Hashawha Environmental Appreciation Area (see page 169), and you'll see Big Pipe Creek on the right. Paralleling the creek, you'll come to a beautiful open area—a tremendous old maple tree shades a picnic bench that's surrounded on all sides by the semicircular sweep of the creek. Take a right on the boardwalk over the creek and up the woods—you'll pass a sign alerting you that you are "Leaving Hashawha."

You will climb a hill that is steep and rocky but relatively short, less than a third of a mile. At the top of the hill, take a left. You're now on a portion of the trail that you took at the beginning of the hike, but this time, take a left at the white blazes at the group of pine trees at 6.1 miles. Follow this short switchback through the pines and emerge at the edge of a pond. Take a right, and you will find your car ahead on the left.

Note: Union Mills offers approximately 8 miles of trails. The hike described here attempts to pull together the diverse hiking opportunities presented by the many trails and the numerous offshoots and connectors. Be aware that this hike includes several creek crossings where the paths are muddy and eroded from equestrian use; expect to get your toes wet. These Union Mills trails have heavy equestrian traffic; be prepared to yield to horses, and, of course, keep an eye out for manure on the trails.

▶ NEARBY ACTIVITIES

The Union Mills hiking area includes the Hashawha Environmental Appreciation Area and Bear Branch Nature Center. See page 169 for a description of hiking opportunities at Hashawha. To reach Bear Branch Nature Center, follow the directions above for Union Mills, but pass the stables and the sign for "Equestrian Trail Parking" and continue another 0.7 miles until you see the "Welcome to Hashawha and Bear Branch Nature Center" sign. Turn here and then take a right at the sign for the nature center. For sustenance after the tough hike at Union Mills, head south on MD 97 into downtown Westminster, which if full of restaurants, antiques shops, and museums. The Maryland Wine Festival takes place each September at the Carroll County Farm Museum grounds in Westminster; for information, call (800) 654-4645, (410) 876-2667, or (410) 848-7775.

CECIL COUNTY

ELK NECK STATE FOREST

KEY AT-A-GLANCE INFORMATION

LENGTH: 6.9 miles

CONFIGURATION: 2 intersecting loops

DIFFICULTY: Moderate to strenuous

SCENERY: Mature forest, marsh, Plum Creek Pond

EXPOSURE: More shade than sun

TRAFFIC: Light

TRAIL SURFACE: Sand, gravel, packed dirt

HIKING TIME: 2.5-3 hours

ACCESS: Sunrise to sunset daily

MAPS: USGS North East; you can get a detailed trail map of both Elk Neck State Forest and Elk Neck State Park at the Elk Neck State Park headquarters as well as online at **www.easycart.net/Maryland DepartmentofNaturalResources/ Central_Maryland_Trail_Guides.html.**

FACILITIES: Shooting range, primitive campsites (closed as of March 2005—future opening uncertain)

SPECIAL COMMENTS: Elk Neck State Forest is popular for hunting; if you hike during hunting season (generally during autumn months), wear orange and/or hike on Sundays when hunting is prohibited; for a hunting schedule, call the Maryland Department of Natural Resources at (877) 620-8367 or visit **www.dnr.state.md.us/ huntersguide.**

Elk Neck State Forest

UTM Zone (WGS84) 18S

Easting   421371

Northing 4381620

IN BRIEF

Hike through diverse wooded flatland, rolling hills, and marshlands in Elk Neck State Park's lesser-known cousin.

DESCRIPTION

Identified on maps as Trails 1, 2, and 3, the "trails" are actually wide forest roads, flanked by thick woods (mixed deciduous trees and evergreens) and allowing only limited vehicle access. You might feel a bit unnerved at the beginning of the hike—in addition to having occasional cars pass you, you'll hear gunshots from the handgun and rifle shooting range you'll pass at 0.6 miles. Once you pass the shooting range, the trail becomes more pleasant and isolated. Vehicles are prohibited from going farther than this point, and the landfill (out of sight of the trail) beyond the shooting range offers good habitat for whippoor-wills and a variety of owls.

Now that the road is all yours, the encroaching forest of pine, maple, oak, sassafras, ash, hickory, and poplar seems to crowd in even more. On the left at 1.3 miles, you will see the blue-blazed Mason-Dixon Trail, a 190-mile trail that runs through Pennsylvania, Delaware, and Maryland. Pass it for now, and continue on Trail #1.

DIRECTIONS

Take I-95 north from Baltimore to Exit 100, MD 272 south. Go 2.5 miles through the town of North East, and then turn left on Irishtown Road. You will see the entrance to Elk Neck State Forest 1.7 miles on the left; turn into the forest and continue 0.4 miles to the parking area on the left in front of the water tower. The sand and gravel road you just turned off is actually Trail #1; head left on it. (If you're interested in seeing nesting hooded warblers, walk down the hill behind the tower before you start the hike.)

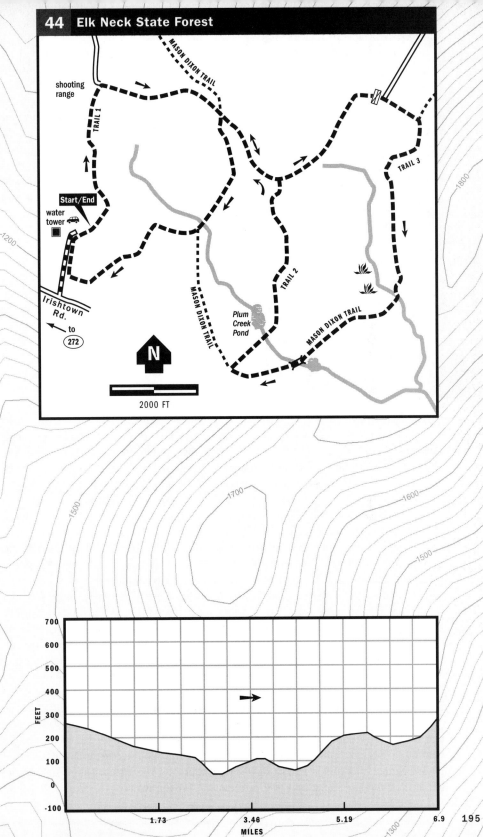

MASON DIXON TRAIL

shooting range

TRAIL 1

Start/End

water tower

Irishtown Rd.

to 272

MASON DIXON TRAIL

TRAIL 3

TRAIL 2

Plum Creek Pond

MASON DIXON TRAIL

N

2000 FT

FEET

700
600
500
400
300
200
100
0
-100

1.73   3.46   5.19   6.9

MILES

Mason Dixon Trail

You will come to a Y intersection at 1.6 miles. Trail #2 goes to the right; continue straight ahead on Trail #1, identified here as Mountain Laurel Lane. The road begins to narrow a bit, and during the summertime the strong aroma of cedar fills the air. An understory of mountain laurel, azalea, fern, and other native shrubs fills out the forest.

When you reach a gate at 2.1 miles, take a right onto Trail #3. At 2.3 miles, take a right into the woods on the narrow, blue-blazed Mason-Dixon Trail, a very woodsy and tightly packed-dirt trail. At 2.9 miles, tall grass overtakes the trail (hike up your socks to protect against ticks); after 100 feet the trail returns to packed dirt. Be on the lookout for frogs and snakes lurking in the grass here. A little farther, the trail hugs the edge of a big marsh, where I passed a great heron rookery. At the sound of my approach, some dozen birds took flight; their massive wingspans and odd guttural calls were both startling and magnificent to behold.

Cross a tiny marsh outlet and then head back into the woods on the very narrow trail. For a little stretch, the trail is barely discernible, but you'll soon see white blazes and then the trail widens. You will see many path offshoots, but continue straight on Trail #3. You will come to trees over the trail every 100 feet or so, and you will have to do lots of climbing, but this strenuous exercise serves as a reminder that things are pretty much left alone here, enhancing the heady sense of isolation you find at Elk Neck State Forest.

When you come to an earthen dam spanning a little pond, look for the tiny cut path, with a footbridge, to the left. At 2.8 miles, you will emerge onto Trail #2; take a right, and you'll soon come to Plum Creek Pond, a beautiful open spot ringed by aquatic plants. This marshy area and the surrounding thick forest make the perfect spot for birding. Depending on the season, some of the birds you may see include kinglets, thrushes, nuthatches, woodpeckers, vireos, and the occasional scarlet tanager.

A word of caution: the trail bridge spanning a pond feeder up ahead has collapsed; enough earth has clogged the feeder so you can cross, but you have to scale precipitous cliffs on both sides. If you feel it's not worth it, turn around and look for the path to the right before the pond. Once you're beyond the pond, take another right and go around the pond that way; you'll link up just on the other side of the cliffs.

Once you've moved past the pond, continue straight on Trail #2. When you reach the intersection of Trail #1 and Trail #2 (the spot where you went straight before), take a left and begin to backtrack. When you see the Mason-Dixon Trail you passed earlier (this time it will be on the right), look for the Mason-Dixon Trail on the left at 0.1 mile later. Take that trail now back into deep woods.

When you cross the next stream, no doubt you will notice that the water is the color of iced tea; I hope it's colored by tannins and not pollution. When the trail splits, keep going straight and stay straight until you come to a T intersection, and then take a right. At a little over 6 miles, you'll emerge onto Trail #1 that you used to enter the forest in your car. Take a right, and you will find your car just up ahead on the left.

▶ NEARBY ACTIVITIES

You might want to spend a few hours in the nearby pleasant town of North East where you can visit Upper Bay Museum, two big buildings on the North East River that house an extensive collection of hunting, boating, and fishing artifacts; call (410) 287-5909 for information. Heading back to I-95, continue past the exit and follow the signs to Plumpton Park Zoo in Rising Sun, which houses a collection of indigenous animals as well as African creatures. Visit **www.plumptonparkzoo.org/index.html** or call (410) 658-6850 for information.

ELK NECK STATE PARK

KEY AT-A-GLANCE INFORMATION

LENGTH: 13.5 miles total hike-bike-drive (8.7-mile hike including 0.7 miles on White Trail, 1.7 miles on Red Trail, 1.9 miles on Blue Trail, 2.1 miles on Green Trail, and 2.3 miles on Orange Trail, plus 2.5 miles biking and 2.3 miles driving)

CONFIGURATION: Loop for Green, White, Orange, and Red Trails; out-and-back with loop for Blue Trail

DIFFICULTY: Easy to moderate

SCENERY: Beach, Elk River, Chesapeake Bay, Turkey Point Lighthouse, mature forests, marshes, ponds

EXPOSURE: Shade on the Green, Red, and White Trails; more shade than sun on the Blue and Orange Trails

TRAFFIC: Light on Green, Red, and Orange Trails; moderate on White Trail; moderate to heavy on Blue Trail

TRAIL SURFACE: Packed dirt with sand and gravel on Green and Orange Trails

HIKING TIME: 1 hour for Red and Blue Trails, 1.5 hours for Orange and Green Trails, 0.5 hour for White Trail; 6 hours total including transit time

ACCESS: Sunrise to sunset daily

MAPS: USGS Earleville, Spesutie; you can get a detailed trail map of both Elk Neck State Park and Elk Neck State Forest at the state park headquarters and online at **www.easycart.net/MarylandDepartment ofNaturalResources/Central_Maryland_ Trail_Guides.html.**

FACILITIES: Picnic pavilions, snack bar at swimming beach beyond Red Trail; campsites; camp store, mini golf, laundry between Green and White Trails; vending machines; playgrounds; boat launch

Elk Neck State Park

UTM Zone (WGS84) 18S

Easting   413444

Northing   4368265

▶ IN BRIEF

Do it all at Elk Neck State Park in one long day of hiking and biking. If it's summer, leave time for swimming as well.

▶ DESCRIPTION

Head straight away from the parking area on the wide, packed-dirt Blue Trail. You will have great views of Chesapeake Bay on the right on this section of the trail; eventually thick woods will block out distant views. The trail splits at 0.6 miles; go left and you will see a raptor viewing area. Depending on the season, you'll see vultures, eagles, ospreys, buteos, hawks, harriers, kites, kestrels, merlins, and falcons.

You will reach Turkey Point Lighthouse at 0.8 miles. The highest of the bay's 74 lighthouses, Turkey Point Lighthouse was built in 1833; for more information about the lighthouse, visit **www.caracove.com/tpls.** Sheer cliffs drop down from the lighthouse into the bay, and even though many signs warn of danger, you can go right to the edge—be careful. With the lighthouse behind you, head right and back into the woods onto a narrow trail that eventually leads you to water level. Walk along the water for a few hundred feet and then turn back into the woods at a little beach, following the Blue Trail back to the parking area.

Back in your car, drive north on Old Elk Neck Road; continue about 1 mile, and turn right on Rogues Harbor Road (look for signs to the boat launch). You'll come to a parking lot on the left; go all the way to the farthest end, where you'll see

▶ DIRECTIONS

Take I-95 north from Baltimore to Exit 100, MD 272 south through the town of North East. Continue on MD 272 south (Old Elk Neck Road) 12 miles until it ends; the Blue Trail starts here.

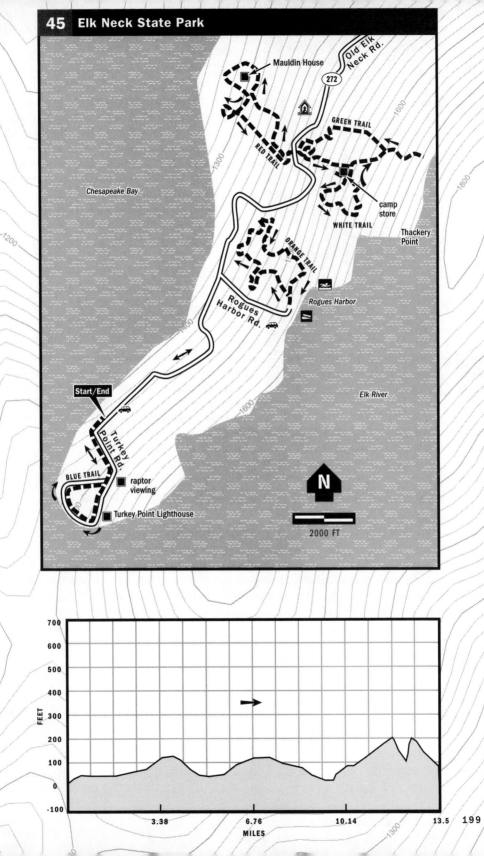

Old Elk Neck Rd.

Mauldin House

272

GREEN TRAIL

RED TRAIL

camp store

Chesapeake Bay

WHITE TRAIL

Thackery Point

ORANGE TRAIL

Rogues Harbor Rd.

Rogues Harbor

Elk River

Start/End

Turkey Point Rd.

BLUE TRAIL

raptor viewing

Turkey Point Lighthouse

N

2000 FT

FEET

700
600
500
400
300
200
100
0
-100

3.38   6.76   10.14   13.5
MILES

Green Trail beach on Elk River

the trailhead for the Orange Trail. The trail splits for the first time soon after it starts; go left, and you'll come to the edge of a marsh, where you might see herons. The extraordinarily beautiful Orange Trail, wooded with poplar, hickory, and oak, supports an abundance of wildlife including deer, squirrels, and owls. The trail feels quite isolated until it runs near a campground; you probably won't see the campground through the thick woods, but you'll probably hear the noise from it during summer months. When you reach the beach at 2 miles, take a right and walk toward the rock jumble in the distance. Climb along the rocks and reenter the woods just before the trail split you took left coming in; this time go straight ahead to the parking area. It's time to unlock your bike.

Bike back out to Old Elk Neck Road and go right. Take the first right, follow signs to the camp store, go to the registration booth, and purchase an interpretive guide for $1 for the White Trail. Lock up your bike at the camp store and go across the road to the White trailhead.

Wooden posts mark the start of the short, pleasant White Trail. Along this loop, you'll see poplar, three varieties of oak, maple, holly, two types of dogwood, birch, serviceberry, paw paw, beech, hickory, mountain laurel, two types of blueberry, sassafras, gum, witch hazel, sycamore, pine, cherry, and locust, and you can read descriptions in the corresponding guide. You'll exit the White Trail on the camp road a bit farther east than where you entered. Head back left, and when you get to the camp store, walk behind it to pick up the Green Trail.

Take a left at the top of the trail; don't worry about the lack of blazes—you're actually on a secondary path that connects to the Green Trail. When you reach a split, take a right (if you don't turn, you'll end up on a park road). When you reach the wide Green Trail just ahead, turn right; after 0.4 miles, you'll come to a beaver pond stocked with bass and sunfish (if you want to fish, you will need to get a Maryland Non-tidal Freshwater Fishing license). If you're hiking here in the winter, look for mallards, black ducks, and teal at the pond.

Take a left at the Y intersection at the end of the pond, and follow the trail to the camp loop; go left and hike to the end of the loop, where you'll see a little path heading to a beach. This beach abuts Elk River just north of Thackery Point. Backtrack to the pond, and go left. The trail becomes very tight and close here. When you come to a T intersection, take a left away from the water and climb up the hill; you'll quickly come to the back of the camp store. Time to grab the bike for the final trail.

Head back out to Old Elk Neck, and take a right. Almost immediately, take a left; the Red Trail starts just ahead on the left. Lock your bike to a tree. The Red Trail follows the contours of the North East Beach Access Road until it splits toward a picnic area; the trail loops around the picnic area, passing the Mauldin House near the top of Mauldin Mountain (a hill, to be more precise), which rises almost 300 feet above the surrounding land.

The Red Trail, which is listed as "difficult" on the Elk Neck State Park map because of its ups and downs, doesn't have any sections that are very strenuous, but if this is your last hike of the day and you've completed all the others described above, you will probably feel a little pushed. The tall canopy of locust, beech, maple, poplar, hickory, and oak promises to inspire you, and you will enjoy the truly beautiful thriving understory, which includes wildflowers as well as springtime dogwood blooms. Look for red-breasted nuthatches, cedar waxwings, and pileated woodpeckers here. When you reach your bike again, pedal back to the Orange Trail parking lot at the end of Rogues Harbor Road at the boat launch signs.

Note: There is no fee to enter the park, but there is a $5 toll bridge on I-95 crossing into Cecil County. The suggested hike described here incorporates all five of Elk Neck's trails; none of the trails intersect, which makes bringing a bike for going from one trail to another (all fairly close) an easy and pleasurable option. You can just as easily walk or drive from one trail to another; be aware there is no available parking for the Red Trail—the closest parking is at the Park Office, across Old Elk Neck Road from the Green Trail.

▶ NEARBY ACTIVITIES

You might want to spend a few hours in the nearby pleasant town of North East where you can visit Upper Bay Museum, two big buildings on North East River that house an extensive collection of hunting, boating, and fishing artifacts; call (410) 287-5909 for information. Heading back to I-95, continue past the exit and follow the signs to Plumpton Park Zoo in Rising Sun, which houses a collection of indigenous animals as well as African creatures. Visit **www.plumptonparkzoo.org/index.html** or call (410) 658-6850 for information.

HARFORD COUNTY

GUNPOWDER FALLS STATE PARK: LOST POND TRAIL

▶ IN BRIEF

Stroll through the floodplain along Gunpowder River and then traverse upland forest to the sight of an abandoned millpond, now lost to the forest floor.

▶ DESCRIPTION

You'll see many people with fishing poles heading away from the bulletin board and going under the bridge on the right. You can head left here and follow the trail along the water's edge, or you can take official Lost Pond trailhead, which has blue blazes, that begins at the edge of the woods near the other parking lot. The two trails closely parallel each other and eventually connect. I took the water's-edge trail, but during heavy rains, mud and maybe even a few inches of water may cover it.

As you walk along the floodplain, you'll pass a massive sycamore that seems to have long outlived its expected life span. Soon after, you'll see another large sycamore jutting over the water. Someone (for good or ill) has nailed wooden steps into its trunk. The result is that you can climb up to a nice river perch with its attendant views of the swiftly running water.

Continuing on, you'll see American beech trees with their roots spread over a nice rock outcropping; they look somewhat tropical. You will ford a small creek at 0.4 miles, where you can head left to the yellow-blazed Sawmill Trail; this trail leads north to the site of the early 19th-century Carroll Sawmill ruins and millrace.

Continuing on the blue-blazed Lost Pond Trail, you'll soon see an enormous tulip poplar

▶ DIRECTIONS

Take I-695 to Exit 32, MD 1 north (Belair Road), and go 5.5 miles; look for the parking lot straight ahead after crossing Gunpowder River. If the lot is full, park on the right near the bulletin board that has the trail map. The trails start at the edge of the far parking lot just behind the bulletin board.

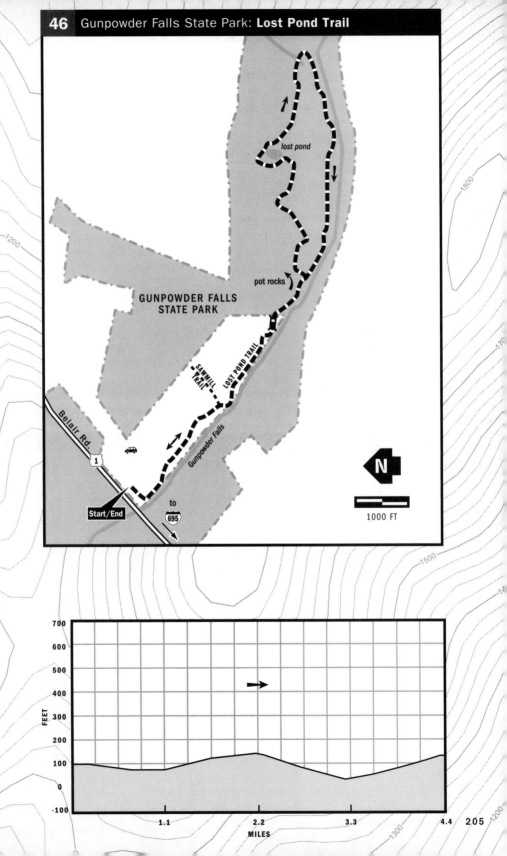

lost pond

GUNPOWDER FALLS
STATE PARK

pot rocks

SAWMILL TRAIL

LOST POND TRAIL

Belair Rd

1

Gunpowder Falls

Start/End

to
695

N

1000 FT

FEET

700
600
500
400
300
200
100
0
-100

1.1   2.2   3.3   4.4

MILES

with a hollowed-out trunk, which would make quite a den for some large rodent or snake. You will cross a little footbridge at 0.7 miles; as you continue along the trail you will hear the wonderful sound of rapids on the right from the large rocks in the river. Just before you reach the 1-mile mark, head right to the "pot rocks," so called because of the deep potholes created in the bedrock from the river erosion; a wooden signpost points the way. This is an excellent place to sit a while and take in the sounds of the noisy river.

When you've had your fill, head back up the hill and continue to the right. The trail leads uphill through an upland forest of mature mixed hardwood trees, mostly oak, poplar, sycamore, and maple. When you get to the top of the hill, you'll begin skirting an open farm on the left through the woods.

Continue walking until you reach the lost pond at 1.8 miles. If you were expecting water, you'll be disappointed. What's left of this abandoned pond is merely the shape and indentation of an oval body of water. Still, it's an interesting sight since it sits in the middle of the woods and clearly looks out of place in its current incarnation: a grassy marshland surrounded by tall trees.

It gets a bit confusing here; there appears to be a well-maintained trail up the hill to the left of the pond, but that quickly peters out. Instead, head around the pond, keeping it to your right; when you come out on the other side, head away from the pond by going left up the wooded hill. At 2.25 miles, you'll cross a small stream using rocks in the waterway as stepping-stones. Head back to the section of trail where you came in, which you'll reach at 3.1 miles, and follow it back to your car.

▶ NEARBY ACTIVITIES

Rocks State Park in Harford County is close by; to get to the park, continue on MD 1 north, turn left onto MD 24 north, and you will come to the park entrance approximately 5 miles north of Forest Hill. You will find plenty of places to eat, in all price ranges, in Bel Air, which is off MD 1.

GUNPOWDER FALLS STATE PARK: SWEET AIR AREA

▶ IN BRIEF

An amazing amount of variety in a relatively short hike—the scenery changes every mile or so.

▶ DESCRIPTION

It's almost a crime that this exceedingly beautiful 1,250-acre section of Gunpowder Falls State Park is so lightly used—but what a treat that is for hikers seeking solitude! The bulk of traffic in the Sweet Air section comes from equestrians.

From the trailhead, follow the path as it merges into a wide farm road. You'll soon pass an open field on the left. You'll come to a cornfield—and the first trail split—straight ahead, at 0.1 mile. Head left to stay on the yellow-blazed Barley Pond Loop. Follow the tree line around the cornfield, turning right at the "You are here" sign, at 0.3 miles; you will reach the edge of the woods at 0.6 miles. Wooden sign here reads: "The woods were made for the hunter of dreams." You will come to many spots along the trail where similar painted signs offer inspirational, nature-oriented quotations. There's a certain irony here: although the quotations are pleasant, this hike is so beautiful that it doesn't need any embellishment. The views are plenty to inspire grand thoughts.

To the left of the sign you will see the red-blazed hikers only trail, and to the right you'll see

▶ DIRECTIONS

Take I-83 to Exit 20, Shawan Road east until it ends at York Road. Take a right on York Road and then the first left onto Ashland Road (which becomes Paper Mill Road). Go 6 miles until Paper Mill crosses Jarrettsville Pike and becomes Sweet Air Road. Go 2.7 miles and turn left onto Greene Road. Go 1.8 miles to a left on Moores Road and another 0.5 miles to a left on Dalton Bevard Road; you'll see a gravel parking area ahead on the right and a sign marking the trailhead for Barley Pond Loop at the leftmost point of the parking area.

ⓘ KEY AT-A-GLANCE INFORMATION

LENGTH: 5.1 miles

CONFIGURATION: Jagged loop

DIFFICULTY: Easy to moderate

SCENERY: Upland forest, Little Gunpowder River, Barley Pond, pine plantations

EXPOSURE: Mostly shade

TRAFFIC: Light

TRAIL SURFACE: Packed dirt, mowed grass

HIKING TIME: 2 hours

ACCESS: Sunrise to sunset daily

MAPS: USGS Phoenix, Jarrettsville; stationary trails map at the parking area

FACILITIES: None

SPECIAL COMMENTS: Alternate directions to those given below: Take I-695 to Exit 27, Dulaney Valley Road north; cross the Loch Raven Reservoir bridge and merge left onto Jarretsville Pike (MD 146 north). Once you cross into Harford County, take the first right onto Hess Road, make a U-turn right onto Park Road and then turn left onto Moores Road. Turn right into the park on Dalton Bevard Road.

Gunpowder Falls State Park: Sweet Air Area

UTM Zone (WGS84)   18S

Easting   370682

Northing   4377315

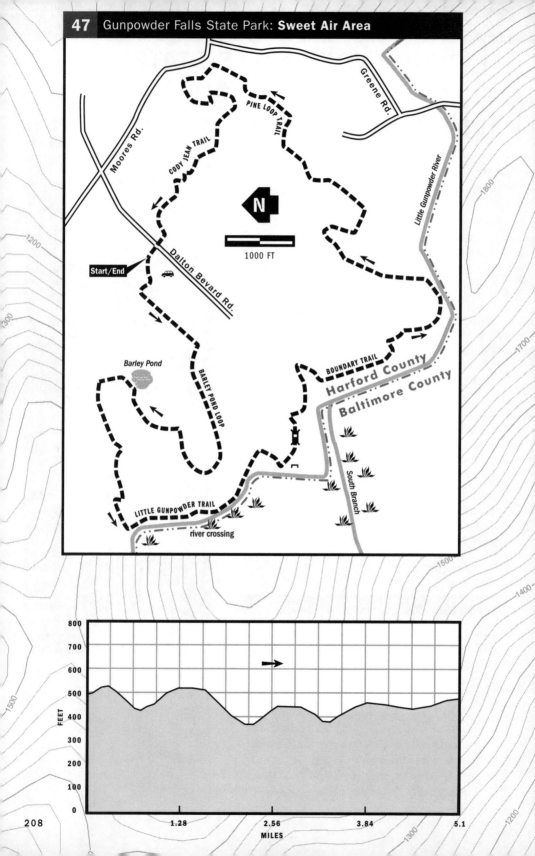

the Barley Pond Trail; take the Barley Pond Trail. (Take the red-blazed trail if there are bikers and horses afoot; it will eventually lead you to the trail for the hike described here, and you'll more than likely have the trail to yourself.) Several varieties of ferns cover the ground here, and mostly oak, maple, and tulip poplar with spicebush and mountain laurel round out the mid-level growth.

Cody Jean Trail

The trail splits again at 0.75 miles; the left path heads to the river, while Barley Pond Trail goes straight. Since you will eventually reach the river on Barley Pond Trail, continue on it; it soon narrows and zigzags, turns into a foot trail, and crosses a tiny stream that supports skunk cabbage and lilies. The scenery is very typical of piedmont northeastern Baltimore–Harford County. At the top of the hill at 1 mile, you will come to Barley Pond, a reflective and beautiful spot with great visibility. I sat and stared for a long time at the largest red fox I've ever seen as it regarded me from the other side of the water.

Head left around the pond, watching for water snakes, frogs, and small fish, mostly bluegills. The trail splits again immediately after the pond; head left to stay on Barley Pond Trail. At the top of the hill, look for the massive oak tree that has split at its base into five separate, very tall trees, a process that replicates throughout the forest. You will reach the end of the Barley Pond Loop at a T intersection at 1.1 miles; take a left to pick up the white-blazed Little Gunpowder Trail.

The twisty Little Gunpowder Trail is full of green vegetation. Little streams wind throughout the landscape amid rolling hills studded with red maple trees. These riparian streams provide perfect cover for many birds, evidenced by an almost constant chorus of song.

The trail splits again a quarter-mile later. The left path leads to the blue-blazed Boundary Trail, which eventually goes to and through the river. For now, take the path to the right, where you'll see both blue and white blazes. The trail soon turns back to only white blazes, and it winds around gradually and easily, following the contours of the hills, which reach like the fingers of an outstretched hand down to the river.

By 1.5 miles, multiflora rose, which can crowd the trail, dominates the landscape. You will reach the river at 1.6 miles; this hike is entirely in Harford County, but the river forms the dividing line between Harford and Baltimore counties. Take a few minutes to sit on the bench at the little wooden resting area and listen to the river's babble, interrupted perhaps by a white-headed woodpecker in a tree above you.

You will see the other end of the red trail you passed at the hike's beginning, but head left along the river. Many long flat rocks extend into the water where you can vie with the snakes and turtles for a spot to sit and sun yourself.

After you cross a footbridge, you'll come to the wide blue-blazed Boundary

Trail; you can cross the river here, but if you're not on a horse, it's a bit of a challenge since it's about 30 feet across and can be 3 to 4 feet deep. (If you do cross and walk the Boundary loop, you'll add approximately 2 miles to the total hike.) For now, continue on the white Little Gunpowder Trail, but pause at the bench below the John Muir quotation. You will see a fallen sycamore in the river where water eddies into a pool; the sycamore has sprouted five new trees, a testament to nature's regenerative power. Moss covers many of the trees in this area, and wildflowers, including asters, bloodroot, boneset, Jack-in-the-pulpit, jewelweed, joe-pye weed, and woodland sunflower, abound. Across the river sits a striated rock outcropping supporting some oaks.

As you continue on Little Gunpowder Trail, you'll pass several orange-blazed cuts running vertically along the hills; these paths connect the upland and river trails. You will pass a grove of beech trees with pristine bark free of graffiti scrawls. When you reach the next trail split, pass the connector yellow trail and head toward the river and the blue-blazed trail instead.

At 2.8 miles, you will be walking parallel to a cornfield; at 2.9 miles go through a pine plantation and cross a stream. Immediately after, you will come to an intersection; head left up the hill through the mixed hardwoods. Along with the trees already named, you'll also find some locust and ironwood. When the trail opens into a big field, head right and the trail becomes mowed grass. After another tenth of a mile, the trail splits; head right and then back into the woods (you'll see blue blazes again). The trail emerges from the woods back onto mowed grass after another tenth of a mile, following the park boundary line past a private backyard. As you walk along the fence and trees, look for the trail heading slightly to the left.

Head right toward the cornfield, where dogwood and pine line the edge. At 3.8 miles, you'll see signs for the Pine Loop Trail both straight and left—go straight. The trail splits, with the blue-blazed Boundary Trail heading left, and the yellow-blazed Pine Loop going right; take the Pine Loop, and you'll soon see the reason for the name. Take the discernible cut to the left into the thick of the white pine plantation; you'll pass a footbridge donated by the Chesapeake Trail Riding Club.

At 4.4 miles, you'll see a cairn with a hiker icon. Take this green-blazed hikers-only Cody Jean Trail; it moves through the white pines from the top of the hill, giving you a nice vantage through the wide spaces between the trees. When you come to a picnic table and another cairn, cross the Pine Loop to stay on the Cody Jean Trail and follow it as it zigzags through mixed hardwoods, crosses a stream, and heads back into the pines (where the air becomes especially aromatic). You will emerge from the pines onto the opposite side of the trail where you turned right earlier to park; you'll see blue and yellow trailheads to the left. Cross Dalton Bevard Road, passing the training area for Chesapeake search dogs on the left.

▶ NEARBY ACTIVITIES

You may enjoy visiting the nearby Ladew Topiary Gardens, dubbed the "most outstanding topiary garden in America" by the Garden Club of America. This fascinating and inspiring destination has earned its listing on the National Registry of Historic Places. To reach it from Gunpowder Falls State Park, reverse the alternate directions under "Special Comments" above, turn right onto Jarrettsville Pike, and follow the signs to Ladew Topiary Gardens on the right.

ROCKS STATE PARK

Explore 85 acres of dense forest and massive boulders rising above Deer Creek, culminating in the main attraction: King and Queen's Seat, 90-foot rock outcroppings once the ancestral meeting place of the Susquehannock Indians.

▶ DESCRIPTION

The first thing you'll see at the trailhead is the yellow sign that reads: "Caution: climbers have been seriously injured while attempting to free climb." This applies to the King and Queen's Seat, which you'll visit at the end of the hike. For now, there's enough to occupy you on the extremely steep and rocky approach to the main loop trail. Fallen tree trunks, 2x4s, and well-placed rocks make the climb a little easier, but it's very strenuous regardless. During the first 900 feet of trail, you'll gain 200 feet in elevation.

This purple-blazed section of trail leads up a hillside covered with rocks as well as tall, straight oaks, ferns, and sumacs. At times the trail itself becomes a series of large slabs of rock, and massive rock outcroppings surround you. At the top of the hill, you'll come to a T intersection; if

▶ DIRECTIONS

Take I-695 to I-95 North (Exit 33B). Go 11 miles to Exit 77B, MD 24 north toward Bel Air, and continue through the towns of Bel Air, Rock Spring, and Forest Hill. After 13.4 miles on MD 24, you'll see a sign for Rocks State Park; continue another half-mile, and you'll see signs pointing to the park office on the left (you can find trail maps and parking there). Pass this entrance and continue another 0.2 miles to the gravel parking area on the left across from Deer Creek; the trail begins at the edge of the woods in front of the parking area.

❶ KEY AT-A-GLANCE INFORMATION

LENGTH: 3.4 miles

CONFIGURATION: Irregular loop

DIFFICULTY: Moderate to very strenuous

SCENERY: Rural northern Harford County, mature upland forest

EXPOSURE: Shade

TRAFFIC: Light on trail, moderate to heavy at King and Queen's Seat

TRAIL SURFACE: Packed dirt, rock

HIKING TIME: 2 hours

ACCESS: 9 a.m. to sunset daily

MAPS: USGS Fawn Grove, trail maps available at park office

FACILITIES: Restrooms and water at the park office, open Monday–Friday, 7 a.m.–3 p.m.; public phone in parking area

SPECIAL COMMENTS: Rock climbing is allowed, but use caution. Regardless of whether you're climbing or merely hiking, wear sturdy boots.

Rocks State Park

UTM Zone (WGS84) 18S

Easting 378777

Northing 4388536

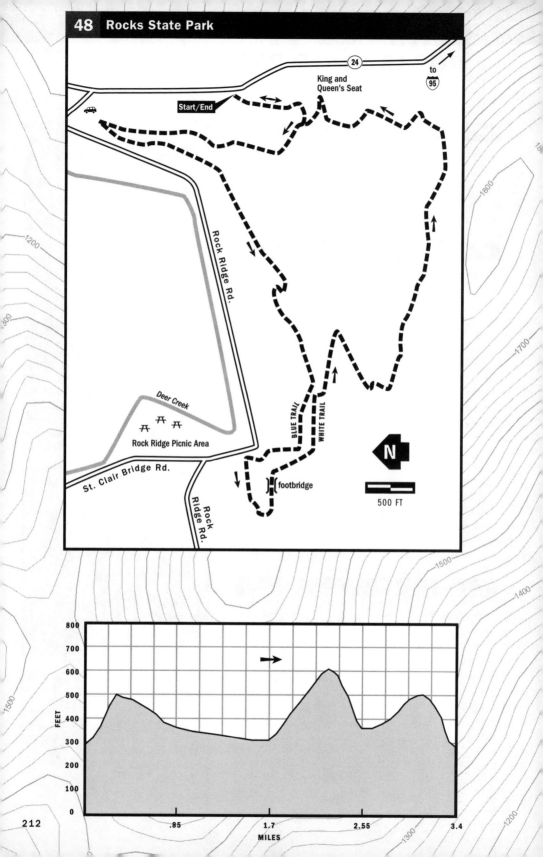

24

to 95

King and
Queen's Seat

Start/End

Rock Ridge Rd.

Deer Creek

Rock Ridge Picnic Area

St. Clair Bridge Rd.

Rock Ridge Rd.

BLUE TRAIL

WHITE TRAIL

footbridge

N

500 FT

1200

1300

1800

1700

1600

1500

1400

1300

1200

800
700
600
500
400
300
200
100
0

FEET

.85   1.7   2.55   3.4

MILES

you're short on time, head left to the King and Queen's Seat now, but for a good hike go right and come back to this attraction later.

You'll appreciate the fairly level, wide, well-maintained packed-dirt trail surrounded by ferns and sassafras at the top of the hill. The blazes turn to white in this section. After 100 feet, you'll come to another T intersection. Take a right, and you'll see a bench immediately on the left. The trail heads downhill and then levels out at 0.3 miles. You will walk along the middle of a flat ridge, which falls off about 20 feet on both sides. At 0.6 miles, you'll see a wooden post with a small orange dot on it: Don't take the green-blazed trail straight ahead (it will take you to a parking area on Saint Clair Bridge Road); instead head left. The white blazes return as you gradually head up the hill; you'll see lots of nice spongy moss along the trail, and a rock outcropping to the right gives good views of Deer Creek below. (You can tube and swim in the creek, but be aware that there are no lifeguards; you can also fish here if you have a freshwater fishing license and trout stamp).

Squirrels, chipmunks, and white-tailed deer accompany you as you continue uphill, winding among the huge slabs of rock along the path. You will have an overwhelming impression of moisture—moss and lichen cover the rocks, and the area is awash in ferns. At 1 mile, you'll come to a small asphalt road that leads to the Rock Ridge Picnic Area from St. Clair Bridge Road. Cross the road and pick up the trail in the woods on the other side at the brown wooden post. At 1.1 miles, look for an oak tree with its trunk growing over a rock; it looks like spilled wax and is absolutely beautiful.

At 1.2 miles, the trail splits; head right onto the blue-blazed trail, which offers a slightly different view. It runs a little lower down the hill closer to Deer Creek, and the red oaks crowding above provide welcome shade on hot days. You'll continue to see a profusion of rocks covered with moss and spilled tree roots. At the T intersection at 1.4 miles, take a right through a big grove where ferns carpet the ground. After you cross the wooden footbridge here, the trail gets a bit confusing—the well-worn path straight ahead leaves the park property, but if you turn around and look to the right, you'll see a rusted thresher and a wooden post marked #1 and another trail barely visible in the tall grass. Follow this trail through the tall grass and occasional sections of flattened grass; you'll soon come to a wooden post marked #2, which will let you know you're on the right path. You will soon begin to see blue blazes, and the path will become more prominent.

A representative working at the Rocks State Park office told me that this area is a recovering farm and the wooden posts correspond to an old trail brochure. Since the area has changed drastically, the park rangers no longer distribute that guide. As of early 2005, all six of the posts still stood, but the park rangers were planning to remove them.

You will cross over another wooden footbridge at 1.5 miles and another 150 feet farther down the trail. You will see an open bog just beyond and lots of azalea and mountain laurel on either side of you. The wooden post marked #6 sits in a big field of ferns with a slight indentation in the ground next to it; you will reach the end of this half-mile loop soon after you see this post. Turn right to head back to the white trail. When the trail splits, you can either go straight or keep to the right to return via a higher elevation than you came and to make another loop so you don't backtrack. Either way, you'll reach another trail split at 1.7 miles and rejoin the white trail at 1.8; take a right, and you'll see white blazes right away.

King and Queen's Seat

The trail runs as a switchback, ascending quickly over the ubiquitous rock. A well-placed bench on the left at 2 miles provides a welcome resting place. At just over 2 miles, you'll reach an intersection with a sign pointing in different directions. If you go right, you'll leave the park; if you go left, you'll come to the picnic area; and if you go straight (actually diagonally right), you'll stay on the white trail. Go straight, and you'll come to another intersection at 2.25 miles. Here you can cut left on the orange trail to head to the picnic area, or stay straight to remain on the white trail, which becomes quite level as it winds through mature upland forest.

At the two wooden posts on the left (they look like ski slaloms), turn left. Go up the hill, which is a moderate climb, and when you reach the top, at 2.8 miles, take a right; you will soon come to the King and Queen's Seat on the right. Be very careful here—people have fallen off these vertical rock faces, some of which are 94 feet above the ground. Many of these slabs have been carved with graffiti, which at first seems to detract from the sanctity of this place so highly valued by the indigenous Indians. I found it sort of nice to see the older scrawls, some of them dating back to the mid-1800s. You might find it interesting that David has been in love with Esther for well more than 100 years now.

The King and Queen's Seat provides a rather stunning vista of the rolling farmlands of northern Harford County sprawling out and Deer Creek running below. In spring and summer, you will see an almost unbroken ribbon of green, and the autumn foliage puts on a spectacular show. In winter months, when you should take extreme caution if you're hiking in snow and ice, the leafless view stretches even farther than it does in summer. In short, it's an amazing spot.

After you've taken it all in, go right off the rocks, and on the right you'll quickly rejoin the purple-blazed trail you used walking earlier. Remember that this is a very steep section; go slowly since going down can be more difficult and tough on the knees than coming up.

Rocks State Park also includes the Falling Branch Area, home to Maryland's second-highest vertical waterfall, Kilgore Falls. To reach it, continue north on MD 24 for another 4.2 miles and turn left onto Saint Mary's Road. Go another 0.4 miles and turn right onto Falling Branch Road. Park on the right at the "Rocks Falling Branch Area" sign. You may also want to visit nearby Eden Mill Park and Nature Center, at 1617 Eden Mill Road in Pylesville; it offers many short hiking trails perfect for small children as well as picnicking, and canoe launching and fishing on Deer Creek. The nature center, which is housed in a restored gristmill, features a hands-on area for children; for more information visit **www.edenmill.org** or call (410) 638-3616 or (410) 836-3050.

ROCKS STATE PARK: FALLING BRANCH AREA

LENGTH: 1.1 miles

CONFIGURATION: Out-and-back with a spur

DIFFICULTY: Easy

SCENERY: Kilgore Falls, mixed hardwoods

EXPOSURE: Shade to the waterfall but mostly sun on the extension along Falling Branch

TRAFFIC: Moderate

TRAIL SURFACE: Packed-dirt after an initial small section of crushed rock

HIKING TIME: 15 minutes to the waterfall and 30 minutes adding the extension

ACCESS: 9 a.m. to sunset daily

MAPS: USGS Fawn Grove, trail maps available at the Rocks State Park central office (see "Directions" below)

FACILITIES: None on the trail; restrooms and water at the Rocks State Park central office (see "Directions" below)

SPECIAL COMMENTS: A proposed sale of the Falling Branch Area by the Maryland Department of Natural Resources in 2004 roused much public opposition, and fortunately the sale was scrapped. For information on the area, call the Rocks State Park office at (410) 557-7994.

Rocks State Park: Falling Branch Area

UTM Zone (WGS84) 18S

Easting 377972

Northing 4394346

▶ IN BRIEF

Take a short hike with a grand payoff: Kilgore Falls, Maryland's second-highest vertical waterfall.

▶ DESCRIPTION

The relatively small (67 acres) Falling Branch Area of Rocks State Park remains environmentally sensitive. Once a meeting place for Susquehannock Indians, local hikers and nature enthusiasts didn't know about it for many years because it sat on private property. Fortunately, in 1993, the state, with the help of many local activists including Harford County public-school children, bought the land and turned it over to Rocks State Park officials for administration. It has become one of the most attractive parcels for many miles around.

From the trailhead, you will wind through a well-exposed section of the trail with thick underbrush of mostly goldenrod and spicebush; a stand of pines provides welcome shade. The path soon runs downhill. You'll see lots of poison sumac on mature red oak trees, as well as an abundance of tulip poplars, beeches, sassafras, hollies, and mountain laurels.

▶ DIRECTIONS

Take I-695 to I-95 North (Exit 33B). Go 11 miles to Exit 77B, MD 24 north toward Bel Air, and go through the towns of Bel Air, Rock Spring, and Forest Hill. After 13.4 miles on MD 24, you'll see a sign for Rocks State Park. Keep going another half-mile; you'll see signs pointing to the park office to the left, but to reach the Falling Branch Area, pass the office sign and proceed another 4.2 miles and turn left onto Saint Mary's Road. Go another 0.4 miles and turn right onto Falling Branch Road; park on the right at the "Rocks Falling Branch Area" sign. The trail starts at the left end of the parking lot.

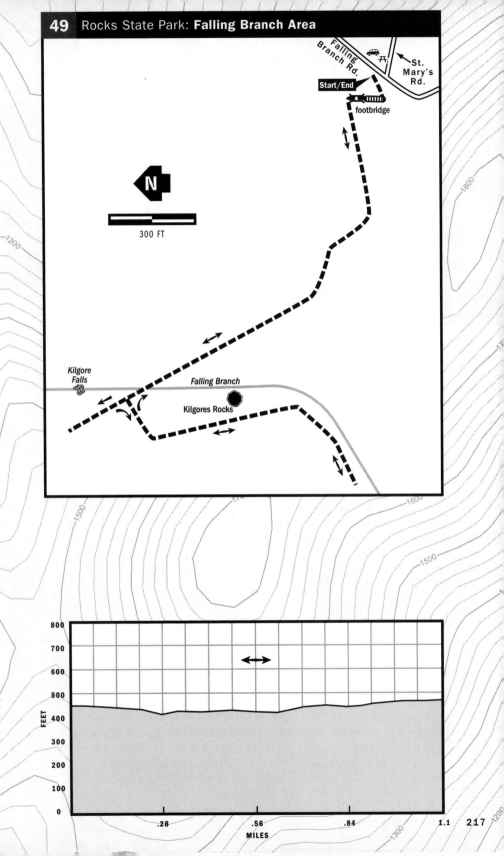

Falling
Branch Rd.

St.
Mary's
Rd.

Start/End

footbridge

N

300 FT

Kilgore
Falls

Falling Branch

Kilgores Rocks

800

700

600

500

400

300

200

100

0

FEET

.28   .56   .84   1.1

MILES

Kilgore Falls

You'll reach a wooden boardwalk and footbridge at 500 feet. The trail turns to packed dirt on the other side, and red cedars abound as the trail rises above a little valley on the left. This area, as well as the woods on the other side of Falling Branch, provides prime habitat for red fox, white-tailed deer, and a multitude of woodland birds, including wild turkey. You'll soon hear the rumble of Kilgore Falls; Falling Branch comes into view on the left, and you'll parallel it upstream. Also to the left, at 0.2 miles, you can see the remains of an old kiln or stone chimney, as well as the stone foundation of a long-abandoned house. On the right of the falls below sits the foundation of a stagecoach rest stop.

When the trail splits at 0.25 miles, head left toward Falling Branch. (You can also go right, which will take you above the waterfall, but the views of its cascade are obstructed from there). You will see other trail cuts here and there, but avoid these; with the exception of the trail described here, all of them invariably lead to private property, and the smallness of the area ensures encroachment. Cross over the Falling Branch on the stepping-stones. Be extra careful in winter; the stones are not set very high out of the water, and ice and snow can make them very slippery. Heavy rains will also cover and/or make the stones slippery. In general, though, the water remains pretty shallow, but if the water is high and the trail on the other side, which runs just alongside Falling Branch, is covered, you can take another trail higher up the hill, which has a wooden footbridge.

At 0.3 miles, you'll reach Kilgore Falls, which sits in an absolutely gorgeous spot—a rock amphitheater known as Prettyboy Schist. Over the schist, the water spills into a deep pool, where actress Sissy Spacek swam in the movie *Tuck Everlasting*. You can climb the rock wall to the left to get to the top of the falls; it doesn't require much experience in rock-climbing, but it does require some nimbleness, to be sure. Be sure to sit down and take in the views of the falls. While it certainly can't compare to Niagara or Angel Falls, if you're lucky enough to have it to yourself, you'll find the wildness of the area to be very inspiring.

When you head back, you can extend the hike by staying on this side of Falling Branch and going diagonally uphill to the right—you'll come to this portion of the trail just after you pass a bench and just before you reach the Falling Branch crossing. This trail initially follows the old stagecoach route away from the falls; you'll be walking downstream and see lots of ferns, moss-covered rocks, and evergreens decorating the hill on the right. About 100 feet from the Falling Branch crossing, be on the lookout for a fascinating sight: up the hill on the right, you can see a decayed tree trunk that bears an amazingly uncanny resemblance to the silhouette of an elephant (albeit a small one).

Continuing on, the trail becomes almost overgrown here as it sees relatively little traffic, but it soon opens up into a field of mostly blackberry bushes and goldenrod. Turn around, at 0.5 miles, when you see the "Trees at Work. Alliance for the Chesapeake Bay" sign. Walk back toward Kilgore Falls, cross over the Falling Branch, and head back to your car.

▶ NEARBY ACTIVITIES

In addition to the main section of Rocks State Park (see page 211), you may want to visit nearby Eden Mill Park and Nature Center, at 1617 Eden Mill Road in Pylesville; it offers many short hiking trails perfect for small children as well as picnicking, and canoe launching and fishing on Deer Creek. The nature center, which is housed in a restored gristmill, features a hands-on area for children; for more information visit **www.edenmill.org** or call (410) 638-3616 or (410) 836-3050. If more nature isn't on your agenda, head into downtown Bel Air for shops and restaurants.

SUSQUEHANNA STATE PARK: RIVER TRAILS

KEY AT-A-GLANCE INFORMATION

LENGTH: 7.5 miles

CONFIGURATION: Out-and-back with a jagged loop

DIFFICULTY: Moderate

SCENERY: Susquehanna River, Deer Creek, historic sites, mixed hardwoods

EXPOSURE: Shade

TRAFFIC: Moderate to heavy on Lower Susquehanna Heritage Greenways Trail, light on alternate Greenways Route and Woodland Trails

TRAIL SURFACE: Gravel, packed dirt, some asphalt

HIKING TIME: 2.5–3 hours

ACCESS: Sunrise to sunset daily

MAPS: USGS Conowingo Dam, Aberdeen; you can get a trail system map at the headquarters building at Rocks State Park, which administers Susquehanna State Park (see page 211 for directions to Rocks State Park); you can also purchase the *Trail Guide to Susquehanna State Park* online at **www.easycart.net/Maryland DepartmentofNaturalResources/ Central_Maryland_Trail_Guides.html.**

FACILITIES: Restrooms and water at the Rock Run Historic Area, campground, Steppingstone Museum, Deer Creek Picnic Area, and Lapidum Boat Launch; public telephone at Rock Run Historic Area

SPECIAL COMMENTS: Tours of Conowingo Dam are available; for more information, call (410) 457-5011.

Susquehanna State Park: River Trails

UTM Zone (WGS84)   18S

Easting   400126

Northing   4386571

IN BRIEF

Follow the mighty Susquehanna River upstream to Conowingo Dam—then return via an obscure wooded foot trail.

DESCRIPTION

If any Baltimore outdoor enthusiast needs a reminder why he or she is lucky to live in this area, Susquehanna State Park provides it. Just consider the Susquehanna River's impressive statistics: 444 miles long, a 13 million-acre drainage basin, the second-largest watershed in the eastern United States. The river begins as an overflow of Otsego Lake in New York and runs through three states before draining into Chesapeake Bay, just south at Havre de Grace, Maryland, pouring 19 million gallons of fresh water into the bay every minute.

The native Susquehannock Indians had been hunting and fishing in the area for centuries before explorer John Smith arrived in 1608. Smith's assessment of the area remains applicable today: "Heaven and earth seemed never to have agreed better to frame a place for man's . . . delightful habitation." European businessmen successfully established trading posts on the

DIRECTIONS

Take I-95 to Exit 89, MD 155 west. Go 2.5 miles and turn right onto MD 161. Go 0.3 miles, turn right onto Rock Run Road, and continue into the park. Follow the signs to the camping area; at the intersection of Craigs Corner Road and Wilkinson Road, turn right, and then turn left onto Craigs Corner Road just before the campground gate. After you pass a private road on the left, look for parking on both sides of Craigs Corner Road before you reach Stafford Road Bridge over Deer Creek. Walk across the bridge and turn right to reach the trailhead of the Lower Susquehanna Heritage Greenways Trail.

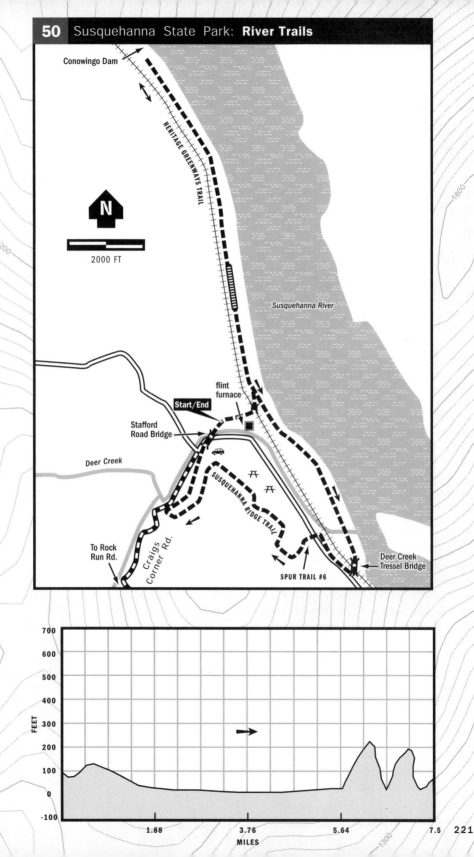

Conowingo Dam

HERITAGE GREENWAYS TRAIL

N

2000 FT

Susquehanna River

flint furnace

Start/End

Stafford Road Bridge

Deer Creek

SUSQUEHANNA RIDGE TRAIL

To Rock Run Rd.

Craigs Corner Rd.

SPUR TRAIL #6

Deer Creek Tressel Bridge

700
600
500
400
300
200
100
0
-100

FEET

1.88   3.76   5.64   7.5

MILES

Susquehanna River from the
Lower Susquehanna Heritage
Greenways Trail

Susquehanna River as early as 1622, and by 1658, enough people had arrived to establish the settlement that would become Havre de Grace.

You will pass Stafford Flint Furnace, just off the trail on the right as you cross Stafford Bridge. Even though the furnace has stood here for more than two centuries, it wasn't one of the area's first structures; it is, however, all that remains of the once-thriving town of Stafford, established in 1749 and destroyed by an ice gorge in 1904. You will be paralleling Deer Creek on a wide gravel trail lined with wild strawberries; fishing in this freshwater creek requires a nontidal fishing license. The creek provides habitat for the federally endangered Maryland Darter and the short-nosed sturgeon. In summer months, you'll see people swimming and tubing the clear waters.

As you head down to this pretty waterway, you'll pass several cutoff paths, but stay on the main trail. Notice the wealth of understory flora surrounding you—you'll see literally hundreds of species of shrubs, including honeysuckle, multiflora rose, raspberry, staghorn sumac, swamp rose, winterberry, and trumpet vine. Trillium, recognizable by its three-petaled flowers and three-leafed stems, abounds on the hillsides. You'll also see Dutchman's-breeches (rarely found in Maryland), Virginia bluebells, dogtooth violet, windflower, and spring beauty as well as some rare and endangered plants including sweet-scented Indian plantain and valerian.

At 0.4 miles, you will cross a footbridge over the site of the Susquehanna Tidewater Canal, built between 1835 and 1839 to link Havre de Grace with Wrightsville, Pennsylvania. Take note of the little footpath to the right of the bridge; you'll take it on the return trip. For now, continue left on the wide Heritage Greenways Trail. At 0.75 miles, you'll see the first cut to the right leading to the Susquehanna River; take this path down to the riverbank, where you'll inevitably see fishermen standing on the many decent-sized rocks that dot the edge of the river. Many regard the Susquehanna as the best fishing grounds on the East Coast. If you come here in early spring, you might catch sight of the annual shad and herring runs. You'll need to get a tidal license to try your hand at catching smallmouth bass, largemouth bass, channel catfish, carp, American shad, alewife, blue backed herring, striped bass, pike, and perch.

You will find that just standing on the alternating sand-mud-rock bank of the striking Susquehanna is inspiring. And if the river alone isn't enough, remember that the woods behind you present one of the most biologically diverse ecosystems in North America. In addition to the flora listed above, you'll see yellow poplar, birch, red oak, black oak, white oak, chestnut oak, American beech, black cherry, white ash, black gum, hickory, sycamore, and red maple dominating the overstory. The myriad creatures that thrive here include wood frogs, eastern painted turtles, river otters, raccoons, white-tailed deer, white-footed mice, eastern chipmunks, and red foxes.

If birds are more your fancy, the river hosts many of them as well, including lots of kingfishers, gulls, ospreys, herons, and bald eagles; for a comprehensive list of more than 100 birds that have been spotted in and around the area of Conowingo Dam, see **www.harfordbirdclub.org/conowingo.html.** The dominant birds in the surrounding woodlands include red-headed woodpeckers, wild turkeys, pileated woodpeckers, winter wrens, house wrens, wood thrushes, sapsuckers, downy woodpeckers, and screech owls.

At 1 mile, you'll come to a very long boardwalk that helps protect especially sensitive wetlands; river floods often reach this area, which is barely above sea level. The hills on the left abruptly rise very steeply; these are gneiss columns, many of them at a 90-degree angle to the ground. The trail soon runs alongside railroad tracks, part of the defunct Philadelphia Electric Railroad Company, and ends at a gate at almost the 3-mile mark. Just ahead you will see Conowingo Dam, constructed in 1926; it is almost 4,500 feet long and 100 feet high, and full-capacity flows approach 40 million gallons a minute. If you're lucky enough to catch a release, you'll see an extraordinary sight.

Turn around here and head back, taking advantage of one of the cuts leading to the river if you haven't already walked down to the riverbank. When you get back to the trail split you passed earlier (this time at 4.2 miles), take the packed-dirt foot trail that heads into the thick woods. Vegetation crowds this stunning, beautiful trail, which runs close to the riverbanks. Look out for poison ivy as well as nettles, which can give you what feels like an intense jellyfish or bee sting that can last up to half an hour; if you get "stung," try hard not to rub the area—that makes it worse. If the water level of the river isn't too high, you'll see a great little beach sitting across from a large jumble of rocks.

At 5.5 miles, cross the Deer Creek Tressel Bridge and head right on Stafford Road, pass the parking area, and go another quarter-mile. You'll see a hiker icon and Mason-Dixon Trail post to the left; this marks Spur Trail #6, blazed in silver (like the rest of the spur trails in the park system), which will lead you to the red-blazed Susquehanna Ridge Trail. The spur is a bit tough, but worth it as it winds uphill through mixed hardwood and a chorus of birds. After 0.1 mile, you'll reach Ridge Trail; take it to the right. It crosses a stream at 6 miles and passes a grove of pines; a sign explains that these trees were planted as a timber crop, but they have had the unfortunate effect of shading out and killing the native poplars. Next you'll come to a cleared area that has been allowed to grow back naturally. You will cross a footbridge and see Deer Creek Picnic Area through the woods to the right; the trail soon ends at the green-blazed Deer Creek Trail. Continue on Deer Creek Trail until it splits at 7 miles—you will hear Deer Creek just preceding the split; head downhill to Craigs Corner Road, a gravel park road. You will emerge from the woods across from the private road you passed earlier in your car; walk along Craigs Corner Road for 0.3 miles to the parking area.

▶ NEARBY ACTIVITIES

You might want to visit the Steppingstone Museum before you leave the park; it features the rural arts and crafts of the 1880–1920 period; call (410) 939-2299 for more information. At nearby historic Havre de Grace (MD 155 east) you will find museums, lighthouses, and the town's famous promenade, which extends 2,400 feet along Chesapeake Bay from City Marina to the Concord Point Lighthouse, rebuilt after Hurricane Isabel destroyed it in 2004. In Aberdeen, check out minor league baseball at Ripken Stadium, home of the Ironbirds; for more information visit **www.ironbirds baseball.com/stadium** or call (410) 297-9292. You can also visit the nearby Army Ordnance Museum, on the grounds of Aberdeen Proving Ground; for more information visit **www.ordmusfound.org** or call (410) 278-3602.

SUSQUEHANNA STATE PARK: WOODLAND–FARM TRAILS

▶ IN BRIEF

Experience the wilder side of Susquehanna State Park as you walk in blissful solitude through woods full of old growth.

▶ DESCRIPTION

Before you begin the hike, you might want to walk down to the Susquehanna River, just behind Rock Run Mill. This beautiful river boasts very impressive statistics: 444 miles long, a 13 million-acre drainage basin, the second-largest watershed in the eastern United States. The river begins as an overflow of Otsego Lake in New York and runs through three states before draining into Chesapeake Bay, just south at Havre de Grace, Maryland, pouring 19 million gallons of fresh water into the bay every minute.

From behind the mill, you can see narrow Wood Island in front of you. The larger Roberts Island sits behind it, with Spencer Island to the right. You can also see Cecil County across the river.

Built in 1794, Rock Run Mill continued to operate well into the 20th century; now it is open weekends from May to September from 10 a.m. to 6 p.m., with grinding demonstrations from 1 p.m. to 4 p.m. A bridge once spanned the river near the mill, but it was destroyed by ice floes in 1856. The toll keeper's house, however, still remains in its position to the left of the mill;

▶ DIRECTIONS

Take I-95 to Exit 89, MD 155 west. Go 2.5 miles and turn right onto MD 161. Go 0.3 miles and turn right onto Rock Run Road and continue into the park. Follow the signs to the historic area; the road ends at the parking area to the left of Rock Run Mill. Walk up Stafford Road, keeping Rock Run Mill on your left. The trail starts 600 feet ahead and leads into the woods to the right.

ⓘ KEY AT-A-GLANCE INFORMATION

LENGTH: 8.3 miles

CONFIGURATION: Jagged loop

DIFFICULTY: Moderate to strenuous

SCENERY: Susquehanna River, mixed hardwoods, Rock Run, historic sites

EXPOSURE: More shade than sun

TRAFFIC: Moderate to heavy at the historic area, picnic area, campgrounds, and river; light on the trails

TRAIL SURFACE: Packed dirt with small sections of gravel and asphalt

HIKING TIME: 3–3.5 hours

ACCESS: Sunrise to sunset daily

MAPS: USGS Aberdeen; you can get a trail system map at the headquarters building at Rocks State Park, which administers Susquehanna State Park (see page 211 for directions to Rocks State Park); you can also purchase the *Trail Guide to Susquehanna State Park* online at www.easycart. net/MarylandDepartmentofNatural Resources/Central_Maryland_Trail_ Guides.html.

FACILITIES: Restrooms and water at the Rock Run Historic Area, campground, Steppingstone Museum, Deer Creek Picnic Area, and Lapidum Boat Launch; public telephone at Rock Run Historic Area

SPECIAL COMMENTS: See the note at the end of the hike description for more about trails at Susquehanna State Park.

Susquehanna State Park:
Woodland–Farm Trails

UTM Zone (WGS84)   18S

Easting   401939

Northing   4384858

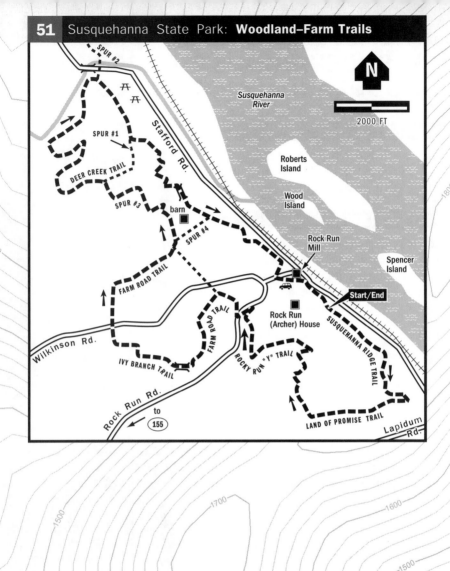

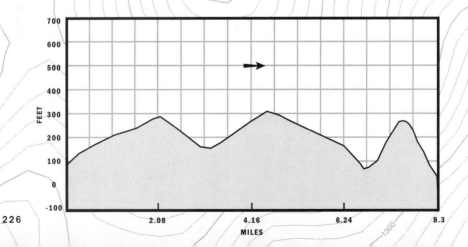

it now houses an information center for the park. The miller once lived in the house across the road.

Noted for birding and wildflower viewing, the narrow red-blazed Susquehanna Ridge Trail (initially blazed in both red and blue) runs along a western ridge facing the Susquehanna River, a few hundred feet above the water. Soon after you start walking, you'll cross a tiny stream and see a little cairn next to it with a hiker icon. The abundant raspberry bushes in this area bear loads of delicious berries in summer; you'll be able to enjoy the berries, but you won't be able to see the river—the leaves in the thick woods will block the view.

At 0.6 miles, you'll cross an intact stone wall, evidence that someone once cleared this land. That's not surprising since Lapidum, which traces its history to 1683, is close by. When you see the white-blazed Land of Promise Trail at 0.9 miles, you'll notice the Susquehanna Ridge Trail continuing straight ahead; it ends a short way later at Lapidum Road, the entrance point to the Lapidum Boat Launch (the launch is open 24 hours a day for a $5 usage fee). Instead of hitting the dead end, turn right onto the Land of Promise Trail, an isolated path that more or less follows that same stone wall.

At 1.1 miles, continue following the stone wall as it skirts the edge of a cleared field. The trail opens into a field, a favorite of songbirds, and moves through chest-high grass. More raspberry bushes await you when the trail reenters the woods at 1.4 miles, but you'll quickly come back out into the field. At 1.5 miles, you will cross a tree-lined road, and you will see Steppingstone Museum on the right. The museum features exhibits on the rural arts and crafts of the 1880-1920 period; call (410) 939-2299 for information. Continuing the hike on the other side of the road, you'll soon notice a little stream down the hill on the left. At about 2 miles, you will come to a fascinating area full of grapevine, trumpet vine, honeysuckle, and some invasive Chinese *Ailanthus altissima* trees, recognized by everyone who lives in Baltimore as those pungent (read: stinky) trees that grow *everywhere*: cracks in the concrete, glass-strewn vacant lots, unruly urban "green spaces." People often snidely refer to it as the "ghetto palm." The somewhat unexpected combination of these trees with the vines creates a little landscape that appears downright semitropical.

At 2.1 miles, turn left onto the yellow-blazed Rock Run "Y" Trail, noted for grapevines, raspberry bushes, and briar patches. Be sure to take the trail split to the right when you see the "1A" sign in the pine plantation—otherwise, you'll end up at Quaker Bottom Road. The trail serves as the access point to the place where Rock Run meets the Susquehanna River at the historic area. To avoid going back to where you began, go left when the trail splits at Rock Run, cross the stream at 2.7 miles (take care on the loose rocks), and join the blue-blazed Farm Road Trail. The area around Rock Run is full of mountain laurel and mature beech trees.

Once across Rock Run, go to the right; you will likely see many brown wood frogs with their characteristic black "raccoon masks" around their eyes. Cross over the stone wall and immediately go left. At 2.8 miles, you will emerge from the woods onto Rock Run Road; go left for about 50 feet and then back up into the woods to the right—a series of log steps and a log handrail mark the trail. You will pass the orange-blazed Ivy Branch Trail on the right, and in another 10 feet, you'll see the same trail on the left; take it to the left (taking it earlier to the right will bring you directly to the road leading to the historic area, where you've parked).

You will see a multitude of enormous trees along Ivy Branch Trail; it's stunningly beautiful and very peaceful, especially around 3.5 miles. You will pass a bog filled with many frogs as well as skunk cabbage, which, contrary to popular belief, doesn't really stink all the time—just when it is bruised or cut. Next you will cross a rocky stream shaded by hay-scented and Christmas fern; their combined aromas will remind you of cedar. You'll see a trail split up the hill: Spur #5 heads left and dead-ends at Rock Run Road; go right to stay on Ivy Branch Trail. You will cross a little footbridge and then skirt a pine plantation on the right before you reach Wilkinson Road at 3.8 miles. You will see the maintenance complex straight ahead—keep it on your right as you walk along the tree line at the edge of the farm field. Continue in the same direction as the little gravel road at 3.9 miles. As you pass the entrance to the maintenance complex, watch for the spot where the groove in the grass, which is the trail, cuts left away from the tree line; the top of the gradual hill affords a wonderful view of undeveloped land for miles in the distance.

When the trail splits at 4.5 miles, head left and you'll be back on the blue-blazed Farm Road Trail. The cut to the right is Trail Spur #4, which you can take if you're short on time, tired, or want to see an abandoned barn, silo, and stable that all look very spooky in their dark, overrun state; the other end of this trail spur links to the red-blazed Susquehanna Ridge Trail, which you can take to the right, back to the parking area. To continue hiking, skip Trail Spur #4 and continue on the blue-blazed Farm Road Trail—you can see the barn later when you're on the red-blazed trail.

Farm Road Trail cuts straight across an open field in waist-high grass full of grasshoppers, dragonflies, and green beetles in the summer. You will reenter the woods for good at 4.8 miles; take note of the little stream on the left. At 5.2 miles, take Trail Spur #3 and cross the stream to link to the green-blazed Deer Creek Trail. This trail winds through mature forest, noted mostly for what the trail guide calls "two giant specimens of native trees, the white oak and American beech." Indeed, the girth of some of the trees is very impressive.

At the trail split at 6 miles, keep heading right, up the hill; going left will take you to Craigs Corner Road. Deer Creek runs on the other side of Craigs Corner Road, and you'll hear it for a while until you turn away and pass Trail Spur #2. Go past Trail Spur #1, across from the Deer Creek Picnic Area through the woods on the left; the trail soon links with the red-blazed Susquehanna Ridge Trail again, this time at 6.9 miles.

Next you'll cross a footbridge and a forest buffer, where a clear-cut area has been allowed to grow back naturally. As you walk along the Ridge Trail, you will see a profusion of wild mint and honeysuckle, which offer a very nice aroma in summer; if you're hiking in winter and miss experiencing the mint and honeysuckle, you will get great river views instead. If you didn't check out Trail Spur #4 earlier, look for it to the right and take it now to see the abandoned barn.

You will reach Rock Run at 8 miles; cross it and go left when you reach the park road. You're now reentering the Rock Run Historic Area, passing to the right the Rock Run House, the 1804 home of Brigadier General James Archer, who resigned from the U.S. Army to join the Confederate Army; he was wounded and captured at Gettysburg in 1863. Several rooms in the mansion have been restored and stocked with period antiques. After passing the house, go right; you will find the parking area straight ahead.

Note: This hike stitches together major portions of each of the trails in Susquehanna State Park except the Lower Susquehanna Heritage Greenways Trail, which is described in Susquehanna State Park: River Trails (see page 220); you can vary the length of your hike by taking the spur trails noted on the trail map. Susquehanna State Park is home to a dizzying array of varied flora and fauna; for descriptions, see Susquehanna State Park: River Trails.

▶ NEARBY ACTIVITIES

You might want to visit the Steppingstone Museum before you leave the park; it features the rural arts and crafts of the 1880–1920 period; call (410) 939-2299 for more information. At nearby historic Havre de Grace (MD 155 east) you will find museums, lighthouses, and the town's famous promenade, which extends 2,400 feet along Chesapeake Bay from City Marina to the Concord Point Lighthouse, rebuilt after Hurricane Isabel destroyed it in 2004. In Aberdeen, check out minor league baseball at Ripken Stadium, home of the Ironbirds; for more information visit **www.ironbirds baseball.com/stadium** or call (410) 297-9292. You can also visit the nearby Army Ordnance Museum, on the grounds of Aberdeen Proving Ground; for more information visit **www.ordmusfound.org** or call (410) 278-3602.

HOWARD COUNTY

CENTENNIAL PARK

ℹ️ KEY AT-A-GLANCE INFORMATION

LENGTH: 3.3 miles

CONFIGURATION: Loop

DIFFICULTY: Easy

SCENERY: Centennial Lake, Wildlife Management Area, Centennial Arboretum

EXPOSURE: Mostly sun

TRAFFIC: Moderate to heavy

TRAIL SURFACE: Asphalt with a short section of packed dirt

HIKING TIME: 1 hour

ACCESS: 7 a.m. to dusk daily

MAPS: USGS Savage; you can download a map at **www.co.ho.md.us/RAP/RAP_ HoCoParksCentennial.htm#anch6461.**

FACILITIES: Restrooms at the pavilion in the parking area and water fountain in front of the tennis courts; other restrooms and water are spread out at various parking areas around the lake; ball fields, playgrounds, pavilions

SPECIAL COMMENTS: For park information, call (410) 313-7256, or the Howard County Recreation and Parks Headquarters at (410) 313-4700.

Centennial Park

UTM Zone (WGS84)   18S

Easting   340273

Northing   4345039

▶ IN BRIEF

Stroll around man-made Centennial Lake, an oasis in the middle of Columbia, and enjoy the diversity of foliage in Centennial Arboretum.

▶ DESCRIPTION

You will pass a volleyball court and playgrounds at 150 feet on the right. A thick stand of trees on the left buffers the trail from MD 108. On the right you'll see a large patch of wildflowers, a mélange of purple, yellow, and white; a hill rises beyond it. Centennial Lake lies on the other side of the hill.

As you head around to the right, the lake comes into view fairly quickly. You'll probably see in-line skaters, walkers, bicyclists, and people pushing strollers, making it obvious that Centennial Park serves as a recreational haven. You will pass a parking area and a pavilion on the left before you reach the boat ramp at just under 0.6 miles. To the left of the boat ramp, you'll see a little wooden post with a hiker icon, denoting the trail, which heads into the woods. This packed-dirt and cedar chip path winds through a stand of tall oaks. At 0.6 miles, still in the woods, go left and you'll see lots of flowering dogwood, white oak, beech, and tulip poplar. When this trail ends at a parking area, take the asphalt trail to the right toward the lake.

At just under 0.8 miles, take a left up the hill; you'll pass more wildflowers on both sides of

▶ DIRECTIONS

Take I-695 to I-70 west; continue to MD 29 south and then MD 108 west toward Clarksville. Go 0.8 miles and turn right into the park on Woodland Road; immediately turn left at the sign for the pavilion and continue to the parking area in front of the pavilion. The trail, marked by two brown posts, starts between the pavilion and the tennis courts.

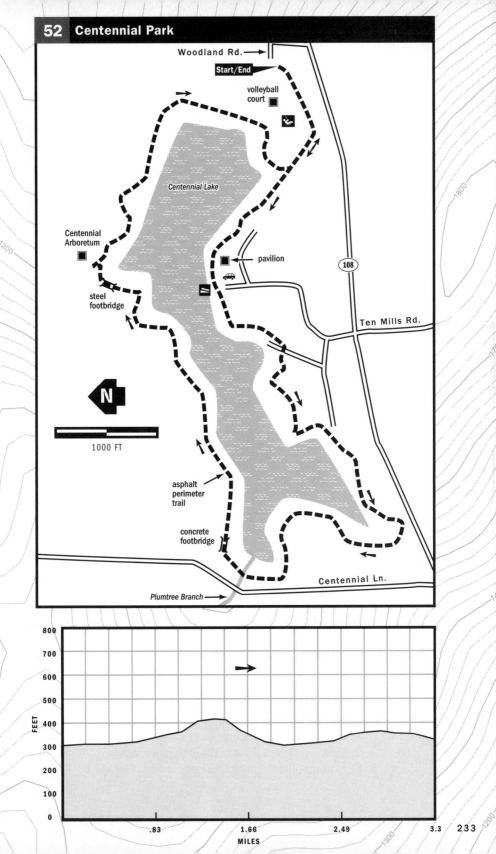

Woodland Rd. →

Start/End

volleyball court ■

Centennial Lake

Centennial Arboretum ■

pavilion

108

Ten Mills Rd.

steel footbridge

N

1000 FT

asphalt perimeter trail

concrete footbridge

Centennial Ln.

Plumtree Branch →

800				
700				
600	→			
500				
400				
300				
200				
100				
0				

FEET

.83   1.66   2.49   3.3

MILES

Wildlife Management Area

the trail. When you reach the next parking area, go right and then quickly left at the playground, heading around Pavilions A and B. Go right, away from the parking area, and cross the little wooden boardwalk at just over 1 mile. More wildflowers as well as cattails flank the boardwalk, and the crowds thin out considerably. Although the woods stand thick on either side, this section of the trail is entirely exposed.

The trail splits at a stand of pines to the left, at 1.2 miles; head to the right and cross another wooden boardwalk. Interestingly, the ecology changes drastically and becomes marshy wetland—willows and cattails sway in the breeze for a few hundred feet before yielding once again to mixed hardwoods. Squirrels and chipmunks run across the path as butterflies flitter about. If you are hiking here in the winter, you will be able to see the Plumtree Branch of the Patuxent River where it opens into Centennial Lake on the right.

The trail splits again in about a half-mile; head left. In this section of the trail, Centennial Lake is a maintained wildlife management area; algae and lily pads fill the water, and lots of ducks and the occasional gray heron live here. You can see the rest of the lake from here, and the contrast is striking—beyond this natural area, the lake is kept quite free of plant growth. (*Note:* Fishing is not allowed anywhere on the lake.)

Continue around the lake to the right and cross over a concrete footbridge. You will pass tennis, basketball, and volleyball courts on the left up the hill. You'll soon come to the first section of the asphalt perimeter trail that is shaded by a canopy of mature trees. At 2.3 miles, you'll cross a burgundy-colored steel footbridge; when you reach the other side, spend some time in the Centennial Arboretum, where you'll see a wide variety of trees, including black walnut, eastern red cedar, persimmon, redbud, scarlet oak, red maple, sassafras, bitternut hickory, black gum, beech, sweet cherry, black cherry, tulip tree, hornbeam (blue beech), staghorn sumac, post oak, dogwood, and black oak. Each immaculately maintained tree bears an identifying label.

When the trail splits at 2.6 miles, head right; you'll have a nice view of the entire lake on your right. When the trail splits again at 3.1 miles, go left; you've now made a circuit of the lake. When the trail splits yet again at 3.2 miles, head left to return to your car; if you go straight, you'll walk parallel to MD 108 for another half-mile and the trail will abruptly end.

▶ NEARBY ACTIVITIES

For good restaurants and shopping, head to the Columbia Town Center and Lake Kittamaqundi (see page 236) by going west on MD 108 to MD 29 south and following the signs to "Town Center." For more hiking opportunities, head to the Middle Patuxent Environmental Area (see page 240), a 928-acre natural area that's home to 150 species of birds, more than 40 species of mammals, and numerous amphibians, reptiles, fish, butterflies, plants, and other wildlife; continue west on MD 108. Go past Centennial Park, and turn left onto Trotter Road between MD 108 on the north and MD 32 on the south, just east of Clarksville.

LAKE KITTAMAQUNDI

KEY AT-A-GLANCE INFORMATION

LENGTH: 3 miles

CONFIGURATION: Loop with an out-and-back spur

DIFFICULTY: Easy

SCENERY: Lake Kittamaqundi, Patuxent River, mixed hardwoods

EXPOSURE: Half sun and half shade

TRAFFIC: Moderate to heavy

TRAIL SURFACE: Asphalt, packed dirt, and a short section of brick

HIKING TIME: 1 hour

ACCESS: Open 24 hours a day, seven days a week; dirt path not recommended after dark; Maryland Transit Administration (MTA) bus #311 runs to downtown Columbia, including Columbia Mall across from Lake Kittamaqundi; for a complete MTA schedule, visit **www.mtamaryland.com** or call (866) RIDE-MTA.

MAPS: USGS Savage

FACILITIES: Food, drink, restrooms in restaurants along the west side of the lake

SPECIAL COMMENTS: The mileage markers included in the hike description below start at the entrance to the trail loop behind the Sushi Sono restaurant, but the abundance of parking in a variety of areas surrounding the lake make it possible for you to start your hike at another place.

Lake Kittamaqundi

UTM Zone (WGS84) 18S

Easting 339835

Northing 4342402

IN BRIEF

Take an easy stroll around Lake Kittamaqundi and, for contrast, finish with a hike through the woods between the lake and Little Patuxent River.

DESCRIPTION

Sandwiched between Little Patuxent Parkway and MD 29, the 27-acre man-made Lake Kittamaqundi bears the name of the first recorded Indian settlement in Howard County. Kittamaqundi means "meeting place," appropriate for the lake's position adjacent to the Columbia Town Center.

From the back of the Sushi Sono restaurant, head left onto the asphalt path down the hill, keeping the lake on your right. You'll see a small buffer of trees between you and the lake and some apple trees on the left. At a quarter-mile, you'll have a good view of Nomanizan Island, reachable only by boat; during the summer months you can rent a canoe, rowboat, or paddleboat at the pier.

You will cross a footbridge and enter the woods at 0.3 miles; the little creek below connects Lake Kittamaqundi with Wilde Lake, a few miles to the northwest. On the left, you'll see the beginning of the Parcourse fitness circuit. Cross the creek on a wooden footbridge and head left. The woods here are thick and mature, full of sassafras, maple, beech, sycamore, oak, gum, tulip poplar, and sumac; these fantastic foliage trees turn the path into a rainbow of color in fall.

DIRECTIONS

Take I-695 to I-70 west and continue to MD 29 south (toward Columbia and Washington, D.C.). Take Exit 20B, MD 175, toward Columbia Town Center. Go 1 mile and turn left onto Wincopin Circle; park anywhere in the nearby lots or garages and walk east toward the lake. The trail described in this hike starts roughly behind the Sheraton Hotel, in front of the Sushi Sono restaurant.

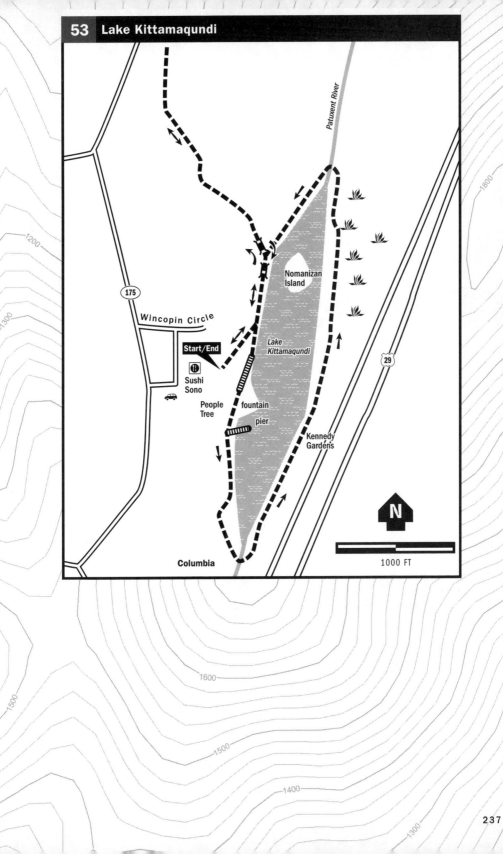

Patuxent River

Nomanizan Island

175

Wincopin Circle

Lake Kittamaqundi

29

Start/End

Sushi Sono

People Tree

fountain

pier

Kennedy Gardens

Columbia

N

1000 FT

View from the pier

Unfortunately, you can hear Little Patuxent Parkway as it comes into view at 0.6 miles. This section of the trail has a nice mix of fairly short, immature trees alongside centuries-old walnuts, which soar hundreds of feet above. At just under 0.75 miles, the trail connects to a sidewalk and ends unceremoniously at a bus stop on a busy intersection; turn around here.

When you see the back of the Sushi Sono restaurant again (where you began your hike), head left; you will be closer to the lake, and at 1.2 miles you'll be on a wooden boardwalk. You will see Clyde's Restaurant (a local institution) and the Tomato Palace on the hill above the lake; I have some great memories of walking off heavy meals with my father on this lake loop. Down the hill a bit, to the right of the lake, you'll see a pagoda and the People Tree, a sculpture that has come to symbolize Columbia. The boathouse here has a ramp for launching boats and canoes and a wooden pier, which offers nice views of the lake, which provides good habitat for hundreds of ducks and geese. Facing the lake to the right is a fountain inspired by the one in Tivoli Gardens in Rome, Italy.

Walk back toward the fountain and take a left up the concrete steps; then take another left onto a brick walkway, which turns to asphalt after about 10 feet. This section of the lake looks more aquatic, with a few cattails and willow trees. At 1.6 miles, the trail splits at a popular fishing spot. A short distance later, the trail splits again; continue heading left, keeping close to the lake. When you cross a creek, you'll be on the opposite end of the lake from where you started. A decent-sized wooded buffer separates you from MD 29, which is not far to the right; between runs Patuxent River. You won't be able to see the river here, but you will a little farther down the trail.

As you walk, you'll pass through the Kennedy Gardens, dominated by black-eyed Susans, maple trees, and ornamental bushes and grasses; you'll find plenty of benches here to sit and soak in the peaceful beauty. The trail splits into a loop at 2 miles; you can head either way, but be on the lookout at the far end of the loop for a small dirt path that heads into the woods and affords a really nice hike. Note that the dirt path is not lighted so it can't be taken at night; also it can get quite muddy after rains. Although the dirt path is easily discernible, it is a bit tight and not many people travel it; expect tall grasses on both sides of the path to sweep your legs. The Little Patuxent River runs on the right, and you'll see the remains of—or perhaps intact—beaver dams. You will be amazed at the contrast between this section of the hike and the beginning. Here white-tailed deer run in the woods; fish, turtles, frogs, and snakes make homes in the river; and you'll probably have the trail all to yourself. The only downside is that it's brief.

At 2.3 miles, townhouses come into view on the right, but just beyond you'll see a path to the left that circles the lake and provides a nice view. When the trail ends at a field behind the houses, zigzag through the oak trees, staying close to the lake on your left. Look for a barely discernible path that cuts abruptly to the right away from the lake; follow this path and head left over a feeder creek into the woods. The path will dump you out onto the asphalt trail in front of the wooden footbridge and Parcourse fitness circuit close to where you began; head left and continue to the start of the trail just ahead.

▶ NEARBY ACTIVITIES

Check out what's happening at nearby Merriweather Post Pavilion, the "Mid-Atlantic Fillmore East," which has hosted everyone from Jimi Hendrix and Janis Joplin to Metallica and Incubus; you will find it just southwest of Lake Kittamaqundi across Little Patuxent Parkway; for more information visit **www.merriweathermusic.com** or call (410) 715-5550. You might also want to visit the nearby African Art Museum of Maryland, which has a collection of more than 200 works of art covering a variety of cultures and styles; take MD 175 north and turn onto Vantage Point Road; continue approximately 0.2 miles to the "Oakland" sign on the right; turn right and continue to the parking area. The large building with the white columns on the left is Oakland; the museum is on the second level.

MIDDLE PATUXENT ENVIRONMENTAL AREA

KEY AT-A-GLANCE INFORMATION

LENGTH: 4.7 miles

CONFIGURATION: Combination

DIFFICULTY: Easy to moderate

SCENERY: Varied flora and fauna, the Middle Branch of the Patuxent River

EXPOSURE: Slightly more shade than sun

TRAFFIC: Light to moderate

TRAIL SURFACE: Initially crushed rock and then mostly packed dirt

HIKING TIME: 1.5 hours

ACCESS: Dawn to dusk except during the restricted deer hunts (see "Special Comments" below)

MAPS: USGS Clarksville; trail maps and informational brochures available at the trailhead bulletin board

FACILITIES: None

SPECIAL COMMENTS: Middle Patuxent Environmental Area holds restricted deer hunts; call (410) 313-4700 for more information. Note that the area is closed during hunts—these times are minimal, scheduled usually for very early morning hours and only on a few weekend mornings.

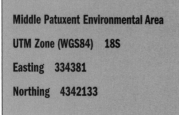

Middle Patuxent Environmental Area

UTM Zone (WGS84)   18S

Easting   334381

Northing   4342133

IN BRIEF

Search for varied wildlife among a swath of buffer woods around the Middle Branch of the Patuxent River.

DESCRIPTION

Pick up an informative trail brochure at the bulletin board before you head out. At 900 feet, you'll come to a clearing with a picnic table, and you'll see wooden post #1; many species of butterflies congregate here, including monarch, banded hairstreak, pearl crescent, great spangled fritillary, American lady, and a variety of skippers. The wooden post marks the beginning of the interpretive wildlife loop; to follow the numbers sequentially—and add a nice out-and-back with a loop in the other section of the Middle Patuxent Environmental Area—go straight.

You'll soon come to wooden post #2 in an area of field habitat being managed for indigo buntings, prairie warblers, American goldfinches, yellow-breasted chats, blue-winged warblers, American woodcocks, and other birds. Head right on a path off the wildlife loop; you'll pass a bench made from the slab of what was once a very wide tree. You'll walk through a field of mid-level growth (blueberry, sweet cicely, azalea, and mountain laurel) with a few pines beyond as you head toward the Middle Branch of the Patuxent River.

The trail in this section is easy to spot but fairly wild, with much encroaching grass; it's

DIRECTIONS

Take I-695 to I-70 west; continue to MD 29 south and then MD 108 west toward Clarksville. Go 5 miles and turn left onto Trotter Road; go half a mile to the gravel parking area on the left. The trail starts behind the wooden posts at the edge of the parking area next to the informational bulletin board.

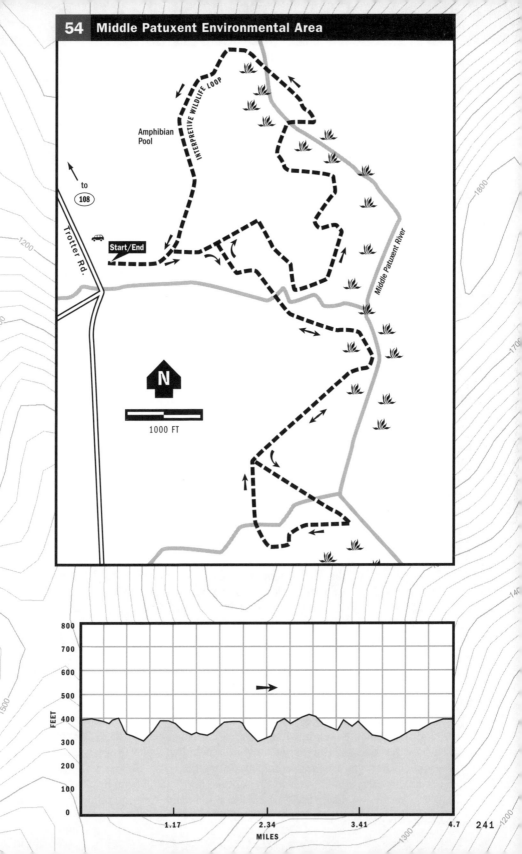

enough to feel very isolated but not so much to require a bushwhack. This very lovely spot in thick woods shows no sign at all of humanity. When the trail opens up at 0.5 miles, it takes on a very Appalachian feel with ferns, big hunks of rock, moss, and the river winding its way through the big trees. You will cross the Middle Branch at 0.7 miles; on the other side look for a hiker icon indicating the blue-blazed trail and follow it. The icon will help you locate the trail, which gets lost here in tall grass.

At 0.75 miles, head right into the mowed section of an open field. You'll gradually head uphill following the tree line as you walk along the mowed path. When I hiked here, I was lucky to see a beautiful red fox prancing up the path ahead of me. As usual in open spaces, hawks wheel above as they look for prey.

When the trail splits at 1 mile, go straight to extend the hike; a few private homes will shatter the isolation for a while, but as you continue on the trail you'll soon regain the feeling of seclusion. Go past a cut off path to the left, and keep going straight; turn left at the mowed path at 1.2 miles and another left 200 feet later. In autumn, you will smell a fantastic sweet, earthy aroma from decaying leaves, tree trunks, and moss that haven't been disturbed for years.

The trail splits again at 1.3 miles; go left. Suddenly, the wide, open trail becomes very narrow and crowded with woods. As you parallel a stream on the right, you'll begin to see numbered wooden posts again. If you have the wildlife loop trail brochure, you may find the numbers a bit misleading since they don't correspond to the map; that's because you aren't on the wildlife loop trail yet—but you will be soon. As you hike a big curve up the hill and wind through mature upland forest, you'll begin to climb above the trail you were on earlier but now in the opposite direction. The trail peaks on a narrow ridge with water below on both sides; at 1.8 miles you will be back on the trail you hiked coming in earlier. This time head right; the trail will take you past the private houses and the field before it begins running parallel to the river, this time on your right. At 2.25 miles, go left—be on the lookout for this turn because it's very easy to miss. (If you do miss it, you'll parallel the river for another quarter-mile before the trail ends, and then you'll have to turn around and come back). Once you've turned left you will backtrack before you rejoin the wildlife loop at 2.7 miles.

Once you're on the wildlife loop, the numbered wooden posts that correspond to the trail brochure come in quick succession. Wooden post #3 sits in a cluster of Virginia pines, which are being crowded out by deciduous, canopy trees. Soon after you'll come to a deer enclosure marked with wooden post #4. At just under 3 miles, wooden post #5 points out the varieties of grapevines in the area: fox, summer, and riverbank. Wooden post #6 sits on one of the highest points in the Middle Patuxent Environmental Area, more than 400 feet; the floodplain below sits at about 275 feet. When you come to the T intersection, head right to continue on the main section of the wildlife loop.

You will see wooden post #7 in a mature upland forest dominated by oak, hickory, and tulip polar. Next you will come to a cluster of spicebush, at 3.3 miles; the bush provides food for a variety of songbirds including wood thrushes and veeries. Immediately after you will see several cuts along the hills—these are drainage areas that indirectly carry runoff water to Chesapeake Bay. The topography changes by the time you reach wooden post #10 in the floodplain. Correspondingly, the flora changes as well, and you'll see more skunk cabbages, cardinal flowers, monkey flowers, mad-dog skullcaps, green dragons, buttonbushes, and American sycamores.

At 3.5 miles, you'll see a small tributary that forms an oxbow (probably once part of the Middle Branch of the Patuxent River); after you cross it, you'll come to wooden post #15—marking dogwoods that are dead or dying due to fungal diseases. At just under 4 miles, you'll come to a concrete wading pool that has been converted into an amphibian habitat. Look to the right to see a bizarre sight: an old car of indistinguishable make; only the hulk of the body, impaled by the trees growing through it, and clearly discernible tail fins remain.

As you continue on the trail, you'll pass a clearing on the left, the home of the Middle Patuxent Environmental Area's outdoor classroom for Howard County students in grades K through 12. Just beyond, at 4.2 miles, you will rejoin the first part of the trail, with wooden post #1; go right and follow the trail back to the parking area.

▶ NEARBY ACTIVITIES

You might enjoy seeing Centennial Lake just 4 miles to the east on MD 108; take time to walk through the park's Centennial Arboretum, an immaculately maintained treasure trove of diverse tree species (see page 232). For good restaurants and shopping, head to the Columbia Town Center and Lake Kittamaqundi (see page 236); go east on MD 108 to MD 29 south and follow the signs to "Town Center."

PATAPSCO VALLEY STATE PARK:
HOLLOFIELD AREA WITH PICKALL AREA ADD-ON

▶ IN BRIEF

Take in one of Patapsco Valley State Park's most popular areas—and then combine it with one of its least visited areas.

▶ DESCRIPTION

The Hollofield Area, which is very popular, especially with families, has three main trails: Peaceful Pond, Ole Ranger, and Union Mill. These three trails combined with an impressive overlook and abundant facilities make it a fine place to spend the day; if you also want to rough it, add the Pickall Area hike; be aware that it requires crossing Patapsco River on the busy MD 40 bridge.

Peaceful Pond Trail begins as a narrow dirt path studded with anthills as it winds among pine, holly, tall grasses, and short stubby trees. When the trail splits at 500 feet, head left; you'll see a sign pointing to the pond. The trail splits again 100 feet later; go left again and you'll find a bench and observation deck. Although "peaceful pond" seems something of a misnomer with MD 40 nearby, it's still a nice spot and provides habitat for many frogs, snakes, turtles, and herons.

Moving away from the pond, head left and then back up the hill the way you came, but this time when the trail splits, go in the opposite direction. You will pass an area full of vines that looks like something out of *Flash Gordon*. At 0.3 miles, at the top of a steep hill, you'll see an odd-shaped oak tree with an appendage at the bottom

▶ DIRECTIONS

Take I-695 to Exit 14, MD 40 west toward Ellicott City. Go 2 miles, cross the Patapsco River, and turn right into the park. Take the first left toward the park headquarters and park your car. With the headquarters to your back, walk down the hill and to the left until you see the brown Peaceful Pond Trail sign and orange blazes.

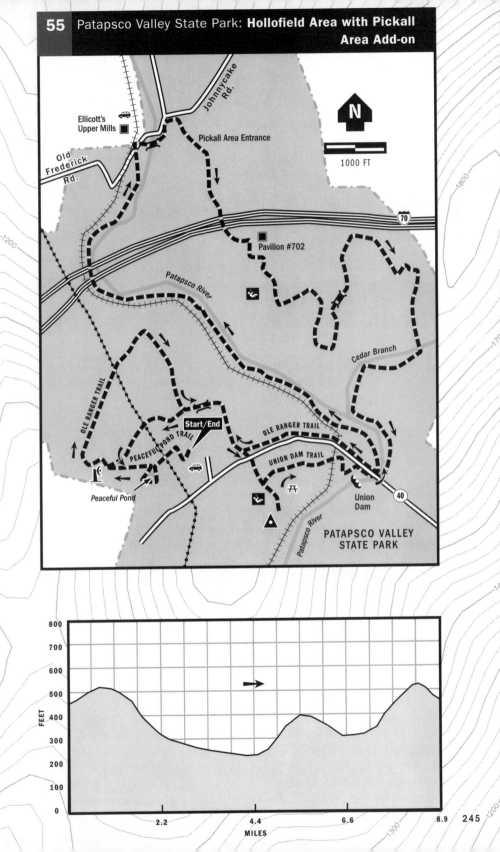

N

1000 FT

Ellicott's
Upper Mills

Pickall Area Entrance

Old
Frederick
Rd.

Johnnycake
Rd.

70

Pavilion #702

Patapsco River

Cedar Branch

OLE RANGER TRAIL

PEACEFUL POND TRAIL

Start/End

OLE RANGER TRAIL

UNION DAM TRAIL

Peaceful Pond

Union
Dam

40

Patapsco River

**PATAPSCO VALLEY
STATE PARK**

FEET

800
700
600
500
400
300
200
100
0

2.2   4.4   6.6   8.9

MILES

Remnants of Union Dam

that runs horizontal for about 6 feet to another mature tree; one of the connected trees bears an orange blaze (Peaceful Pond) and the other a light-blue blaze (Ole Ranger Trail).

Take the blue-blazed Ole Ranger Trail; it winds through tulip poplars, white pines, and multiflora roses. You'll soon come to an old radio transmission tower, where in the 1940s women employed by the Maryland Forest Service kept a lookout for fires. Just past the tower, the trail becomes a crushed-rock fire road. At 0.4 miles, the road splits—turn away from the trail to the left, which runs out to Church Lane Road, and take the one to the right and head deeper into the woods. You'll be walking on rutted, decaying asphalt over sloping, wooded hills rising above the Patapsco River gorge. Oak, hickory, and ash trees dominate here, with spicebush and witch hazel at eye level, providing perfect habitat for songbirds.

You will come to a power-line cut at 0.75 miles; pass the paved road that runs toward the transmission lines, and continue straight ahead on the packed-dirt Ole Ranger Trail. You will cross a little stream at 0.9 miles—notice the zigzag of the stream as it runs in a series of S-curves. The trail becomes rocky before it splits at 1.1 miles; for now, cross the footbridge—you'll head in the other direction on the return hike. After crossing the bridge, head toward the paved park road, and turn left under MD 40; continue straight, pass the tollgate, and head straight to the overlook, described by park literature as "arguably the most breathtaking [vista] in the park." Each season offers its own splendid view from this spot.

To access the final trail in this section, head left from the overlook and pass the tollgate and playgrounds on the left and picnic pavilions on the right. At the end of the paved road, you'll see the sign for the white-blazed Union Dam Trail, which immediately crosses a picnic area and goes downhill toward the river on a twisty, rock-strewn path. Notice the CSX rail line below heading into the hill you're hiking. You'll reach the dam (or what's left of it after numerous floods) at 2.3 miles. You will come back on the blue-blazed Ole Ranger Trail; if you are short on time you can head to your car, which is just up ahead on the paved road to the left. Head left when the trail splits, at 3.2 miles, and follow the sign reading "Tower .5 mile." Go left at the orange arrow pointing to the pond and backtrack to the park headquarters; you will reach it at 3.8 miles.

If you do want to hike the Pickall Area Add-on, head left from Union Dam and follow the trail along the river. You'll pass under the MD 40 bridge. Unlike the people you probably met along the trail in the Hollofield Area of the state park, in this section you're likely to share the path only with geese.

At 3.4 total miles (the miles you hiked in the Hollofield Area plus the distance you have hiked since leaving Union Dam), you'll come to the railroad tracks. You will see a path to the right alongside the tracks, but whenever possible, walk along the river on the sand and dirt bank instead; you will almost feel like you're on an abandoned tidewater beach. Whenever the trail runs directly into water or disappears in vegetation, just head back up to the tracks.

At 4.3 miles, you will pass under I-70, and at 4.9 miles you will come to a little gravel parking area beside the river. You will be standing on Old Fredrick Road and the site of Ellicott's Upper Mills (1775), where the Ellicott Family lived in Fountaindale, the family manor. Cross the steel bridge, which connects Howard and Baltimore counties. On the other side, head left for about 500 feet and then turn right onto Johnnycake Road. You will see the Pickall Area entrance on the right; this section of the state park is open to vehicle traffic only on weekends, 9 a.m. to sunset, from May to October. So if you're here at other times, you'll probably have it all to yourself.

As you head up the paved park road, you will see a little stream below you on the left. At 5.5 miles, you will cross I-70 and then pass a power-line cut before swinging up to the left. When you get to the parking area on the right and pavilion #702, take a right and pick up the footpath in the woods to the right. The footpath arcs around the picnic and playground areas, winding through a forest of oaks, pines, poplars, and dogwoods. A footbridge at 6.1 miles gives way to a mowed section of field rising between the woods. You will approach I-70 again at 6.6 miles, but before you reach the interstate, take a right at the power-line cut. In about 500 feet, you'll reach the park boundary; turn onto the very narrow foot trail and head right back into the woods. The white-tailed deer that populate this area feast on backyard gardens at night.

At 6.8 miles, the trail heads left toward houses; go right instead onto the barely discernible trail. Make your way straight toward the crest of the hill and then head down toward Cedar Branch. The trail sort of disappears here, but the going is easy. Cross Cedar Branch and you'll come to a wide fire road that runs parallel to the water; you'll see a few sporadic blue blazes as you walk to the right. The fire road eventually narrows to a foot trail. At 7.7 miles, Cedar Branch empties into the Patapsco River; at this point, take a left and head downstream.

You will be on a narrow and lightly used trail that courses over rocks and fallen trees. When you see the MD 40 bridge, climb the hill and cross the bridge. Follow the road you drove on when you entered the park; admittedly, it isn't very pleasant, but the shoulder is wide. Across the bridge, go back down the hill and pick up Union Dam Trail; follow the directions above to return to the blue-blazed Ole Ranger Trail.

PATAPSCO VALLEY STATE PARK: ORANGE GROVE–AVALON AREAS

ⓘ **KEY AT-A-GLANCE INFORMATION**

LENGTH: 5.3 miles

CONFIGURATION: Loop

DIFFICULTY: Moderate

SCENERY: Cascade Falls, historic ruins, abundant wildlife, mature forest

EXPOSURE: Shade

TRAFFIC: Light

TRAIL SURFACE: Packed dirt

HIKING TIME: 2 hours

ACCESS: 10 a.m. to sunset daily

MAPS: USGS Relay; you can purchase an excellent map of the entire Patapsco Valley State Park trail system at the park headquarters or online from the Maryland Department of Natural Resources online at **www.trailmapsetc.com** or **www.dnr.maryland.gov.**

FACILITIES: Restrooms and water at the trailhead

SPECIAL COMMENTS: The state park charges a $2 per day use fee, which is usually collected by the honor system; place the money in an envelope at the tollgate.

Patapsco Valley State Park:
Orange Grove–Avalon Areas

UTM Zone (WGS84)   18S

Easting   348989

Northing   4344967

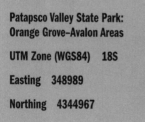

▶ IN BRIEF

See waterfalls, rivers, streams, upland forest, historic structures, and entire herds of deer in one of the more diverse hikes in Patapsco Valley State Park. This hike begins in the Orange Grove Area and takes in the Avalon Area before returning to the Orange Grove Area.

▶ DESCRIPTION

The 300-foot suspension Swinging Bridge provides one of the few places for easy access across Patapsco River. You can cross it to go to the paved Grist Mill Trail and the Hilton Area of the state park, but if you want to hike in the Orange Grove Area, turn around and head up the hill on the stone steps to the blue-blazed Cascade Falls Trail. It winds uphill, taking in a little switchback, before quickly coming to Cascade Falls, at 0.3 miles. Ferns, mossy rocks, and oak surround a narrow ridge where the falls spill over; the trail becomes a series of rocks that lead across the falls and give you an unobstructed, obviously fantastic view. It's a superb way to start your hike.

On the other side of the falls, you'll see the orange-blazed Ridge Trail on the left; you will take

▶ DIRECTIONS

Take I-95 to Exit 47 (BWI Airport), and travel east on I-195 to Exit 3 heading toward Elkridge. Turn right on US 1 heading south, and then take the next right onto South Street; you will see the park entrance immediately on the left. Follow the park road past the "Welcome to Orange Grove Scenic Area" signs and turn left onto Gun Road followed by an immediate right onto River Road. Continue to the parking area on the left across from the Swinging Bridge over Patapsco River; you will find restrooms here. The trail starts at the "Cascade Falls Trail" sign up the hill from the parking area.

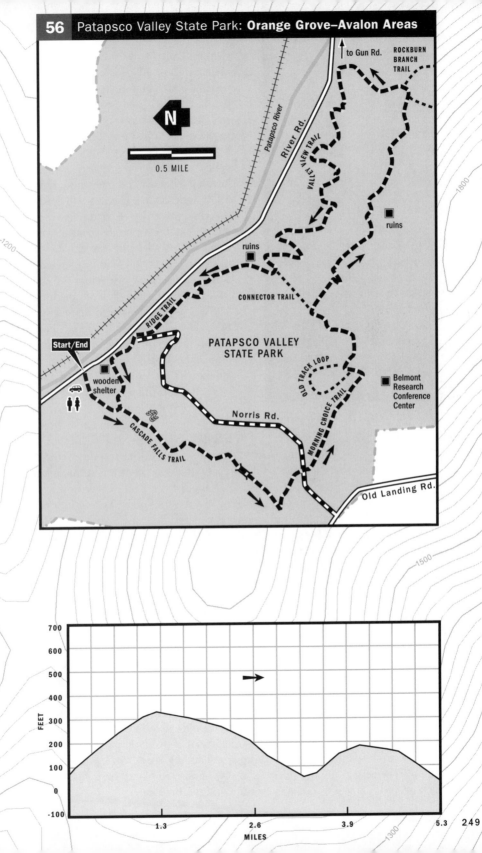

Swinging bridge

that trail on the way back, so head right instead. The trail becomes very rocky as it winds through mature beech, oak, dogwood, maple, redbud, and sassafras trees; you'll see and hear the stream that feeds the falls to the right. At just over 0.25 miles, you will cross the water again. Soon after, the trail splits; you can go either way, but I suggest heading left since the trail to the right forms a loop and after 0.8 miles will lead you to the same place you're heading now by going left. Cross the water once again and continue to parallel the stream by heading upstream. You will come to a creekbed and small footbridge at just under 0.5 miles followed by a little gully full of moss and ferns. You will see a few eastern hemlocks visible; look for plant species more commonly found in mountains, including erect trillium, false hellebore, and wild sarsaparilla, among the underbrush. Lots of rocks and fallen trees in the water to create pools and small rapids that produce a pleasant babble. Cross the water again, this time on a wooden footbridge and again, on another wooden footbridge, soon after (just before you come to the second footbridge you will see the spot where the other side of that initial loop connects to the main trail).

At 0.75 miles, the trail levels out and quiets down a bit. You're now away from water, walking among beech and oak trees in a mature forest. When the trail splits, go left up the hill heading toward the yellow-blazed Morning Choice Trail (if you go straight, you would be hiking much closer to the park boundary and public roads). In the middle of the hill, the trail splits again—stay on the Morning Choice Trail on the left; you will head uphill where you will see more vines and smaller trees. Lots of birds will be flitting around the tall, thin oaks and poplars; during spring and fall migrations, you might see bluebirds, scarlet tanagers, and Baltimore orioles. At 0.9 miles, you will cross Norris Road, a gravel park road. When you come to a T intersection, take a left into a natural drainage area; it's usually muddy here, but boards placed at the lowest points in the trail will help keep your boots dry.

After walking through a small stand of holly, you will come to the red-blazed Old Track Loop Trail, at 1.1 miles. For a short section the red- and yellow-blazed trails run together. On the right you will see a huge cluster of bamboo that measures about 25 feet high and 75 feet across. When the trail splits, head left on the red-blazed path. You can take the yellow-blazed path, which eventually leads to a nice stream crossing where wood thrushes congregate, but it's impassable in all but the lowest water levels; the trail ends abruptly at Landing Road, where you'll have to turn around. The better option, I think, is to stay on the red-blazed trail; you'll soon hook back up with the yellow one so you can continue the loop.

On the red-blazed trail, you'll soon come to an open field to the right through the woods; you will see Belmont Research Conference Center up the hill. Stay within the woods for a while longer, passing evergreens and oaks covered in ivy—a nice spot of green in winter. At 1.6 miles, rejoin the yellow-blazed trail. Take a left up the hill; at the top you'll see an orange-blazed trail, which is a connector trail to the yellow-blazed one. You can take this if you're short on time, but to extend the hike and make a bigger (and very pleasant) loop, take a right and stay on the yellow-blazed trail heading toward the Avalon Area of Patapsco Valley State Park.

The path becomes a cut groove along the tree line of the field before winding back through the woods at 1.9 miles; you will pass the ruins of old houses on the left. Both houses have paths running to them, but it's not safe to poke around inside. Once past the house ruins, you will come back to the field again, where you'll follow the tree line. Look across the field for deer; I've never seen fewer than two dozen in this area, and the last time I hiked here, I saw no less than 50 of them. As a bonus, you will see loads of jays, cardinals, blackbirds, and cedar waxwings flitting about the mountain laurel and holly on the edge of the field.

At 2.4 miles, you will come to the purple-blazed Rockburn Branch Trail; if you take a left you will return to the orange-blazed Ridge Trail. If you take Rockburn Branch Trail, you will make a 1.2-mile loop that runs along Rockburn Branch for approximately 0.3 miles and through forest. This loop, added to the rest of the hike described here, will increase your total mileage to 6.4 miles.

In either case, you have the options in this area of taking the Rockburn Branch, Valley View, or the southern sections of both the Morning Choice and Ridge trails, all in the Avalon Area of the state park. I suggest going left for 100 yards on the purple-blazed Rockburn Branch Trail and then going straight down the hill on the orange-blazed Ridge Trail toward Valley View Trail, which parallels the much higher Ridge Trail before the two eventually link (taking Valley View Trail provides more diversity). At the bottom of the hill, you will come to a wide gravel path; head left and cross a stream. Then walk left toward a wooden stone shelter, where you'll see a sign pointing to the white-blazed Valley View Trail straight ahead; on the right you will see the orange-blazed Ridge Trail and a footbridge.

Valley View Trail begins as a narrow ridgeline in the middle of the hill following the valley (thus the trail's name) amid a plenitude of evergreens. Initially you'll parallel River Road, which doesn't provide the best scenery but does allow good views of the valley and Patapsco River beyond. The trail soon rises away from the road and very quickly climbs the hill; in winter you can see across the entire valley from this spot. Valley View Trail provides a good sense of the topography—hills rising and falling all around, with the piedmont river valley below. You won't want for grand, sweeping views along this trail.

At 3.2 miles, take a right at the T intersection, and you'll be back on the orange-blazed Ridge Trail, which winds along a series of drainage cuts. You've lost your valley views, but you'll gain a level area in mature upland forest, with abundant groves of mountain laurel. Head downhill and at 3.5 miles, pass the connector to the yellow-blazed Morning Choice Trail you hiked earlier. You will still see lots of mountain laurel and now also an abundance of beech trees. The ruins of a series of stone houses, some with collapsed wooden roofs still visible, mark the trail after 3.8 miles. At

4 miles, you will cross a little stream running over beautiful pink-hued, striated rocks; you will see a wooden shelter ahead. At 4.4 miles, you will see a cut that leads down to River Road; turn the other direction and head uphill to the left. You will soon hear Cascade Falls and, at 4.8 miles, you'll reach the cut to the right that leads to the falls. When you reach the falls, cross the water, and head back to your car.

▶ NEARBY ACTIVITIES

Satisfy your thirst for history by driving (or walking) on River Road through the developed part of the Avalon Area of Patapsco Valley State Park. All that remains of Avalon, a thriving mill town until wiped out by a massive flood in 1868, is one stone building that now houses the visitor center, which features exhibits about 300 years of history in the Patapsco Valley. You will find the 704-foot-long Thomas Viaduct about 1.5 miles south of the Swinging Bridge; completed in 1835, the viaduct ranks as the world's largest multiple-arched stone railroad bridge. Less than a mile north of the Swinging Bridge on River Road, you will come to Bloede's Dam, which contains the world's first submerged electrical generating plant.

PATAPSCO VALLEY STATE PARK:
UNMAINTAINED AREA–GRANITE–WOODSTOCK

Make a loop in a section of Patapsco Valley State Park on trails that take you over tough, but rewarding, terrain.

▶ **DESCRIPTION**

Many developed areas inside Patapsco Valley State Park provide amenities for family outings, camping, and picnics, but the state park also offers huge tracts where you're on your own. Since the area for this hike runs through unmaintained areas of the state park, it promises solitude and a vigorous walk. Be aware that you will come to places where the trail seems to disappear, but I assure you that you can get through the entire hike described below.

From the trailhead, follow the path down a steep ridge to the river, where you'll probably scatter mallards and wood ducks; head left and walk upstream. The trail, which initially is difficult to discern, becomes clearer as you walk along the river. The path, which is actually a horse trail, winds along the water's edge; it's very rocky, so

▶ **DIRECTIONS**

Take I-695 to Exit 18, Liberty Road west toward Randallstown. Go 1.9 miles and turn left onto Old Court Road. Go 5.7 miles, pass through historic Granite, past the Maryland Job Corps, and cross Patapsco River. As soon as you cross the river and the railroad tracks, park on the right in the gravel parking area (be careful not to park in front of the wooden hitching posts—these are for horses). You can also take I-695 to Exit 22, Greenspring Avenue south; take the first right onto Old Court Road and go 12 miles to the parking area above. The trail starts behind you over the tracks and to the left down the hill.

ⓘ KEY AT-A-GLANCE INFORMATION

LENGTH: 7 miles

CONFIGURATION: Loop with an added out-and-back depending on water level

DIFFICULTY: Moderate to strenuous

SCENERY: Patapsco River, wildlife, railroad accoutrements

EXPOSURE: Mostly shade

TRAFFIC: Light

TRAIL SURFACE: Packed dirt, potential railroad track in added out-and-back

HIKING TIME: 2.5–3 hours

ACCESS: Dawn to dusk daily

MAPS: USGS Ellicott City, Sykesville; you can purchase an excellent map of the entire Patapsco Valley State Park trail system at the park headquarters or from the Maryland Department of Natural Resources online at www.trailmapsetc.com or www.dnr.maryland.gov.

SPECIAL COMMENTS: This is an unnamed, unmaintained section of Patapsco Valley State Park; I call it Granite–Woodstock above due to its location between those two towns. Beware that this hike involves a river crossing (with an alternate path if crossing isn't feasible) and a potentially frightening railroad bridge crossing if water levels are high.

Patapsco Valley State Park: Unmaintained Area–Granite–Woodstock

UTM Zone (WGS84)   18S

Easting   338720

Northing   4355244

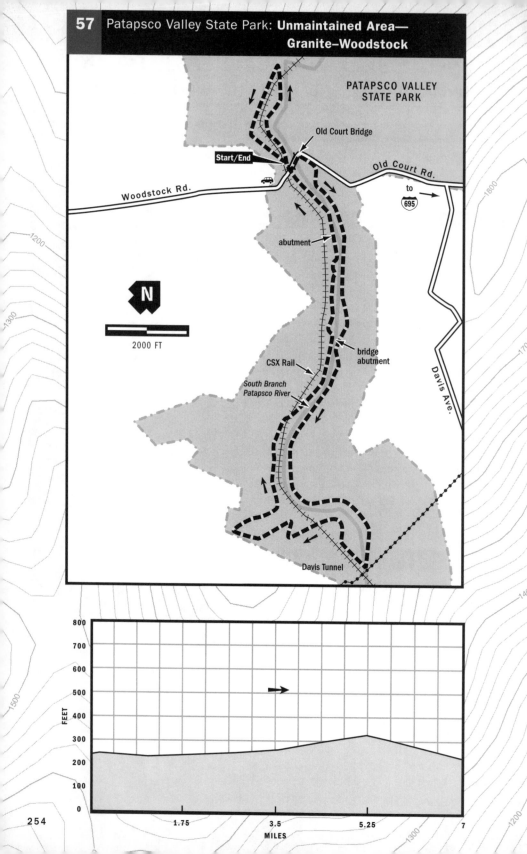

PATAPSCO VALLEY
STATE PARK

Old Court Bridge

Old Court Rd.

Start/End

Woodstock Rd.

to
695

abutment

N

2000 FT

bridge
abutment

CSX Rail

South Branch
Patapsco River

Davis Ave.

Davis Tunnel

FEET

800
700
600
500
400
300
200
100
0

1.75   3.5   5.25   7
MILES

unless you too are wearing horseshoes, be extra careful. You'll have to climb over the large trees that have fallen across the path.

You will come to an oxbow tributary at 0.25 miles; it's only about 6 inches in depth, but it's about 20 feet across, and there are no rocks to use as stepping-stones. If you want to keep your boots dry, head up to the left and circle around until you find a better place to cross. On the other side of the oxbow, you'll be able to see the trail more clearly as a narrow groove in the grass. Horses cross the Patapsco River and you can do the same (if the weather is warm and you take your shoes off) at 0.5 miles; the river is fairly shallow here and only about 100 feet across with a sand-and-rock bank that cuts into the water. After you cross the river, follow the obvious trail on the other side back toward the bridge on Old Court Road.

I hiked here in winter and didn't want wet feet, so instead of crossing the river, I climbed the hill and walked along the railroad tracks back toward the trailhead. Whichever route you choose, you'll reach Old Court Road at about 1 mile. The Old Court Road bridge has a wide shoulder, and you will have no trouble picking up the obvious trail on the Baltimore County side. You will have a pleasant and easy stroll through primarily beech and oak trees with briars lining the path. Generally speaking, the equestrian traffic usually makes the trail fairly muddy in places, and you'll probably see lots of deer prints in the mud as well as a few deer scampering about.

At just under 2 miles, the trail swings away from the river a bit, and you will cross an old abutment. If you look across the river to the Howard County side, you'll see corresponding abutments leftover from the old bridge destroyed by a flood. The trail splits here; keep going straight instead of taking the path to the left, which is a half-mile spur that dead-ends at Davis Avenue. You will cross over a little brook in this section, which is marked by low growth plants, mostly grapevines and mountain laurel. At 2.25 miles, look for a huge gash in the ground, almost like a sinkhole. A trickle of water pours into it from the hillside, creating a beautiful mini-waterfall that's maybe 8 feet in height.

Soon after, you will come to huge rock outcroppings; enormous oak and walnut trees, covered in poison sumac, dominate the left side of the trail here, and the river runs alongside you on the right. When you see an island in the river, the trail will head uphill. At 2.8 miles, you will come to a grove of tulip poplars with gnaw marks at their bases, evidence of beaver activity; look in the river here and you're bound to see beaver dams as well. A number of fallen trees cover the path here, and as a result, the horse trails veer to the left onto higher ground; I recommend staying on the path along the river—it makes for more difficult hiking involving climbing and weaving around rocks and trees, but it's quite wild and strenuous and invigorating.

Every now and then when you think you might have lost the trail, it reappears as an obvious alleyway weaving between the trees. After 3 miles, you'll walk along a narrow ridge that falls off about 10 feet to the right with a wall of jagged rock on the left; you'll have nice views of the river here. Loads of grapevine, ivy, and briars dot the hillside as you make your way toward the pine forest on top of the hill. At 3.4 miles, the river curves around to the right, and you'll see a bridge in the distance— keep heading toward it. If the path gets too rough, you can always backtrack a bit and take one of the three or four cuts to the path that will eventually loop back toward the bridge (if you take one of the paths to the left, head back to the right toward the

Patapsco River south of Davis
Tunnel

river when you come to a power-line cut so you don't go past the bridge). Staying
along the river requires some scrambling over rocks, gaining and falling in elevation
as you cross drainage areas and gullies, but it's a great way to go. If the sun is out and
hitting at the right angle, your view will be pleasantly obstructed temporarily by the
reflection of mica chips on the rocks as you climb upward.

You will come to a grove of holly; take care to avoid getting caught on the many
briars and prickers along the way. You'll reach a few rock promontories that provide
great views, making it well worth the strenuous climb. The path comes back down to
level land toward the bridge. Over the years the bridge supports have blocked sedi-
ment and rock, making the river crossing easier; in fact, it might be quite easy
depending on conditions. I recommend crossing the river by foot in all but the most
difficult conditions because crossing the railroad bridge above the river can be
scary—it certainly isn't for children or anyone afraid of heights. Big gaps in the railroad ties make it a bit forbidding, and trains still run on the tracks, albeit infrequently. You'll certainly hear one coming in plenty of time to either get across safely
or wait until the train has passed.

Standing on the bridge tracks, you can see Dorsey Tunnel almost a mile in the
distance behind you and Davis Tunnel a few hundred feet ahead; you'll be heading
toward Davis Tunnel. Once you're on the other side of the bridge, look down the hill
to the right for a stream culvert that remains from the old railroad bed used by the
famous *Tom Thumb*, the steam-powered engine that raced a horse and came up short
due to a slipped belt. Walk toward Davis Tunnel and head to the right; you'll walk up
the hill on deer trails, which look like lanes through the trees. Many layers of earth
and forest sit atop the train tunnel now, and you'll see a prominent path made by
mountain bikes and hiking boots rather than deer. When you reach the top of the
hill, the river will be a few hundred feet below on the right; every now and then the
trail opens up, giving you opportunities to see the whole valley. The trail splits several times at about 4 miles; every time it splits, take the paths (many of them single-

track paths made by mountain bikes) to the right to stay close to the river. You will walk over a carpet of moss and also see some climbing up the trunks of beech and oak; azaleas also grow along this section of the trail. You'll go gradually downhill toward a little brook; cross the brook and head again toward the river. At 4.5 miles, you will cross Davis Branch. As you continue on the path, stay as close to the river as possible—often this means simply staying in sight of it.

At 4.7 miles, you'll see a ridge to the right; when you see it, head toward the railroad tracks. When you reach the T intersection, take a left at the rock escarpment; at first you'll walk in the buffer of woods alongside the tracks, but soon you emerge at the tracks, and the wooded path ends. When I reached this point, I was a bit bummed to be out of the woods, but the sight of a bald eagle following the river downstream, a victim of its hunting prowess hanging from its talons, tempered my disappointment. You can also see hawks and turkey vultures in this open area, and Canada geese, green herons, and kingfishers populate the area year-round.

As you walk along the tracks, you will see lots of lamb's ear and skunk cabbage. At 4.8 miles, the pathway suddenly gets very narrow against the tracks, so cross over and go down the hill where you'll see a groove along the river—this is the continuation of the trail. Few people use this path though, and you may lose it occasionally, but the wide wooded area helps make the way easy; a few gullies and brooks pose potential snags, but you will probably be able to cross them in one big jump or by using a decent sized rock or two for stepping-stones.

At 5.3 miles, the trail widens and becomes easy to follow; from here you'll be able to see the trail you walked on the other side of the river. The sweet gum trees in this area give off an enticing aroma, and you will see lots of squirrel, deer, raccoon, beaver, opossum, and fox tracks in the muddy riverbank. After another quarter-mile, the trail gets rough and passage becomes difficult as the hill drops to the river's edge; if the trail becomes impassable, just go back up the hill, walk along the tracks until you see the trail reemerge below, and then walk back down the hill to join it. The best place to climb back up to the tracks is right after the stone abutment of an old bridge; go back down to the river at the #21 sign on the tracks. At 6.2 miles, the trail gets lost in jumble of fallen trees, but make your way best you can, keeping the river close by, and the trail will soon reemerge. Once back down along the river, look for a section of trees that have been felled, indicating another beaver area; when I hiked here, I scared one of the poor unsuspecting creatures—he ran into the river, swam to the other side, and regarded me from a safe distance.

At 6.6 miles, you can begin to see the Old Court Bridge when the river bends to the left. This time, don't climb the hill; instead keep under the bridge, and you will reach the trailhead up ahead on the left at 7 miles.

▶ NEARBY ACTIVITIES

If you prefer maintained trails, pavilions, ball fields, and picnic areas, as well as facilities, head a short distance north to the McKeldin Area of Patapsco Valley State Park. Take Woodstock Road west until it ends at Old Frederick; take the first right onto Marriottsville Road, and continue until you reach the entrance to the McKeldin Area.

PATUXENT BRANCH TRAIL

KEY AT-A-GLANCE INFORMATION

LENGTH: 10.4 miles

CONFIGURATION: Out-and-back with an added lake loop

DIFFICULTY: Moderate due to length

SCENERY: Patuxent River, Lake Elkhorn, historic bridge

EXPOSURE: More shade than sun

TRAFFIC: Moderate on trail; heavy at lake

TRAIL SURFACE: Asphalt, packed dirt, crushed rock

HIKING TIME: 3–3.5 hours

ACCESS: Dawn to dusk daily; Lake Elkhorn open 6 a.m.–10 p.m. daily

MAPS: USGS Savage; trail maps available at the parking areas along the route

FACILITIES: Restrooms and water at Lake Elkhorn and Savage Park

SPECIAL COMMENTS: You can shorten your hike by parking at any of the three areas along the route, and you can make the hike one way by setting up shuttles at Savage Park and Lake Elkhorn.

Patuxent Branch Trail

UTM Zone (WGS84) 18S

Easting 341887

Northing 4334106

IN BRIEF

Hike a scenic forested river valley along the Patuxent River through a portion of an old B&O rail bed from Savage Park in Savage north to Lake Elkhorn in Columbia.

DESCRIPTION

Inaugurated by a ribbon-cutting ceremony on November 2, 2002, Patuxent Branch Trail connects many sections of Columbia's extensive pathway network. From the asphalt trailhead, you will go immediately into a stand of mature trees—mostly oaks and tulip poplars. Be on the lookout for white-tailed deer, which congregate in this area. At 250 feet, the trail splits; follow the sign pointing to the right that give the mileage to Vollmerhausen Road, the Pratt Railroad Bridge, and Lake Elkhorn.

At 0.2 miles, you will cross over a wooden bridge marked "B1." You will see the Panther Branch of the Patuxent on the left and lots of beautiful beech trees in this section. After 0.5 miles, the trail opens up and runs behind Patuxent Middle School and Bollman Bridge Elementary. You'll reach Vollmerhausen Road at 0.7

DIRECTIONS

Take I-695 to Exit 11, I-95 south toward Washington, D.C. Take MD 32 east toward Fort Meade (Exit 38) and a quick exit onto MD 1 south toward Savage. Stay in the right lane and take an immediate right onto Howard Road, which soon turns into Baltimore Road. Follow Baltimore straight until you see Savage Mill Manor; then turn right into the park and go as far as you can to the left. The trail starts at that farthest left point at the edge of the parking lot across from the baseball and soccer fields; you'll see a map of the Patuxent Branch Trail on a bulletin board there.

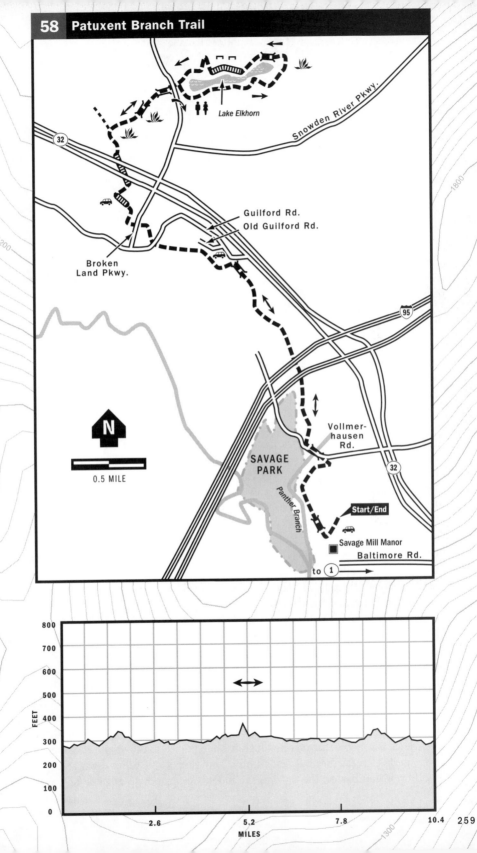

Patuxent River

miles; turn left and walk along the sidewalk. Admittedly, walking along the road isn't very nice, but you'll soon be back in the woods; cross Panther Branch on the bridge at just under 0.9 miles and take a right across Vollmerhausen Road. Go 200 feet to the left and then turn right at the trail map sign and head into the woods.

You'll no longer be on asphalt, but rather crushed rock and dirt. Patuxent River runs on the right as you walk upstream; mature walnut, sumac, sassafras, oak, and tulip poplar trees flank this section of the trail, which runs along the rail bed of the main line of the B&O railroad. The B&O, the nation's first passenger line, ran between Baltimore and Ellicott City beginning in 1830; this particular spur of the B&O's Washington Branch served the textile mills and quarries between Savage and Guilford until 1928.

This may not be the best hike for solitude, but it gives you the chance to marvel at the existence of a long stretch of thick woods running through a heavily populated suburban center. In addition, the scenery is often very lovely; for instance, you will see lots of ferns along the trail at 1 mile. On the downside, it's almost impossible not to hear cars along the route even though you will rarely ever see them; the traffic noise grows especially loud at 1.2 miles when you walk under the two I-95 bridges soaring several hundred feet above your head. This area also provides an interesting perspective for people on I-95; while they're driving along at more than 70 mph, they see a nice ribbon of thick woods stretching away from the interstate. On the trail under the interstate, you can see the river, the mature trees, and the occasional deer, all up close.

The woods grow especially thick along the trail away from the I-95 bridges. You will see lots of cut paths to the river; head down to the river to see for yourself why it was named "Patuxent," the Algonquian word for "rapids." The big rocks in the river create eddies and pools that make enough babbling noise to drown out the traffic above.

At 1.7 miles, the trail leads uphill and comes out to an open area, providing good opportunities on the right to see birds; from the high angle here you can look into the tops of the trees and see finches, cardinals, blue jays, red-winged blackbirds, and bluebirds flit around the branches.

At just before 1.9 miles, the trail splits at another mileage marker indicating 2 miles to Lake Elkhorn; follow the trail in that direction, and you'll soon come to and cross over the Pratt Through-Truss Railroad Bridge, built in 1901. The second parking area option for this hike is just beyond this bridge on the left. (To begin your hike here, from MD 32, turn south off Guilford Road onto Old Guilford Road and then turn left into the parking lot.)

You will follow Old Guilford Road, which is now closed to westward traffic, for a while before it reverts to a narrower asphalt path. This section of the trail will remind you that you're walking through suburban Columbia; every so often a building or house will pop into view, but just as often, thick stands of woods will crowd both sides of the trail. The result is a strange battle between the sounds of moving cars and birdcalls. You will cross a power-line cut at 2.4 miles and then walk under Guilford Road Bridge. Lots of deer live in this area; if you don't see any of them, you'll at least see thousands of their hoofprints in the mud along the trail. At 2.7 miles, you will pass under Broken Land Parkway as the trail winds through an area with a little creek. A 3,000-foot wooden boardwalk takes you across the boggy, marshy, very thickly wooded land. You will come to another wooden boardwalk at 2.9 miles; go straight here, following the sign to Lake Elkhorn, where a big stand of beech and tulip poplar decorate both sides of the trail.

Another wooden boardwalk at 3.1miles will take you across a marshy area and under MD 32. Despite the highway above, you will enjoy this spot, which if full of cattails and aquatic life; in addition, the white wildflowers here attract a multitude of butterflies. When the trail splits at 3.5 miles, head right toward the lake through thick woods and underbrush. Another wooden bridge carries you past a little creek bed on the right. You will come to a steel bridge at 3.8 miles, just before you reach the Broken Land Parkway underpass; Lake Elkhorn is on the other side. (To begin your hike here, take Broken Land Parkway south from MD 29 and turn left onto Cradlerock Way and then turn right onto Dockside Lane).

The man-made 37-acre Lake Elkhorn, created in 1974, averages only 8 feet in depth, but its watershed stretches some 2,500 acres. Since the lake trail is a loop, you can head in either direction; to follow the mileage in the hike described here, go to the right. One of the first things you'll see is a warning sign about the northern copperhead snake; the sign tells of two dogs that died after being bitten. Generally speaking, the chances of being bitten by a northern copperhead are slim to none, but take proper caution; if you see a snake and it has an hour glassed-shaped head, give it a wide berth.

At 4.2 miles, you will see a pavilion, which has restrooms, on the right. A fishing pier juts into the lake, which is stocked each spring with trout and bass. Waterfowl that live on and around the lake include trumpeter and mute swans, Canada geese, white Chinese geese, mallards, and great blue herons. As you continue around the lake, you'll see many path offshoots; these head into the residential areas surrounding the lake. Sometimes these houses sit right next to the lake; other times you will barely be able to see them through the thick buffer of red oak, tulip poplar, and maple trees.

You'll reach the farthest edge of the lake at 4.8 miles. You will cross a small footbridge here on the right at the lake's edge, and you will see lots of lily pads and other aquatic plants. Generally speaking, the majority of the waterfowl live at this end of the lake. Houses get closer to the trail here, but so does the lake itself; in a few places the trail has only 5 feet of open space on either side. At 5.4 miles, the trail turns to a wooden waterfront promenade; a platform with benches makes this a convenient place to sit. You will see lots of reeds and rushes on the left, a favorite haunt for red-winged blackbirds. You will come to Lake Elkhorn Dam at 5.7 miles and the lake's entry point from the Patuxent Branch Trail at 6.3 miles, completing your hike.

▶ **NEARBY ACTIVITIES**

Savage Park, the hike's starting point, includes historic Savage Mill, a 19th-century textile mill that has been restored and adapted for use as an arts and crafts retail center. Antiques shops, home furnishings stores, craft galleries, artist studios, specialty shops, restaurants, and an authentic French bakery fill its more than 175,000 square feet. For more information, visit **www.savagemill.com** or call (800) 788-6455.

ROCKBURN BRANCH PARK

A 450-acre park overshadowed by the monstrous nearby Patapsco Valley State Park, Rockburn Branch Park provides a wonderful place to spend the day with friends and family.

▶ DESCRIPTION

Due to its proximity to adjacent Patapsco Valley State Park, Rockburn Branch Park often gets overlooked as a hiking destination, but lots of people take advantage of its lack of entrance fee and many amenities. The variety of available activities makes Rockburn an attractive place to pass the day. Children can spend hours on the playground, toss balls around the fields, and also easily handle the hike described here. Folks who like disc golf will enjoy the course at Rockburn, which ranks as one of the finest in the area. My friend Doug and I hiked and then finished our day with a round on the course; the only casualty of the day was Doug's Blue Crush driver disc, which was swallowed up by a towering pine tree.

From the parking area, you'll see two paths—one asphalt and the other brick and crushed rock. Take the brick and crushed rock trail; you'll immediately pass the Clover Hill House on the right. The house, built in the late 18th century and added on to in the 19th century, is now falling into disrepair. Immediately beyond the house, you will see the burned-out

▶ DIRECTIONS

Take I-695 to I-95 south; take Exit 47, I-195 east to Exit 3, Washington Boulevard toward Elkridge. Pass the signs for Patapsco Valley State Park, and turn right onto Montgomery Road and then right at Rockburn Elementary School. After you pass a soccer field on the right, turn left into the parking area. The trail starts just beyond the bulletin board in front of the Clover Hill House.

ⓘ KEY AT-A-GLANCE INFORMATION

LENGTH: 3 miles

CONFIGURATION: Jagged, intersecting loop

DIFFICULTY: Easy

SCENERY: Rockburn Branch, mixed hardwoods, historic structures

EXPOSURE: Mostly shade

TRAFFIC: Light to moderate

TRAIL SURFACE: Packed dirt, asphalt, crushed rock

HIKING TIME: 1 hour

ACCESS: 7 a.m. to dusk daily or as posted

MAPS: USGS Savage; you can download a trail map at **www.co.ho.md.us/RAP/ RAPDocs/RBPTrails.pdf.**

FACILITIES: Restrooms and water at the parking area off Landing Road, pavilions, ball fields, playgrounds, and disc golf course

SPECIAL COMMENTS: The directions below are to the park's south entrance. To enter the north area of the park, stay on Montgomery Road and turn right onto Ilchester Road and then another right onto Landing Road; the park entrance will be on your right. For general information, call (410) 313-4700.

Rockburn Branch Park

UTM Zone (WGS84)   18S

Easting   348074

Northing   4342459

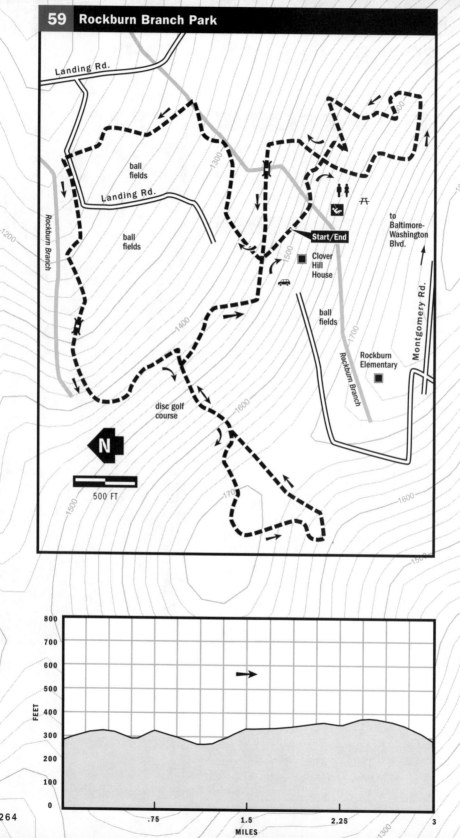

Landing Rd.

ball fields

Landing Rd.

ball fields

Rockburn Branch

Start/End

Clover Hill House

to Baltimore-Washington Blvd.

ball fields

Montgomery Rd.

Rockburn Branch

Rockburn Elementary

disc golf course

N

500 FT

remains of Phelps Log Cabin, which is surrounded by a chain-link fence. Historians believe the cabin was built by settlers at the end of the 17th century and later became slave quarters. The historical significance of both Phelps Log Cabin and the Clover Hill House, saved them from being razed, and they were moved to Rockburn Branch Park; sadly, a fire in September 2001 halted reconstruction efforts on the cabin. These historic structures help preserve pieces of recent history, while Indian artifacts, discovered during the park's construction, help preserve pieces of long-ago times.

About 800 feet from the trailhead, the trail heads right; instead of following it, head straight toward the playground and tennis courts. You'll pass picnic tables, a basketball court, and portable bathrooms on the right. At 0.3 miles, you'll come to another parking area, with a pavilion as well as portable bathrooms. Cross this parking area and pick up the asphalt trail on the other side; now the "hike" begins. When you see the "Authorized Vehicles Only" sign straight ahead, turn right onto the dirt path and enter the woods; you'll see yellow blazes on the trees. Tall oaks and plenty of underbrush flank the pebble and packed-dirt trail, which zigzags as it goes up and down hills.

At just under 0.5 miles, ignore the yellow blazes to the left and keep going straight. You will pass a boggy stretch on the left, where you can spot bluebirds. Just beyond this point the trail cuts to both the right and left; pass the cut off paths and continue going straight. Yellow blazes will reappear on the many beech trees that populate this area. Unfortunately, you'll soon reach the park boundary, and some private homes appear on the right in an opened area with lots of felled trees, but the surroundings become more pristine as you cross a footbridge and head uphill to the right. At 0.7 miles, you will come to a beech tree marking the place where the trail seems to intersect with itself. Keep going to the right here; you'll make a loop and reemerge at this point.

The trail heads gradually uphill over exposed roots and opens up at just under 0.9 miles into a field surrounded by trees. Go halfway around the clearing on the mowed path that hugs the tree line and pick up the trail on the other side. You'll once again see yellow blazes on beech trees. Turn around at the wooden sign at 1.1 miles and loop back so that you're facing a little red hiker icon on a post to your right; follow the path as it switchbacks through the woods, returning to the beginning of the loop you saw earlier, at 1.2 miles.

You'll soon come to a clearing marked off with wooden posts and steel cables; look for the white-tailed deer that congregate here. You will reach another footbridge as the path travels up to the left through lots of brush, mostly briars and sassafras. When you see a parking area on the right at 1.4 miles, head left to stay on the trail. You will come to another trail split soon; head right and then take an immediate right through a stand of very tall, thin oaks. You will emerge onto a cul-de-sac, and you'll see ball fields on the left. Walk straight ahead and then turn right onto the asphalt path, keeping the ball fields on your left.

At 1.7 miles, you'll see a "trail" sign in the woods on the right, but pass it; this trail takes you back to the section of trail you've already walked. Instead, stay on the asphalt path, and you'll soon be back in the woods following the Rockburn Branch of the Patapsco River. During summer months, you won't be able to see the water immediately, but it's on your right through the woods. At 1.9 miles, the trail heads to the right on mowed grass, leaving the ball fields on the left. You will cut through a stand of pines and cross the paved road (this is the park entrance from Landing Road). Head to the left, away from the maintenance building on the right; you will see some private houses through the woods on the right as the trail winds uphill through hanging grapevines.

At 2.2 miles, Rockburn Branch becomes more prominent, and you take another wooden footbridge across it. The shallow water here makes it easy to spot frogs, toads, tadpoles, newts, crayfish, and minnows. Now you're passing through a lovely little stream valley, indicative of the area's location between the Piedmont plateau and the coastal plain.

At 2.4 miles, you will come to a power-line cut buffeted by very tall mature oaks; before you follow the cut, look for circling hawks above the bordering trees. At 2.6 miles, you'll see the pavilion and portable bathrooms you passed earlier. Go to the right on the paved path; at the playground, which is now on the left, take a right where the trail branches at a disc golf bucket. Continue until you connect with the paved trail, and then head left; you will find the parking area is just up ahead.

▶ NEARBY ACTIVITIES

You can easily reach the Avalon, Glen Artney, and Orange Grove areas of Patapsco Valley State Park from Rockburn Branch Park by following the directions above back to Washington Boulevard, and then turning right onto US 1 heading south. Take the next right onto South Street, and you will see the park entrance immediately on the left. Also nearby is historic Ellicott City, a former mill town founded in 1772; the town's immaculately preserved main street now houses shops and restaurants. Follow Landing Road north to its end at Ilchester Road; turn right and then take the first left onto Beech Wood Road. Turn left onto Bonnie Branch Road and then a quick right onto College Avenue; continue on College Avenue to Saint Paul Street and turn right. Turn left onto Maryland Avenue to Frederick Road, which becomes Main Street in downtown historic Ellicott City.

SAVAGE PARK

Take a leisurely stroll through beech, oak, and pine trees before confronting the rapids-filled Patuxent River. End your hike in and around historic Savage Mill.

▶ DESCRIPTION

The Wincopin Trail begins as an asphalt path but quickly turns to packed dirt. Consequently, the trail becomes narrower and tighter, but it's well maintained and easy to follow. Very thick woods—beech, oak, and poplar—crowd either side.

At just under 0.4 miles, the trail splits. To the left is the Beech Grove Trail; you'll take this trail back. For now, remain on the Wincopin Trail by going straight. Very soon after, you'll see another trail split to the left; it leads to the most thickly wooded section of the park and runs along the Middle Patuxent. But for now, continue on Wincopin and then head right on the Pick Rock Trail. The Pick Rock ends at the Little Patuxent River. You'll have plenty of river views ahead, so take a left when the trail splits and link up with the Hogs Neck Trail (passing one more leftward split along the way), a loop that follows the

▶ DIRECTIONS

Take I-695 to Exit 11, I-95 south toward Washington, D.C. Then take MD 32 east toward Fort Meade (Exit 38); take a quick exit onto MD 1 south toward Savage. Stay in the right lane and take an immediate right onto Howard Road, which soon turns into Baltimore Road. Go three blocks and take a right onto Guilford Road. Go five blocks to a left onto Vollmerhausen Road. Continue on Vollmerhausen for another 1000 feet to a parking area on the left. You'll see a sign there that reads, "Savage Park Wincopin Trail Access." There's parking and a portable toilet here, and the trailhead is just at the end of the parking area.

ⓘ KEY AT-A-GLANCE INFORMATION

LENGTH: 2.8 to 8.2 miles (see "Special Comments" below)

CONFIGURATION: Out-and-back with loop, plus a second out-and-back with loop

DIFFICULTY: Moderate

SCENERY: Middle Patuxent and Little Patuxent River, Savage Mill historic sites

EXPOSURE: Mostly shade

TRAFFIC: Moderate

TRAIL SURFACE: Packed dirt, some asphalt and sidewalk

HIKING TIME: 1.5–3.5 hours, depending on length

ACCESS: 7 a.m. to dusk daily

MAPS: USGS Savage; you can download a map at **www.co.ho.md.us/RAP/RAP Images/Savage_Map.gif.**

FACILITIES: Restrooms, water, ball fields, pavilions, concessions in added portion of the hike, near Savage Mill

SPECIAL COMMENTS: A quick and easy hike can be done by following the description below to 2.8 miles. If you want to hike all of the trails in Savage Park, add on the remaining 5.4 miles described below.

Savage Park

UTM Zone (WGS84)   18S

Easting   341482

Northing   4335043

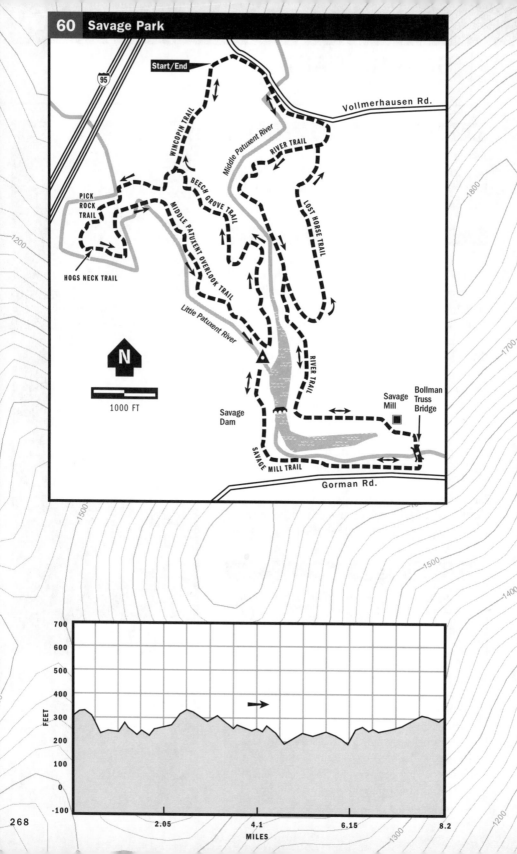

Start/End

Vollmerhausen Rd.

WINCOPIN TRAIL

Middle Patuxent River

RIVER TRAIL

PICK
ROCK
TRAIL

BEECH GROVE TRAIL

LOST HORSE TRAIL

HOGS NECK TRAIL

MIDDLE PATUXENT OVERLOOK TRAIL

Little Patuxent River

N

1000 FT

RIVER TRAIL

Savage
Mill

Bollman
Truss
Bridge

Savage
Dam

SAVAGE MILL TRAIL

Gorman Rd.

FEET

700
600
500
400
300
200
100
0
-100

2.05   4.1   6.15   8.2
MILES

Patuxent River

contours of the horseshoed river. The easternmost portion of the loop runs alongside the river and links with the Middle Patuxent Overlook Trail, which you'll join by going right at the next split at 1.2 miles. In addition to the beech, oak, and poplar you've already seen, pines begin to make an appearance. The trail heads uphill a bit as it winds through the aforementioned trees.

At 1.7 miles, link up with the Beech Grove Trail. Take a right and then another right back onto the Middle Patuxent Overlook Trail. Suddenly, it gets very rocky as the trail heads downhill. When you reach the Beech Grove Trail again in front of the river, take a left and then a quick right at the remains of an old bridge. The trail ends in another 500 feet where you'll be standing high above the confluence of the Middle Patuxent (to your left) and the Little Patuxent (to your right).

Head back to where you took a left and then a quick right just moments earlier. Instead of going back from where you came, take that path you turned left on and stay in that direction so that the Middle Patuxent is on your right and you're walking upstream. Follow the Beech Grove Trail you passed earlier as it follows the Patuxent for less than half a mile and then winds through beech trees before hooking back up with the Wincopin Trail at 2.5 miles. You'll reach the trailhead at 2.8 miles.

To hike the rest of Savage Park's trails, go right alongside Vollmerhausen Road from the original trailhead. Go roughly 500 feet and be on the lookout for the asphalt trail to the right. The trail soon runs behind Patuxent Middle School and Bollman Bridge Elementary. There are lots of beautiful beech trees in this section. At 3.3 miles, the trail splits: right is the River Trail and left is the Lost Horse Trail. For now, take the River Trail; you'll return by taking the Lost Horse. Within a little over a tenth of a mile, you'll reach the Middle Patuxent River, a rapids-filled beauty that sparkles with sunshine. The River Trail is at water level and simply follows the contours of the river, providing many places to stop and take in the beautiful and wild scene. You'll see the other end of the Lost Horse Trail at 3.8 miles. Continue past it on the River

Trail. There are some really beautiful rock formations all around—on the hills and in the water, creating more sections of rapids. The trail then goes up and down very quickly, which creates something of a strenuous hike. At 4.2 miles, look for the path heading up the hill to the left. This is actually the Mill Race Trail, though you'll see no signs telling you that. You'll know you've been on the Mill Race Trail only when you emerge onto a parking lot at the top of the hill. The trail sign will be behind you, at the tree line.

Parallel the parking lot and head into Savage Mill. Constructed in 1822 as a cotton mill, Savage Mill now houses antiques stores, historical displays, restaurants, and specialty shops. Assuming you haven't stopped to shop, go through the main stone mill building and take the metal stairs down to Gorman Road. Follow the sidewalk to the Bollman Truss Bridge at 4.7 miles. A national Civil Engineering landmark completed in 1869, it is the sole surviving example of the bridging system invented in 1850 by Wendell Bollman, a Baltimore engineer. This system was the first bridge system to be made entirely of iron and was used by the Baltimore and Ohio Railroad.

On the other side of the bride is the Savage Mill Trail, which runs beside the river for another half-mile before ending at the Little Patuxent River, on the other side of the overlook where you stood at 1.8 miles of this hike.

Backtrack all the way through the Savage Mill and back down to the River Trail. Once back on the River Trail, when you see railroad ties heading up the hill to the right, take the path and then go left at the top of the hill. When the trail splits, take a left. (Rightward goes to the restrooms, water, ball fields, pavilions, and concessions mentioned in "Facilities" above). You'll see a stone wall covered in moss to the left. This is an old railroad bridge abutment. The trail heads around it to the right up the hill on railroad ties. Stay on the wide path—the cuts to the left head back down to the water. You'll soon come to a small wooden footbridge. The trail heads up the hill. Take a left into a stand of mature trees—oak and tulip poplar mostly. Be on the lookout for white-tailed deer, which congregate in this area. The Panther Branch of the Patuxent runs to the right. Follow this asphalt trail (Lost Horse Trail) all the way until it meets back up with the River Trail at 7.8 miles. Soon, you'll come to Vollmerhausen Road. Take a left and your car will be 500 feet to the left.

▶ NEARBY ACTIVITIES

Time should be saved to explore Savage Mill. Nine buildings remain which date back to 1820. The Mill was placed on the National Register of Historic Places in 1974. It is open Monday to Wednesday, 10 a.m. to 6 p.m.; Thursday to Saturday, 10 a.m. to 9 p.m.; Sunday, 11 a.m. to 6 p.m. For information, call (410) 792-2820 or visit **www.savagemill.com.** For more hiking, the Patuxent Branch Trail runs from Savage Park all the way to Lake Elkhorn, some 4 miles. For a description of this hike, see page 258.

60 Hikes
within # 60 MILES

BALTIMORE
INCLUDING ANNE ARUNDEL, CARROLL, CECIL, HARTFORD AND HOWARD COUNTIES

APPENDIXES
& INDEX

APPENDIX A:
HIKING STORES

Baltimore Scout Shop
800 Wyman Park Drive
Baltimore, MD 21211
(410) 338-0141

Eastern Mountain Sports
Annapolis
Annapolis Harbour Center
2554 Solomon's Island Road
Annapolis, MD 21401
(410) 573-1240

Lutherville–Timonium
2442 Broad Avenue
Timonium, MD 21093
(410) 561-0142

H&H Outdoors
424 N. Eutaw Street
Baltimore, MD 21201
(410) 752-2580

Hudson Trail Outfitters
Annapolis
Annapolis Mall
Annapolis, MD 21401
(410) 266-8390

Towson
424 York Road
Towson, MD 21204
(410) 583-0494

REI
63 West Aylesbury Road
Timonium, MD 21093
(410) 252-5920

Sunny's The Affordable Outdoor Store–Sunny's Great Outdoors
Annapolis
3 Old Solomons Island Road
Annapolis, MD 21401
(410) 841-6490

Bel Air
5 Bel Air South Parkway
Bel Air, MD 21015
(410) 515-2044

Dundalk
1549 Merritt Boulevard
Dundalk, MD 21222
(410) 284-4020

Ellicott City
9291 Baltimore National Pike
Ellicott City, MD 21042
(410) 461-9122

Glen Burnie
7324 Ritchie Highway
Glen Burnie, MD 21061
(410) 761-3511

Parkville
7906 Harford Road
Parkville, MD 21234
(410) 668-8050

Randallstown
8139 Liberty Road
Randallstown, MD 21244
(410) 922-3622

Timonium
2157–B York Road
Timonium, MD 21093
(410) 561-7885

Towson
7 West Chesapeake Avenue
Towson, MD 21204
(410) 825-8050

Westminster
625 Baltimore Boulevard
Westminster, MD 21157
(410) 840-8701

The Urban Adventure Company
1500 Thames Street
Baltimore, MD 21231
(410) 534-4453

APPENDIX B: PLACES TO BUY MAPS

ADC The Map People
6440 General Green Way
Alexandria, VA 22312
www.adcmap.com
(800) ADC-MAPS (232-6277) or
(703) 750-0510

Eastern Mountain Sports
Annapolis
Annapolis Harbour Center
2554 Solomon's Island Road
Annapolis, MD 21401
(410) 573-1240

Lutherville–Timonium
2442 Broad Avenue
Timonium, MD 21093
(410) 561-0142

Hudson Trail Outfitters
Annapolis
Annapolis Mall

Annapolis, MD 21401
(410) 266-8390

Towson
424 York Road
Towson, MD 21204
(410) 583-0494

Passenger Stop Inc.
812 Kenilworth Drive
Towson, MD 21204
(410) 821-5888

REI
63 W. Aylesbury Road
Timonium, MD 21093
(410) 252-5920

United States Geological Survey
(888) ASK-USGS (175–8747)
www.usgs.gov

APPENDIX C: HIKING CLUBS

Chesapeake Hiking and Outdoors Society (CHAOS)
www.chaoshikers.org
marylandchaos@yahoo.com

Maryland Outdoor Club
www.marylandoutdoorclub.org

Mountain Club of Maryland
7923 Galloping Circle
Baltimore, MD 21244–1259
(410) 377-6266
www.mcomd.org

Sierra Club–Greater Baltimore Chapter
(410) 783-0680
maryland.sierraclub.org/baltimore

Sierra Club–Maryland Chapter
7338 Baltimore Avenue, Suite 101–A
College Park, MD 20740
(301) 277-7111
maryland.sierraclub.org

INDEX

INDEX

INDEX